GREAT AMERICAN

CRAFT BEER

A GUIDE TO THE NATION'S FINEST
BEERS AND BREWERIES

ANDY CROUCH

RUNNING PRESS
PHILADELPHIA · LONDON

For The Assistant Brewers

Printed in China

9 8 7 6 5 4 3 2 1

Digit on the right indicates the number of this printing

Library of Congress Control Number: 2010924452

ISBN 978-0-7624-3811-2

Cover and interior design by Ryan Hayes
Typography: Ziggurat, Mercury, and Gotham

Running Press Book Publishers
2300 Chestnut Street
Philadelphia, PA 19103-4371

Visit us on the web!
www.runningpresscooks.com

WHAT'S ON TAP

FOREWORD

If you date the inception of the American craft brewing renaissance back to the opening of the first start-up, small-scale, still-operating artisanal brewery then we are all celebrating this movement along with Sierra Nevada as they celebrate this monumental thirtieth anniversary this year. A lot of credit for the early awareness and enthusiasm for beers beyond the standard light lager style that dominated our national beer landscape back then must go to the homebrewers, beer enthusiasts, and open-minded regional brewers who recognized the potential for small-scale commercial brewing before it got off the ground. Fritz Maytag's visionary efforts in taking over the ailing Anchor Brewery and directing it toward this movement toward better beer were certainly instrumental in setting us all on the right path. Fritz was a mentor and inspiration for many of those early craft brewers like Ken Grossman of Sierra Nevada and Jack McAuliffe of New Albion Brewing. Fritz's altruism and openness in sharing his passion and knowledge with these fledging brewers set the tone for the welcoming, mutually-supportive community that has grown into an international movement toward better-beer.

The giant brewing conglomerates that dominated the marketplace for many decades were nearly successful in stripping all of the color and diversity out of the American beer landscape by marketing and distributing very similar versions of a very approachable, and very innocuous omnipresent beer style: the light lager. They differentiated the beers they produced not by focusing on the distinction of the liquid itself but by the ways and means of marketing and selling their respective liquids. The almighty liquid that is beer was nearly turned into a commodity. All it took was money. Money to buy giant advertising campaigns. Money to buy national sales armies. Money to gobble up smaller regional breweries.

The craft brewing movement has never been about money. Since the first day Ken Grossman visited Fritz Maytag at Anchor Brewery, it has always been about a shared enthusiasm and passion for and knowledge of the wide world of beer beyond the light lager juggernaut. This knowledge and passion moved out in small concentric circles from the founders of this movement as home brewers, early craft brewers, and beer lovers shared information, access to equipment, access to ingredients, and access to the growing ranks of disenfranchised consumers who expected something more out of their beer. Today craft beer still accounts for less than 5 percent of the beer sold in America, but it is the only segment of the beer industry that is growing. Imports are down. Industrial light lager is flat. Craft beer sales are at an all-time high and are gaining moment and traction into the mainstream. We still have a long way to go. The largest American-owned breweries, Yuengling and Boston Beer, each control 1 percent of the domestic beer market. Two giant international brewing conglomerates share over 80 percent control of the domestic beer market. Something is wrong with this picture. Much as it was when our ancestors dumped tea into Boston Harbor, American beer enthusiasts are revolting against foreign control and voting with their wallets to support the hundreds of small, independent craft breweries making beautiful, full-flavored beers; beers differentiated by the quality and distinction of the liquid inside the bottle, not the marketing and aggressive sales tactics that take place outside the bottle. We haven't achieved this minor but expanding success with money. We have done it together with passion and knowledge.

Great American Craft Beer, by Andy Crouch, represents another great leap forward for our movement. Andy's knowledge of and passion for craft beer is infectious and articulate. If we are going to continue to convert more drinkers each day to the world of better-beer, the information we need to share about the beautiful, diverse beers needs to be approachable, methodical, and enticing. This book offers a great overview of the movement and a unique format of segmented, related styles in a way that allows the reader to understand the connections between certain beers while learning about the individual (and very individualistic) breweries that produce them. As I read the book, it was immediately apparent that Andy's approach to analyzing, appreciating, and describing these amazing beers truly comes from the experience of trying them himself and formulating an impression based on his knowledge and his palate. His evocative descriptor language for the nuances of beers like "graham cracker" notes or "cotton candy" hops reminds the reader that he is coming to this book first as a beer lover and second as a beer expert.

This book will give beer lovers—novices and experts alike—an increased level of confidence and knowledge to experience beer as Andy does even if each reader's opinions or favorite beers differ. That's what is so great about craft beer; it's subjective. We each come to it with our own set of reference points and perceptions. And we each find the beers that ring true to us individually. Every one of us has a unique taste biography;

our own internal narrative of evolving palate preferences. Therefore beauty is in the eye of the beer-holder. But having a common language and shared context gives us all a basic platform from which we can move out in our own preferred directions. And incorporating food-and-beer pairing into this journey amplifies the breadth of experiences we can enjoy and build upon. So Great American Craft Beer the book is born some thirty odd years after the movement began. What does our future as beer lovers and beer makers hold? What will the next thirty years look like? What are the next trends, ingredients, and styles that are going to enchant and captivate us? The great thing is that none us knows for sure. Andy's book will share information that will answer your questions about the wonderful Beer Moment we are now in and the path that we took to get here. But where do we go from here? We shall see what we shall see. It kind of feels exhilarating not knowing where our individual palates or the beer world are going next, doesn't it? As beer lovers we are fortunate to have more choices of more beers from more breweries than ever before in the history of our country.

As craft brewers, we take our beer very seriously. At Dogfish Head, our goal is to make world class beer that is outside of every class in the world. Other growing craft breweries may focus on nailing Old World styles and in that way making them their own. Regardless of our individual approaches, we collectively take our passion for and enjoyment of our beer very seriously. But we don't take ourselves too seriously. Because beer is fun. Our community is one of the most joyous and most inviting places around. The example the founders of our community set in sharing their knowledge and passion is alive and well and gaining momentum. When I look behind the beer fest booths at the smiles on the faces of craft brewers and their coworkers, I know they feel the same way about this as we do at Dogfish Head. Whether their brewery focuses on traditional wheat beers or Champgne-bottle-conditioned strong ales doesn't matter; as Andy successfully describes within these pages, the more styles and non-styles of great beer, the merrier. We do a lot of things differently. We contain multitudes. But what bonds us together is our shared obsession with making American craft beer synonymous with quality enjoyment. Compared to many of the other "best" things in life—a new car, a vacation, a world-class bottle of wine —craft brewed beer is an affordable luxury. More and more people are discovering this every single day.

As readers of this book, as beer enthusiasts, as beer evangelists, you should know that when a craft brewer or one of her coworkers looks out across a beer fest floor at a sea of your excited faces smiling back at us, we are very thankful for your contributions to this better-beer renaissance. In terms of market share, we are still a tiny island. But together we are heavy. When we share our beer passion and knowledge gleaned in places like this book, or at a brewpub beer dinner, or at the dining room table with friends and family, we will collectively keep turning a lot more people on to the good stuff. With knowledge and passion, we can nudge friends and loved ones off of light lager terra firma and onto the flavor bridge. We can guide them toward our island. Because there's a party over here. Everyone's invited. The club is open.

— *Sam Calagione,*
President and Founder,
Dogfish Head Craft Brewery

PREFACE

The process of writing a book is usually a pretty lonely one, with countless hours spent staring at a computer monitor, hunting and pecking letters on the keyboard, reorganizing, and editing. Thankfully, the manner of researching and selecting the products profiled in this book was anything but solitary. Following years of tastings, brewery visits, and travels to pubs across the country, Great American Craft Beer is, at its heart, a celebration of the conviviality and kinship of beer. On these travels and experiences, I was usually accompanied by friends and family members and often greeted by passionate and personable brewers and owners who were more than willing to offer assistance, advice, and, most importantly, their beer.

At the outset, this book is dedicated to the assistant brewers, cellar men and women, and those individuals whose creativity and dedication to craft make our pints possible. As always, I am grateful to the brewers and owners who participated in the research process, offered their time freely, and shared their beers and brewing wisdom.

I also raise a pint to the family and friends who attended numerous tasting parties, in which we sampled, discussed, debated, and celebrated the fruits of the brewing artisans whose work I explore in this guide. I especially thank Jennifer Cox, whose unfailing support and boundless optimism helped sustain me through each chapter.

To the talented chefs Sean Paxton and Bruce Paton, whose wonderful recipes grace the beer and food section of this guide, I offer sincere thanks and a growling stomach.

With a book whose subject matter is so extensive, the journey to the project's fruition was ably assisted along the way by several individuals whose interest in the subject matched my own. A couple of pints should be raised to my agent, Scott Gould of RLR Associates, whose enthusiasm for the book was immediate and never waned. The good folks at Running Press, including my editor Geoffrey Stone, have gently guided the project through the editing and design process. I thank them for their interest and assistance in making Great American Craft Beer a better read.

I also want to thank the founders and active participants at BeerAdvocate.com and other beer-related websites for their unmatched love of the subject. Their contributions, ranging from humorous and informative reviews to suggestions about particularly interesting beers, helped bring some new angles to my research.

Finally, I raise a special toast to you, the readers. Be your interest in the subject of beer only a passing one (please keep reading) or that of the most hardened beer geek (also keep reading), I hope you enjoy this guide and that it inspires you to support the talented brewing artisans who bring us all this great American craft beer.

THE
GREAT AMERICAN
CRAFT BEER
EXPERIENCE

With the bounty of amazing beers available in every corner of America, never before has there been a better time or place to be a beer drinker. Whether you love super-hoppy India Pale Ales, lightly fruity Hefeweizens, or dark and soulful Stouts, American craft brewers have you covered. After decades suffering as international laughing stocks, American brewers now rank with and influence the best craftsman that Germany, Britain, the Czech Republic, and Ireland have to offer.

Welcome to your personal guide and companion to the exciting world of American craft beer. In preparing yourself for a passionate and informative journey through the most palate-pleasing ales and lagers produced in America today, keep in mind the inalienable truth that there is a beer out there for everyone. And while viewing grocery store shelves and tap handles packed with beer options may seem daunting at first, don't worry; you already know everything you need to select the perfect beer for you. If you're a coffee drinker, a lover of sweet fruits, or a chocoholic, hundreds of craft beers already await your attention.

Touching upon a wide library of subjects, including beer, food, travel, and history, *Great American Craft Beer* seeks to capture the essence, passion, and dedication of the people who brew America's best beers. Far beyond a mere tasting notebook, this guide finds its origins in a desire to inspire a love of craft beer in everyday drinkers. Advocating a flavor-based approach, *Great American Craft Beer* invites you to connect with craft beers by using the flavors you already enjoy tasting. The beers and brewers profiled in these pages have been selected after years of rigorous tasting and research, and they represent the very best of American craft brewing. After finishing just a few chapters, you'll be ready to step right up to the bar and order your next pint with confidence.

CHAPTER ONE

EXPLORING BEER

Beer has long played an influential role in American history, from its dwindling stock having steered the captain of the Mayflower's hasty decision to come ashore in Plymouth, Massachusetts, in 1620, to its plentiful abundance on tables during the plotting of the American Revolution. Early Americans, especially innkeepers and housewives, plied the craft of homebrewing beers to match those their ancestors enjoyed back in their native lands. Despite its importance in our history, America eventually lost touch with its beer heritage, leading to a culture of uniformity, where the only distinctions in products were in their labels and advertising tag lines. While someone might be a Bud man, reach for the Silver Bullet, or prefer living the High Life, it is unlikely that flavor plays a significant part of the buying decision. And today we find ourselves in this unusual situation, caught between an absence of beer culture and the rich brewing traditions of our ancestors.

My intention is not to decry the practices that brought us to a lamentable state of monotony, but to celebrate what saved us from it, namely the passion, dedication, and hard work of pioneering craft brewers. Slowly growing from a rundown brewery in San Francisco and spreading to Colorado, Michigan, Maine, and all points in-between, brewers started painting with a new palette of colors, from light amber and orange to deep brown and pitch-black. They brewed on stovetops before graduating to sheds and garages and eventually to vacant commercial spaces.

Some wanted to restore beer to its rightful place at the dining table, so they opened restaurant-breweries, called brewpubs. Deemed "microbrewers" by the news media, as much for their diminutive sizes as for their improbable competition with the big macrobrewers, these early craft beer pioneers sought not to blaze a trail to business success, but to provide a few flavorful alternatives to the homogenized beer offerings surrounding them. Their early efforts, the quality of which ranged from undrinkable to similar to today's standards, were often met with derision. Consumers had no idea what to make of beers that were not light yellow in color, beers with real flavor that did not quickly fade after each sip. But these unflappable individuals, who left safe careers as lawyers, carpenters, and astrophysicists, among many others, endured. They scraped together old farm equipment, sourced difficult to find ingredients, and suffered countless rejections as they tried to hand-sell their bottles pub to pub, consumer to consumer. They lived for the few moments when someone's eyes lit up—when the new ales and lagers touched their lips and opened their minds to a new world of beer.

Even though many of these microbreweries have now grown from small, one- or two-person operations into some of the largest breweries in America, one common conviction still binds them together: the dedication to producing highly flavorful beers with traditional ingredients. The "craft beer" name helps distinguish between the consistent yet one-dimensional macrobrewed beers with adjuncts such as corn and rice, and the flavorful products made by craft brewers that appeal to consumers who appreciate the bolder flavors of all-malt beer.

The craft brewing revolution has always been about one beer, a single experience that shatters decades of programming from big brewery advertising and changes the way people perceive beer. No longer is beer a drink of last resort, something to settle for, a mere interchangeable widget easily replaced with another bland, lifeless bottle with a different label. The craft brewing rebellion, part of a broader change in the way people think about the quality of what they consume, has slowly altered the definition of beer and has greatly expanded the consciousness of drinkers. Even in the furthest reaches of the country, gone are the days where macrobreweries were the only option available. In most major cities, even the diveiest of bars are likely to carry Samuel Adams, Sierra Nevada, Fat Tire, or a locally crafted option.

Despite these successes, challenges still remain for craft brewers. At the top of the list lies educating potential converts about the wealth of better beer options available to them without scaring them off. While some breweries choose to inundate consumers with information overload, many appreciate that people already understand the accessible, common, and approachable flavors they enjoy in what they eat and drink every day. The challenge for these brewers is to get consumers to momentarily drop their defenses and check their beer prejudices at the door just long enough to enjoy a palate-changing moment.

At its core, this guide serves as both an invitation and an instrument to learn more about better beer. Instead of tossing reams of information and numbers your way, I focus on what you already know, namely the flavors you prefer, and match them with similarly tasting beers.

In order to prepare you for experiencing the Style and Flavor of Beer, it's important to spend a little time Exploring Beer, including touching upon the history and development of beer styles. I will also detail the process of making beer, laying out each step from the hop and grain farmers through to the filling of a glass.

Any beginner spectator can sit in the stands at Wrigley Field and enjoy a Cubs game, but understanding the rules of baseball adds a new dimension of appreciation and enjoyment to the experience. The same principle applies to beer, where, with even a little bit of knowledge about how beer is made, you can enhance the experience of enjoying a pint and learn to tell different beer styles apart. Armed with this knowledge, you'll be able to distinguish between the styles you enjoy.

HISTORY OF BEER

Volumes have been written about the history of brewing beer and its significance and contributions to the development of culture and society. If you fancy yourself a history buff, cultural anthropologists and beer writers alike have produced some excellent books for your review. If you prefer the nickel tour of beer history, these next few pages should help stoke your interest in the subject.

Although its origins cannot be definitively traced, the practice of brewing dates back many thousands of years to when nomadic men and women discovered, likely through glorious accident, that consuming grain dropped into water and left to ferment resulted in magical, other worldly feelings. Informed by their readings of hieroglyphics and other ancient forms of communication, historians believe that brewing first occurred in parts of northeast Africa near modern day Egypt and the city of Babylon in modern-day Iraq. The Sumerians honored a goddess of brewing called Ninkasi, who now gives her name to a craft brewery in Oregon, and a hymn to the goddess actually contains an early recipe for making beer. When the Sumerians were able to repeat the miraculous fermentation experiment on a regular basis, the first culture of beer came into existence, celebrating a gift deemed to be handed down from the gods. Whether the desire to farm a stable grain crop for brewing really incited the end of the nomadic lifestyle cannot be known, but many historians have so hypothesized.

From the time of the Babylonians, world history is replete with references to beer and brewing, even within the laws of Hammurabi, as well as accounts of ale, Chica, and sake brewing in what is now modern-day Scandinavia, Mexico, and China. These cultures have each celebrated the contributions of mythical gods and kings of brewing, from Gambrinus to Radegast.

With the spread of knowledge regarding the cultivation and fermentation of barley, brewing developed in intriguing and diverse ways across the globe. Used as liquid refreshment in times when water was not safe to

drink, beer has also been employed as a form of currency and a means of bartering for goods and services. Throughout history, beer has cut a wide swath through society. It has been the domain of pharaohs, kings, and queens, and given solace to the working classes.

The dark, sooty fermented grain drinks made by early homebrewers likely bear no resemblance to the clean, flavorful beers of modern brewing. In the first days of brewing, malt was often dried by the warmth of the sun and the air. Some brewers would speed the drying process by placing their grain over a fire, either through direct heat fueled by a wide range of unsavory yet combustible materials or by less direct methods. References in texts of the time suggest that these early beers contained dark colors and acrid, smoky flavors that disgusted

many drinkers. Accordingly, the maltsters undertook substantial efforts to limit the influences of wood, straw, charcoal, and other heating materials on their beers. As kilning technology developed and improved, brewers and early maltsters employed new methods of drying their malts, which resulted in less foul tasting beers.

While usually an activity undertaken in the home, often by women, early brewing was also performed on a commercial basis in many communities. The oldest existing brewery in the world,

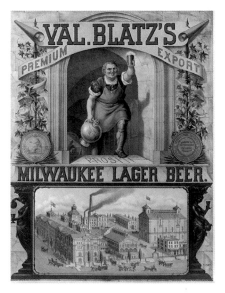

the abbey of Weihenstephan in the Bavarian region of southern Germany, has operated for nearly one thousand years, since 1040.

Long flavored with various herbs and spices, water and barley saw the arrival of their bitter and pungent third partner-in-crime, hops, in the fifteenth century. Within one hundred years, the preservative and flavor contributions of hops became widely acknowledged, and the custom of adding them to beer became widespread. This practice was eventually enshrined in local brewing regulations, including the famed German Purity Law of 1516. Installed as a cross between a tax law and a way to protect ingredients necessary for baking, the Reinheitsgebot (translated as "purity regulation" or "requirement") has long been an influential force in German brewing and a source of pride for brewers who follow it. Its earliest version appeared in Munich in 1447 when the local governing council ordered all brewers to use only barley, hops, and water in the brewing process (the role of yeast not being fully appreciated for another four hundred years). Forty years later, a Bavarian king ordered all brewers in his domain to comply with the purity law. By 1516, the Reinheitsgebot extended to all of Bavaria and later throughout the whole country where it would govern until the European Court of Justice struck it down as anti-competitive in 1987.

With the advances of brewing ingredients and technology, including the invention of the hydrometer gravity measuring tool, the color of beer also changed. From a small town called Plzen in what is now the Czech Republic, a Bavarian brewer named Joseph Groll used a decidedly pale malt to make what is believed to be the world's first light colored lager, named Pilsener after the town.

When it comes to brewing in the United States, beer history does not begin and end with Adolphus Busch, Adolph Coors, and Frederick Miller, the founders of America's largest modern breweries. Long before the new settlers arrived, Native Americans brewed a beer using corn and other ingredients. The first brewery founded by European settlers opened in 1612 in New Amsterdam, modern day Manhattan. In their voyage to the New World, travelers on the Mayflower, who would go on to found the Massachusetts Bay Colony, relied upon a slightly alcoholic or small beer as a means of safe water consumption, solidifying the beverage's role in early American life.

In choosing to come ashore in Plymouth in 1620, the ship's crew determined that their beer supplies would not last them a return journey if their passengers kept drinking. In his journal capturing the scene, William Bradford, later elected governor of the colony, wrote of the dire beer situation on the ship, "We could not now take much time for further search or consideration, our victuals being much spent, especially our beere."

As with their Old World ancestors, the new colonists quickly set out to build brewing systems in order to produce safe drinks for their local communities, with breweries starting to appear in towns along the Atlantic Coast. Local inns from Boston to Philadelphia provided lodging, nourishment, and locally produced beer and cider for their clientele. But by the early part of the eighteenth century, many Americans began to strongly question the wisdom of allowing people to consume alcohol, especially wine and spirits. The voices of temperance started clearing their collective throats and, in 1808, members of a New York congrega-

City Tavern

tional church formed America's first temperance group. The concept of moderation spread to New England, where the Total Abstinence Society formed in Portland, Maine, in 1815, followed by the Boston-based American Society for the Promotion of Temperance in 1826. By 1829, the ASPT claimed a membership of more than 100,000, and within four years, the total number of temperance groups ballooned to more than 5,000 with membership rolls exceeding 1.5 million people. In 1874, a group of women who were disturbed by their husbands' abuse of alcohol organized the Woman's Christian Temperance Union to promote total abstinence from alcohol as a healthy and moral lifestyle.

Long before national Prohibition loomed, a Maine-based temperance group in 1846 successfully fought for the passage of the nation's first alcohol prohibition law. Promoted by Colonel Neal Dow of Portland, the Darth Vader of Prohibition, the law banned the sale of alcoholic spirits except for medicinal and mechanical purposes. Within a decade, all six

New England states fell to Prohibition. Starting slow and building steam, the Maine model traveled to the nation's capital where a Minnesota congressman named Andrew J. Volstead introduced Bill No. 6810, known as the National Prohibition Act, in May 1919. Following the ratification of the Eighteenth Amendment the previous year, America became a dry nation on January 16, 1920. While standing for nearly fourteen years, the move did not appear to prove popular with Volstead's local district, as Minnesotans tossed him out of office in 1922. Following a slow groundswell of opposition and a desperate need for additional tax dollars, the Eighteenth Amendment was repealed in 1933 with the ratification of the Twenty-First Amendment.

Despite the initial excitement over the availability of beer, which started flowing almost immediately upon the repeal of the Eighteenth Amendment, American beer went into a period of slow decline as the many competing breweries struggled to resume their operations following Prohibition. Over several decades, the diversity of American beer styles inherited from German, Czech, Russian, Polish, and many other ethnic groups slowly disintegrated, leaving behind a ubiquitous, pale, and relatively innocuous product known simply as American Pilsner. Regional breweries came and went, with a handful of mega-breweries growing to dominate nearly all of American brewing. This sorry state of affairs set the stage for a renaissance in American brewing.

AMERICAN CRAFT BREWING

For people under a certain age, it's perhaps difficult to remember a time when the beer selection was limited to a few national brands. Until the late 1980s, and perhaps well into the early 1990s in many parts of the country, you would have been lucky to find a couple of upstart craft brands or a struggling regional beer. From the end of the failed national experiment of Prohibition, American beer traveled a long, painful, and declining course in terms of flavor and character. While the nation's biggest breweries succeeded in refining the science and efficiency of their brewing operations, the resulting products managed a level of industrial  uniformity never before experienced. In the process, beer lovers were left with products whose core benefit was consistent, yet uninspired flavor.

During this troubling period, beer lost its character and traded its soul for the sake of quality control and corporate aims. What brewing traditions America had inherited from its forbearers were quickly abandoned. Treated as a prosaic and tired formula that was interchangeable with the next formula, fewer than fifty breweries operated in America by the end of the 1970s, a worrisome forecast for the future.

In this dire, bleak environment, a handful of craft brewing pioneers stood up and decided to try their own hands at brewing the flavorful beers their grandparents described with pride. Even before President Jimmy Carter signed into law an amendment that allowed people to brew up to 100 gallons of beer per year for their own personal use, these homebrewers, the wily instigators of the craft beer movement, rejected corporate beer and struck out on their own.

A New Age of American Beer

The 1980s were an inspired, exciting, and disorienting time for the lowly craft brewing pioneer. Without a business model to follow, these beer lovers plotted, raised money, and slowly pieced together their own makeshift breweries. They personally knocked on legislative doors in order to get laws passed that would allow them to open brewpubs; they sourced the few raw materials available to companies of their tiny size, and they tested and re-tested their new recipes. These pioneers left successful careers for the as yet undefined world of craft beer.

Fueled by the hard work of groundbreakers, new breweries and brewpubs began opening in cities throughout America. West Coast innovators include: Jack McAuliffe of the long defunct New Albion Brewery, Fritz Maytag of Anchor Brewing Company, and Ken Grossman of Sierra Nevada Brewing Company. East Coast pioneers include: Jim Koch of Boston Beer Company, Richard Wrigley of the now closed Commonwealth Brewing Company, and Peter and Janet Egelston of Northampton Brewery. Slow going at first, the popularity of these strange new beers grew as curious novelty seekers showed a willingness to try something new.

Similar to the rush preceding the Dot com era bust, more than 500 breweries operated in the United States by 1995, with three to four new breweries opening every week. That number more than doubled to 1,102 breweries by 1996 and 300 more opened that same year. The craft beer

pioneers suddenly found themselves surrounded by fresh new faces, including many corporate types who saw dollar signs in the new and fast growing industry. A lack of brewing experience or business sense dissuaded very few from the chance to own their own brewery, and some existing breweries quickly expanded well beyond their means. As the number of available brands soared, store shelves became packed with new brands of seemingly unknown origin and often questionable quality. Plagued by brand confusion, consumers new to craft beer found themselves paying a few extra dollars to try stale or poorly made beers. Left with a bad taste in their mouths, consumer anger precipitated a major correction in the industry, where flat, and then negative, growth took root.

Craft Beer Rises Again

Fat with advertising dollars from the big brewers, the mainstream media happily crowed over the misfortunes of craft brewers, often decrying their efforts as a mere fad. Despite this criticism, craft brewers regrouped and refocused their efforts, often targeting local markets as opposed to distant ones they could not service. Underperforming brewers and business owners disappeared from the market, leaving behind increasingly savvy professionals who sought to avoid the mistakes of the past. The highly stable and flavorful beers available now are a testament to their rededicated efforts to improve quality. The brewers you encounter today know that they have to temper their passion by mixing it with a dedication to their businesses and the quality of their crafts.

The more than 1,500 craft breweries operating in the United States today account for more than nine million barrels of beer and contribute more than $6 billion to the economy. As a result of the measured growth programs of craft brewers, consumers can embrace fresh, clean, and well-constructed beers in all parts of the nation. As new generations of drinkers grow up in a world where craft beer is omnipresent, where Samuel Adams has seemingly always existed, craft brewers will hopefully have an easier time connecting with consumers over the values of their  flavorful products versus those of the larger brewing concerns. With craft beer experiencing consistent growth and interest among all age groups, the future is abuzz with hope and optimism for craft brewers.

HERE AND ABROAD

Despite its relatively late start compared to other great brewing nations, America has quickly, over the course of thirty years, become one of the world's pre-eminent brewing nations. Mixing a healthy respect for traditional brewing practices with a New World curiosity for experimentation, bundled together with passion for their craft, American brewers have made this nation the best place to be if you are a lover of good beer. It is now beyond question that American brewers can compete with the best craftsmen of Germany, Ireland, Britain, the Czech Republic, and beyond. And nowhere in the world will you encounter such a diverse selection of flavorful beers, born of hundreds of historic and newfangled styles. Americans no longer have to board planes to travel abroad in search of better beer offerings. In an unusual historical reversal, foreign beer lovers now dream of traveling to America to visit our breweries and patronize our brewpubs.

In many ways, America has developed into a saving grace for many of the world's endangered beer styles. In the past thirty years, this nation has given shelter to many moribund styles, from Porter to Pale Ale, Imperial Stout to Barley Wine. In retrospect, American brewers perhaps seemed the least likely to serve as saviors of anything related to beer. Ensconced in a country with little to no surviving native beer culture, American brewers looked abroad to understand the essence and true character of beer. Our brewers have drawn inspiration from foreign brewers near and far, dissecting their popularity, studying their charms, and extracting the vital characters of their signature offerings.

In all the time that small American brewers have undertaken their studies of European breweries, a curious thing has transpired. Once considered to be the apex of world brewing, European brewers have encountered some very trying times in recent years. In a world dominated by dizzying degrees of brewery mergers and acquisitions, these once proud leaders now tremble before their futures. As corporations continue their conglomerative efforts, fewer and fewer iconic foreign brands remain in the hands of their original owners. Before its purchase of Anheuser-Busch, InBev alone purchased a controlling stake in hundreds of beer brands, including Stella Artois, Hoegaarden, Labatt, Boddingtons,

Beck's, Franziskaner, Lowenbrau, and Spaten. Diageo, the world's biggest wine and spirit producer, also scooped up several classic brands, including Red Stripe, Guinness, Harp, and Smithwick's.

As American craft beer started to rise, and an American beer culture began to develop, our European brethren started watching their own beer histories evaporate before them. Pints of Guinness lightened in color from opaque black to ruby red, Stella Artois became the world's foremost Belgian beer, and the world's biggest breweries became even more inbred. Beer drinkers around the world are still assaulted on a daily basis with various marketing canards suggesting that drinking a particular foreign brand is an exotic experience akin to visiting that nation's beer joints, but in the end, these prefabricated experiences feel much like an airport version of the *Cheers* bar.

That is the unusual thing about beer culture; it cannot be recreated or faked. It remains an organic and fragile thing, a living experience that is easily suffocated if not cultivated under just the right conditions. And while many of the world's iconic brewing nations continue to experience a downward shift in consumer interest in their traditional beers, many still retain a vibrant beer culture. My handy dictionary defines "culture" as a set of values or social conventions associated with a particular field, activity, or group characteristic. When applied to beer, it describes the practice of integrating beer into every day life. This does not mean that Europeans sneak sips during business meetings or church services. Rather, they have long respected beer and recognized its role as an everyday beverage, giving it a spot at the table, be it lunch, dinner, or just a mid-day break with pals. Foreign visitors often get to experience this remarkable beer culture first-hand, whether in a quiet Belgian café or at a shared community table in a Munich beer garden.

Beer has not enjoyed such a cherished role in American life for a long time, if ever. Dating from the earliest days of the nation, continuing through the anti-saloon campaign times, and existing to this day in the form of neo-Prohibitionists, the American populace is often taught to fear alcohol instead of respect it. Beer, wine, and spirits are locked away from young people, cultivating a forbidden fruit phenomenon with their relationships to alcohol. Yet when you travel abroad, you can see societies that maturely manage alcohol without resorting to scare tactics.

The unusual convergence of Europe's grown-up relationship with alcohol and the decline of its breweries has led to a unique opportunity for

American brewers. For a country that has never possessed much of a distinct brewing heritage, America has now taken a leading role in exporting its new take on beer to the rest of the world. With the help of the federal government and brewing trade groups, enterprising American brewers now send over thirty thousand barrels a year of their flavorful and unusual beers to more than a dozen countries in Europe and Asia. If you visit bars from Copenhagen to Tokyo, you may be struck not by the lack of local flavorful beers but by the surprising frequency of American craft brands. Alongside bottles of Carlsberg and Kirin, you can now find Brooklyn Lager, Great Divide's Oak Aged Yeti, and Port Brewing specialty releases.

In these topsy turvy times, American brewers are hoping that they can sweep to the aid of their inspirational brewing elders. American brewers have started plying their trades abroad, in Indonesia, Italy, Britain, and beyond, helping to expose the world to the new American way of thinking about beer. And while this growing sphere of influence is great news for small American craft brewers, this expansion has resulted in an unexpected identity crisis for the world's richest brewing nations. In a reversal of history, American craft brewers have inspired a new generation of foreign brewers in places such as Scotland, Japan, Scandinavia, and Australia, to start their own breweries based on American models. When combined with an emerging generation of global beer geeks, including many rabid European beer raters, a modest but growing international market for big-flavored American beers has developed.

And while it is good news that beer drinkers in countries long dominated by prosaic lager brewers have started to see new beers appear on their store shelves, it remains to be seen whether America will ever learn to truly embrace the traditional beer cultures of more alcohol-friendly nations.

MALT MEETS
THE MASH TUN

Learning about Beer and Brewing

Ialways find that when I know a little bit about a subject, it sparks a desire to learn more. Whether a detail about the playing style of John Coltrane, the brushstroke methods of Georges Seurat, or the hand-eye coordination of Peyton Manning, a little extra knowledge often adds a new level of appreciation and fun to any experience. Learning new pieces of information about beer is like putting together pieces in a puzzle. When you learn about its core ingredients, for example, you can understand how each of the parts fit together to form the foamy final product that sits before you.

At its base, beer is an alcoholic beverage made from a mixture of water and malted cereal grain, such as barley or wheat, flavored with hops, and then fermented with yeast. While creative modern brewers have vastly increased the list of possible ingredients, these four core ingredients comprise the majority of beer made today. A few larger breweries use adjuncts, such as rice and corn, to lighten the bodies and flavor profiles of

their beers, a practice derided by beer geeks and purists who believe such efforts reduce the overall flavor of the beers. And while some craft brewers have gone off the deep end with their esoteric creations, including garlic and beet beers, most brewers restrict their ingredients to the key four with occasional simple additions.

Understanding how the ingredients in beer interact is crucial to differentiating between the many available beer styles. Commonly referred to as the soul of beer, malt is a workhorse that provides the base for all the other ingredients. In comparison to wine, grain replaces grapes as the primary fermentable ingredient in beer. To create brewing malt, maltsters, including Samuel Adams in his time, wet barley until it germinates, then slowly dry it at controlled temperatures, causing the barley's starches to undergo a sugar conversion. Maltsters are able to create different malt types based upon the kilning process length, with longer periods creating darker colored malts and resulting in roasted flavors.

In designing a beer recipe, each brewer carefully chooses among malt varieties in order to select the color and flavor of the final beer. Brewers employ specialty grains, including chocolate and black malts, to create dark beers such as Porter and Stout, while less roasted pale malts lighten Pilsener, Pale Ale, and Amber.

Brewers next add pellet or whole leaf hops, close relatives of the Cannabis plant, to bring a balance of bitterness and earthy aromas to the beer. Hops are often called the spice of beer, providing splashes of flavor against the malt backdrop. As with the use of spices in making a stew, a brewer must artfully select the hops to use and determine the point during the process at which to add them. Early hop additions during the boil impart bitterness, with middle additions contributing flavor, and final additions providing aroma. Hops also work as a natural preservative agent in beer, fighting against spoilage.

While malt and hops each significantly affect the qualities of the final product, the particular character of the brewing water is also important. As water comprises more than 90 percent of beer, the mineral content of a brewer's water supply heavily influences the final flavor. In Burton-on-Trent in England, the high calcium and sulfate content of the region's brewing water provides the qualities needed for strong flavored pale ales. In contrast, the soft water in Pilsen, in the Czech Republic, gave birth to the region's world-famous crisp lagers.

After the brewer develops a recipe and the materials arrive at the brewhouse, the actual brewing process finally begins. The brewer mills the malted grain to finely crush it into grist in order to withdraw the sugars that the yeast will feast upon during fermentation. The brewer then mixes the grist with water in a large brewing vessel, called the mash tun, where the mixture is gradually heated to a set temperature, which converts the malted barley's starches into sugars. This process is crucial to the head retention and body of the resulting beer. The brewer then transfers the mix to another large brewing vessel, called the lauter tun, where the brewer adds hot water to wash the sugars from the malt, resulting in thick, sweet liquid called wort. A false bottom in the lauter tun strains the spent grain from the water and allows the wort to transfer to the brew kettle. In an eco-friendly gesture, many breweries donate or sell their spent barley to local farmers for use in feeding their livestock.

In the kettle, the brewer brings the wort to a rolling boil and then adds hops at select intervals to achieve the desired flavors and aromas. After the boil finishes, the brewer transfers the wort to the fermentation tanks, where yeast is pitched to start fermentation. During fermentation, the yeast eats the sugars in the wort and creates the wonderful byproduct of

alcohol, resulting in beer. For thousands of years, early brewers had no conception of what added that great kick to their drinks, where they unknowingly relied upon airborne yeast strains to inoculate their brews. It took French scientist Louis Pasteur, known more for his work with milk bacteria, to discover that yeast microorganisms held the secret of fermentation. By establishing the existence of yeast cells in his 1876 *Études sur la Bière* (Studies Concerning Beer), Pasteur helped brewers exercise greater control over fermentation and the resulting

products of their efforts.

Another defining moment in the life of beer occurs when the brewer chooses the type of yeast strain to be used, generally either ale or lager. Ales are beers whose yeast collects at the top of the vessel and that best survive fermentation at warmer temperatures. But as with trying to classify a wide ranging art style in a single phrase, no short description can hope to capture the essence of such a broad category of beers. Generally speaking, ale yeasts produce fruitier beers. Lager yeasts collect at the bottom of the brewing vessel and undergo fermentation at cooler temperatures. The cool lagering process generally produces a smoother final product that possesses less aggressive aromas and flavors. The type of yeast used and fermentation temperature also influence the length of the aging process. Ales generally age for one to three weeks, while lagers age for six to eight weeks. Certain high-powered ale and lager styles can age for a year or longer in order to mellow or fully develop their flavor profiles.

ONE BEER

I f you look deep enough into every beer lover's history, you will find a single beer that led to a lifetime of love and dedication to grain, hops, and yeast. I'm not talking about that first sip of Coors Light stolen from a father's temporarily abandoned can or bottle. Rather, I'm referring to that one beer that turned the head, opened the mind, and cracked a world of doubts, stereotypes, and suspicions about the assumedly crude character of beer. Depending upon when you came of drinking age, your One Beer might be a very different offering. For many older drinkers, that beer may have been Anchor Steam, Redhook Ale, or even New Albion Ale. More recent converts to better beer may have been influenced to hit the road to beer enrichment by a hoppy IPA, a fruity Cherry Ale, or perhaps a roasted Coffee Stout.

Now, tens of millions of barrels later, the birth of each craft beer lover from coast to coast can be traced to a single beer. It is important that you never forget this singular experience, a moment you'd think you never could forget. But with all the excitement the craft beer industry has to offer to consumers, it sometimes seems as if the remarkable moments that led to this point have been forgotten.

Sparking an attraction to craft beer is all about finding the right beer for the right moment, the one sip that radically transforms the drinker's conception of beer. After experiencing a constant stream of fizzy, yellow, freezing cold monotony, it takes the gobsmacking power appeal of real color, aroma, and flavor to stop you in your tracks. As the internal cymbal crash within you signifies the breaking of long-accepted beer stereotypes, you end up happily poised with an exclamation point in a speech bubble above your head.

It is difficult if not impossible for recent entrants to craft beer to remember the scary time, seemingly ages ago, when flavorful beers were a scarce commodity. In this time, the occasional pint of Sierra Nevada Pale Ale or bottle of Samuel Adams Boston Lager, now derided by some hardened beer geeks as "mainstream brands," offered hope in a dark time. Now nearly omnipresent, these beers and other locally produced pale ales, Hefeweizens, and Porters, along with larger brands, such as Blue Moon Belgian White by Coors, helped teach people about a new world of beer.

The funny thing about The One Beer is that the experience is likely relived in a series of beer sojourns enjoyed over an extended journey into craft beer. For every beer enthusiast, their drinking life is defined by a series of single beers and special moments. These moments happen in the right pub at the right time, with warm weather and the perfect quenching accompaniment, with celebratory occasions with family and friends, and with stolen minutes of personal solace at the end of a long day, each accompanied by the One Beer.

After a lengthy and near-monogamous relationship with Miller Genuine Draft, my own interest in better beer started with my first sip of the famed Guinness Stout. The polar opposite in terms of body, flavor, and overall perception from the American-style premium lagers I grew up with, this gateway beer encouraged me to take my first brewery tour and then experience an impromptu jaunt through dozens of local and imported brands. Next, I visited a new brewpub that opened in my college town and tried my first sampler, which unexpectedly led to my second beer moment. With the first taste of Court Avenue's Blackhawk Stout, I subconsciously learned the difference between the ubiquitous Irish-style Dry Stouts and the sweeter but less popular Export Stout style. With beers from the Vermont Pub's syrupy Wee Heavy to Capital's malty Blonde Doppelbock to Summit's pleasingly bitter IPA, my interest and beer experiences multiplied. And just when I think that I've seen and tasted it all, another beer comes along, like Sly Fox's wonderfully hoppy German-style Pikeland Pils, a canned craft beer, and the process starts again from scratch.

These singular moments, defined by individual brands, serve as path markers for the evolution of a craft beer drinker, from the early days of inexpensive cases of beer to later travels to distant breweries and pubs. In an era where you can order extreme beers from eBay and some of the world's greatest beers are easily available in your local store, it can be easy to lose track of where your interests developed. Losing this focus can also cause a disconnect between yourself and the overwhelming bulk of folks who do not yet share the enthusiasm for the charming marriage of hops and malt.

As someone who can hearken back to that memory, you now have the chance to give some thought to what One Beer could help give a friend or family member their first beer moment.

HISTORY OF BEER STYLES

From the earliest days of commercial brewing, drinkers have relied upon an informal patchwork of descriptions to differentiate the beers available to them. If one brewer's beers were interminably smoky, people knew and told one another. If another had managed to brew a stable product that could last a few extra days, it was worth telling their friends. As brewers experimented with different herbs and spices or different means of drying or heating malts, the flavors in their beers changed. Over centuries, with much taking place in the last 150 years, historians, writers, and brewers have endeavored to capture and convey these differences in meaningful ways for consumers.

Some styles were developed out of wondrous accident, while others were born of necessity, and still more through experimentation and tightly scripted production. Brewers have developed new beer styles from the earliest marriages of grain sugars and hidden airborne yeasts. In the modern age, the fruits of brewing devolve into two main groups: ales and lagers. As previously discussed, ales are made with yeast strains that rise to the top of the fermentation container and require warmer temperatures during fermentation. The resulting flavors are generally fruity and high in esters. Representative examples include Porter, Stout, India Pale Ale, Barley Wine, and Hefeweizen. Lager beer yeast falls to the bottom of the fermentation vessel and benefits from lower temperatures. The resulting beers are typically clean and less estery and include Bock, Pilsener, Dunkel, and Dortmunder. In each of these families, dozens of individual, needy yeast strains demand very specific circumstances in order to produce the desired results.

In contemplating the differences in beers from around the world, critics and historians eventually sought to define them. Cue the controversy as debate still rages today over how to define the world of beer styles, with little agreement on all the specifics. While many less than comprehensive beer style lists have been suggested, the most widely accepted standards today stem from the works of the Brewers Association and the Beer Judge Certification Program, each of which draws heavily upon historical research and defining examples from world-class breweries. The association's present list contains nearly 150 different styles, each of which include a short description of the expected criteria for a properly styled beer: color, body style, aroma and taste flavors, hop bitterness and aroma levels, and ester levels. The guidelines also provide a mind-numbing array of statistical data, including the acceptable style ranges for the beer's original gravity, final gravity, alcohol level, level of bitterness, and color.

While the guidelines are intended to help give brewers guidance and historical perspective for the creation of their recipes and reviewers some objective criteria for the judging of beers, they offer less help to everyday consumers. And while you can certainly have some geeky fun with the numbers, all the average beer drinker requires is a passing knowledge of the differences between beer styles in order to better prepare themselves to find the right beer for them.

In terms of beer guidelines, many beer drinkers have a passing knowledge that the reason German beer is so good is because there is a law protecting its quality. This law, the Reinheitsgebot (literally translated as "purity regulation" or "requirement"), was created as a cross between a taxation law and a way to protect bakers' ingredients, and has long dominated the German beer scene. German brewers and drinkers alike proudly tout the regulation as singular proof that their brewers top everyone else. The history, meaning, and practical effect of this historic regulation, however, are far from clear. In reality, the Purity Law is a convoluted, confounding, and even antiquated idea, the intricacies of which even German brewers do not always seem to comprehend.

In recent years, the conventional wisdom behind beer styles has started to take hits from new critics, including those who believe its underpinnings to be historically inaccurate and others who believe they restrict creativity and should be abandoned altogether. Some well-researched beer historians now contend that many of the classic narratives that writers have been retelling for years, including the Three Threads tale of the invention of Porter and the storied English practice of sending highly hopped pale ales to India (IPAs), are nothing but fictional, feel-good accounts that constitute pub trivia malarkey. While the history lessons surrounding the origins of beer styles and the specific parameters of early examples are interesting, they are perhaps less relevant than the agreed-upon modern representations. Accordingly, this guide touches upon history where it is relevant and reliable, but always strives to define styles in their modern context, in the way the majority of present day brewers, writers, and drinkers understand them.

The more lively debate, however, can be found amongst the brewers themselves, with young, upstart brewers questioning the old guard's affinity for convention and traditional practices. Led by a group of fearless radicals, this quiet rebellion seeks to overthrow the way brewers categorize their beers. These free-form brewers eschew traditional restriction and seek to change the way people think about tasting beer. In focusing their scorn on the beer style guideposts most brewers use, this small band of brewers refuses to adhere to traditional style parameters in the brewing or labeling of their beers. These brewers have suggested that style guidelines place oppressive and arbitrary restraints on their boundless creativity.

While the radicals quietly conspire around the fringes of the brewing world, traditional brewers remain steadfastly dedicated to promoting the importance of brewing within the existing style network, which they note is pretty massive in scope. Regardless of who will eventually prevail in this debate, beer styles provide a necessary check on the beer industry, allowing consumers to judge a particular beer's quality against similarly styled beers they have had. While pushing the envelope of beer is a defining characteristic of the American craft brewing revolution, so is respect for tradition. The constant push and pull between tradition and invention serves the industry and consumers well, and everyone gets to benefit from the evolution and ever-changing nature of the American palate.

IS CRAFT BEER ANYWAY?

———

From the early days of homebrewing and the first pioneers of better beer in the 1960s and 1970s, Americans blazed a trail with little to guide them. Beer with the character of the kind they dreamed of brewing had not been produced in this country in many decades, if ever. Beyond the technical difficulties of figuring out how to brew the beers they read about in old brewing books, these brewers lacked even a basic lexicon to describe what they were doing. And from the earliest days, the media and the public didn't quite know what to make of these new beers.

As a people, Americans have a compulsion to define things, to create a vocabulary that allows them to distinguish between different groups. The overriding tendency is to draw lines of distinction between favored groups to the exclusion of others. This same attitude can be found within the beer industry, where from the earliest days of small craft breweries, a new generation of brewers endeavored to distinguish their efforts from those of the larger corporate breweries. As these new beers clearly departed from conventional, homogenized American lagers, this goal was pretty understandable.

The trouble developed in how to inform the public about these new beers, where a need quickly developed to give a name to their unusual efforts. Despite the general agreement on the need to distinguish their brands from the well-known national beers, these new brewers could never agree on just the right descriptors for their efforts. Should they be called boutique, cottage, artisanal, or specialty breweries? Considering their small sizes, many brewers simply adopted the moniker of "micro-brewers."

The term "microbrewer" quickly caused some unforeseen problems that the small brewers were actually happy to experience. After initially limiting membership to breweries producing less than 3000 barrels (93,000 gallons) of beer a year (then a massive amount for individuals used to homebrewing in five or ten gallon batches) the microbrewers quickly realized that their success was going to eventually force some fellow brewers out of the club. Despite increasing this production limit to 10,000 and then 15,000 barrels, the microbrewers' scorching rise in the 1990s led to a new identity crisis. As small, regional breweries started to float into double-digit growth rates, with some brands, including Boston Beer Company, making several hundred thousand barrels of beer per year, many brewers questioned whether it even made sense to call themselves "micro" anymore.

These same brewers also worried that using the prefix *micro* might suggest that their efforts were minute in terms of both size and seriousness. As smaller brewers transitioned from struggling to survive to a point of growing stability, they abandoned the term "microbrewer" in favor of "craft brewer." Even a decade after most brewers agreed on the change, they are still arguing about what the term "craft" means. This existential debate has taken on a life of its own within the trade group representing the small brewers, where a long-standing, fiery debate has raged over how to describe and define their efforts. When the Brewers Association's governing board established that an "American craft brewer is small, independent and traditional," few brewers complained about the small and traditional components. The association's definition of "independent," which requires that less than 25 percent of the brewery be owned or controlled by a beverage alcohol company that is not itself a craft brewer, became a center of controversy. Suddenly, breweries such as Brewery Ommegang and Mendocino Brewing Company (both owned by foreign breweries), the Jacob Leinenkugel Brewing Company (owned by Miller), and Widmer Brothers Brewing, Redhook Ale Brewery, and Goose Island Brewing (all partly owned by Anheuser-Busch), suddenly no longer qualified as craft brewers.

For the brewers, writers, and consumers who do not agree with the Brewers Association's selected definition, the line drawn has struck a quiet and rare note of discontent within the industry. For their part, supporters of the definition adopted by the association, whose membership includes hundreds of small, medium, and large-sized breweries from around the country, endeavor everyday to distinguish their efforts from those of the nation's largest breweries. And while most beer drinkers generally understand the difference between the work and products of smaller brewers versus those of the bigger brewing operations, even these lines are starting to blur. With an eye towards the success experienced by craft brewers, Anheuser-Busch InBev, MillerCoors, and other large breweries have ramped up the production of their own flavorful beers to counteract the advances made by smaller brewers. These breweries have even dared to co-opt the language of smaller breweries, advertising their specialty offerings as "crafting a better beer."

And while terms such as *micro* and *craft* conjure up images of tiny garage breweries, the overwhelming majority of brewing operations do not live up to this outdated vision. When it comes to craft beer, no word is thrown around so casually as "handcrafted." From its earliest days, craft brewers have wrapped their brands in romance with allusions to the hands-on nature of their brewing operations. The starry-eyed reference paints a picture of a lone brewer, engulfed in the steam of a boiling brew, gently stirring a heavy mash rake in a smoldering copper cauldron. At just the perfect moment in these fairy tales, the master craftsman carefully and delicately adds a pinch of hops, all the while acting as part artisan, part considerate usher.

These colorful fables endure for many consumers until they finally visit a brewery for the first time, when the mythical land of hop pixies and malt elves quickly dissolves into a semi-chaotic world filled with snaking hoses, water puddles, gurgling buckets of foamy particulates, and the occasional stench of caustic in the air. The genteel notion of handcrafting also takes a bit of a hit as today's brewing operations are generally more akin to an industrial factory or a computer programming suite.

Relieved of this dreamy vision of brewing, it remains important to note that making beer is hot, sweaty, and difficult work undertaken by strong people who also have a creative and passionate side that is reflected in their beers. Without both the technical yin and the artisanal yang, you would be left with some disappointing results. When applied to pottery shaping, model ship building, or log cabin construction, the phrase handcrafted seems apt. When discussing modern brewing operations, handcrafted seems an overly romanticized and at times misleading descriptor, even when applied to America's smaller breweries. And that is for the best, as those romantic old days really stunk for the overworked brewer. If you want to experience such small operations in action today, try stopping by your local brewpub and offer to lend a hand lugging around fifty-pound bags of malt.

As craft breweries mature from tiny micros to small regional players and even larger national operations, their brewing systems and operations should match their improved business practices. Automation is a friend to both consumers and brewers, where stainless steel and computers regulate and stabilize all measures of the brewing trade and eventually result in the improved quality of the pint in front of you. At its best, brewing will always remain one part art and one part science, with the calculus lying between the two resulting in the true beauty of beer.

The questions over how to define craft beer and distinguish the efforts and products of smaller brewers from those that have so long dominated the American beer scene will continue to increase in difficulty in coming years as craft breweries grow more successful. Once one of the smaller brewing businesses in America, the Boston Beer Company now produces around two million barrels of beer per year and stands, after recent industry consolidations, as the largest American owned brewery. Breweries such as Sierra Nevada Brewing Company and New Belgium Brewing Company, now both national brands, continue to grow and expand at steady rates. If a definition of craft beer is anchored to a brewery's size, it remains difficult to figure out how these large craft brewers fit in a category with the 200 barrel producing brewpub down the street.

If you take size out of the equation, then how do you define craft? The oft-cited label of craft beer applying to beers produced by someone other than the biggest brewers tends to quickly degrade when applied to imported beers, such as Guinness, Bass, Hoegaarden, and Paulaner, which are also brewed by corporate behemoths. And if corporate ties are enough to get you booted from the craft club, what about the smaller breweries that are also listed on stock exchanges? Can a difference be drawn between a small brewery that brews beers for Miller and has accepted its money to update its facilities and those craft breweries that enter into partnership deals with larger breweries?

Finally, what can you make of the full-flavored beers produced by the big brewers? Some beer enthusiasts deride such offerings from Anheuser-Busch, Miller, and Coors as 'faux-craft' beers. One beer in particular, Blue Moon Belgian White, draws the particular ire of craft brewers who both fear and covet its meteoric rise in sales. They complain that many consumers don't know that it's brewed by Coors Brewing Company (now Molson Coors and even MillerCoors) and this news does indeed come as a bit of a surprise to drinkers who favor its luminous yellow color and orange slice. For its part, Coors admits that it is not actively trying to key American drinkers into the fact it makes this popular sleeper. Should it matter that the beer, which is a perfectly passable version of the Witbier style, is produced by a company that also makes millions upon millions of barrels of light beer? While consumers have a valid truth-in-labeling complaint, does that change the fact that countless new drinkers have tried the brand, enjoyed it, and gone on to try other beers beyond their familiar light offerings? That Coors has long treated Blue Moon with respect demonstrates that a larger brewery can indeed produce and promote full-flavored beers.

So if a beer is enjoyable when consumed blind to beer politics, should that be the end of the matter? In the end, shouldn't the question always be whether the beer is any good? While many beer geeks deny that such beers qualify as craft, I would doubt their abilities to single out the Michelob Porter, Miller 1880 Barley Wine, or Coors Barmen Pilsner as macro pariahs in a blind tasting of beers. Debating which breweries qualify as craft sometimes seems as futile as questioning whether somebody is punk enough to be a punk rocker. When beer devolves into a game of us versus them, the craft label is rendered an empty, political term. Rather than constantly recalculating production numbers and updating team rosters, consumers should focus more on the character of the aromas and flavors in their pints—and less on classifying the places that brew them.

FOR ALL SEASONS

Another great selling point of beer is its seasonal appeal. For every change in the weather, from warm to cool, sun to snow, there is a beer style to meet the occasion. In the chilling months of winter, frostbitten beer drinkers sooth their shivering souls with dark, hearty beers, including Bock, Porter, and Imperial Stout. With the brightening of days and spirits, the new dance of summer's renewing sunshine requires the selection of new beers, including Hefeweizen, Dortmunder, and India Pale Ale.

Brewers have long embraced the changing consumer drinking patterns that accompany shifting weather patterns, helping fuel the demand for seasonal products. These beers often appear as little known styles, such as Kolsch or Helles, simply to be rebranded by savvy breweries as "summer ales." People usually associate the summer months with the typical 'lawn-mower beer,' often a freezing cold light lager, preferably in a can, with little hop bite, a low level of malt, and not much character to get in the way of refreshment. These beers certainly hit the spot on a hot day and will forever hold a place in the hearts of home gardeners everywhere. For the more discriminating beer drinker, the warmer season offers opportunities to enjoy a wide range of styles and flavors that are equally as refreshing as the can of 'lite.' These Easy Drinkers and Cool and Refreshing beers, including Hefeweizen, Witbier, and Cream Ale, offer crisp, refreshing, and thirst-quenching qualities, all without forsaking flavor.

When the weather turns cold, craft brewers offer a new set of beers to meet the physically and mentally challenging conditions and prospects of summer's distant return. The term "Winter Warmer," or "winter ale," can accommodate several different styles, all providing a robust, hearty drink to cozy up to in colder days. While less popular than the summer beers, these beers, which include dunkels, barley wines, and imperial stouts, help fortify people and lift their spirits.

Eventually, brewers expanded beyond mere summer and winter beers and started offering several different seasonal beers throughout the year. With the demands of wholesalers and retailers, the panoply of offerings has solidified into a routine of particular seasonal styles. Starting in the spring, you'll see the release of bocks and maibocks, or blonde bocks, hearty and malt-forward lagers that help welcome springtime through-out Germany. Following the hefeweizens, witbiers, and golden ales of summer, autumn beholds a plenty bounty of great beers, ranging from malty Oktoberfest-style offerings to spicy pumpkin beers.

As you develop a better understanding of beer styles, your impressions of what constitutes the perfect beer for the moment often changes dra-matically. Where you once might have reached for the refreshing qualities of a banana-filled Hefeweizen in July, now you'll think of perhaps reach-ing for a robust Imperial Stout, matching the sticky thickness of humidity with the terminal viscosity of malt and alcohol. Many breweries, includ-ing the Stone Brewing Company of San Diego, California, now release their biggest beers, such as their Stone Imperial Stout, in the middle of the summer to the cheers of beer enthusiasts. Other beer lovers put aside the comforts of golden ales for the challenges of mouth-puckeringly sour Berliner Weisse, the refreshing spiciness of rye beers, or the tart acidity of an American Wild Ale.

And while breweries love to see the popularity of their seasonal offer-ings, consumers sometimes complain that they cannot get these limited release offerings year-round. In response to this demand, many seasonal beers, such as Magic Hat's Fruity #9 and the Harpoon Brewery's now-flagship IPA, have gone on to secure placement in their brewery's permanent portfolio. These beers and many others succeeded in seasonal test runs only to be called from the bullpen to the regular rotation after positive response from excited consumers.

Despite the occasional crowing for an Oktoberfest in May or a Kolsch in December, everyone agrees that there is something special about antic-ipating all of the joys that accompany each new season, be they the blooming of perennials, the summer solstice, the brilliant colors of falling leaves, or the gleam of a first snowfall. And there is certainly something special about getting to enjoy a special, limited release beer alongside each of these memorable moments. Perhaps there is something to be said about beers that are not available every day.

THE SESSION BEER

Americans don't have much experience in consciously limiting their alcohol intake. Our history has been punctuated with periods of government enforced moderation or prohibition and our doctors repeatedly inform us of the health benefits of limiting alcohol consumption. But as a drinking populace, Americans have not yet embraced the concept of session drinking, or purposely selecting lower alcohol products in order to sustain a lengthier drinking session. Most people have just generally viewed alcohol as a means to a socially lubricating end.

The origins of the term "session drinking," as with all things beer history, are a little hazy, but the concept remains a relatively accessible one. A session beer is one that allows its imbiber to consume several glasses over a few hours without becoming disturbingly and painfully drunk. The term can be applied to many styles of beer and doesn't reference any particular method of production beyond lower booze content. This idea of lower alcohol beer comes with some negative perceptional baggage here in the United States. With the legacy of Prohibition era "near beer," 3.2 beer, and modern non-alcoholic offerings, the concept of session beer can often times be a hard sell. For starters, we're not talking about *no* alcohol, just lower alcohol than usual, which compared to the elevated ABVs (alcohol by volume) of modern craft beers may hardly seem slight. In defining session beers, this can refer to any beer that possesses less than 5 percent alcohol by volume, even though the British tend to apply the term to beers less than 4 percent. While the British definition is certainly a truer acknowledgment of the powerful physiological effects of alcohol, American brewers don't actually make very many beers that weigh in at 3.5 percent. That is a bit of a shame, as many British brewers have demonstrated that their session beers, while small in alcoholic prowess, are anything but diminutive in terms of flavor. When viewed through the bottom of a 20-ounce British Imperial pint, however, it's easy to understand why they felt compelled to shave an extra point or so of alcohol off their session sipping beers.

It can be challenging today for the drinker looking to undertake a session of beer enjoyment without incurring the taxing if pleasant after effects of alcohol. For one, most bars don't list the alcohol levels in the beers they serve unless it is mandated by law. So undertaking a true session might require asking the bartender about his or her selections, or doing a little advanced legwork. With that said, certain beer styles are often safer bets in terms of limiting your alcohol intake. These styles include Mild, Golden Ale, Kolsch, Hefeweizen, American Wheat Ale, Witbier, American Pale Ale, and many fruit beers. But substantial alcohol deviations can appear in individual brands so even this list is anything but a sure bet. The best option is to come armed with a little knowledge, ask the bartender, or patronize better beer bars that provide you with a descriptive menu.

It's important to note that the best session beers provide a focused and complex flavor experience without relying upon the diverse flavors and aromas contributed by alcohol. By selecting high quality and flavorful malts, brewers can produce highly drinkable and nuanced beers that sustain your interest every bit as much as boozier offerings. Hop heads need not worry either, as brewers remain fully capable of brewing less robust beers that still pack the full range of hoppy aromas, flavors, and bitterness levels. For example, the Stone Brewing Company, celebrated by hop and alcohol fans alike, brews a beer called Levitation that gives consumers a rise—not from alcohol, but from prodigious amounts of Amarillo, Simcoe, and Columbus hops. With its snappy hop aroma and pleasant malt flavors, you'd never guess Levitation weighed in at a meager 4.4 percent alcohol. Such American beers result in curious twists on the old session beer concept.

So next time you're getting ready to sit down for a few beers and some conversation, take a moment to think about the alcohol levels in the pints you're drinking and consider experiencing a new side of light beer, with a full-flavored but less boozy craft offering.

CHAPTER TWO

THE STYLE AND FLAVOR OF BEER

Pick a flavor, any flavor, and there is a beer that can match it. Choose any aroma you favor, and an ale or lager exists to mimic its essence and please your palate in the process. Endlessly creative American brewers have concocted all manner of delicious and nuanced beverages, from IPAs chock-full of grapefruit and orange aromas, to Belgian-style tripels that taste like bananas and Wrigley's Juicy Fruit gum, to stouts brimming with smooth, inviting coffee and chocolate notes. Much like young Charlie entering Willy Wonka's Chocolate Factory, if you can imagine the beer you want to drink, inventive brewers can brew it. From clean, subtle, and cool lagers to palate bullying hop monsters and every hint of floral fruit, bready sweetness, or funky flavor in between, the wide world of American brewing creativity is bound only by the imaginations of its passionate brewers and the courage of adventurous consumers.

This chapter seeks to play gustatory matchmaker for the flavors you want to enjoy in your pints. Despite all of the diversity available today, many people fail to try new beers, in part because they do not realize the wide range of flavors available for sampling. Or, you may simply not know what flavors you like in beer. You may be a little afraid of bitterness or shy away from dark colors or roasted notes. All the while, the range of beer styles actually offers you safe, approachable harbors such as the Schwarzbier, a dark, brooding beer that appears menacing but is actually airy light in body and flavor.

When it comes to choosing a can of soda or a scoop of ice cream, you tend to go with the flavors that you enjoy, and the decision is relatively easy because you know what you like. If you already know what flavors you enjoy in other foods and beverages, there is no reason you cannot apply the same approach when it comes to choosing your next beer.

This chapter focuses on familiar, approachable, and easily recognizable flavor sets. When you know how to group styles together based upon their shared characteristics and draw parallels between the flavors of food and drink that you already know and enjoy, you can greatly simplify the experience of choosing the beers you want to drink. When faced with a lengthy tap list in a pub or a cooler full of countless six-packs, you may scan for a familiar name because you have never really understood the differences in the available styles enough to recognize the ones you enjoy. Now, if you know you enjoy banana fruit flavors or happen to be in the mood for something roasted or chocolaty, the selection process gets a lot easier.

While there is no need to understand the complete intricacies of dozens of beer styles, a little knowledge can enhance your enjoyment, like knowing the songs at a concert. It's time to explore a little history about the dozens of beer styles you can find in local stores and bars. By no means meant to be authoritative, definitive, or complete, the brief descriptions here simply give you an easily accessible dose of basic information for exploring the world of craft beer. In the end, however, it will always be easier to understand a handful of common flavor pairings than to remember the subtle distinctions in sixty styles or more.

Creating a list of the best beers from the litany of great American craft brewers turns out to be a pretty daunting and restless task. While the tasting part certainly has its moments, the winnowing process leaves a substantial number of excellent brewers out in the cold. In this guide, I've endeavored to present you with the very best beers from the top breweries in the selected styles. While not always resolute in my devotion to the doctrine of style guidelines, I have attempted to shadow their widely-accepted framework. After pursuing the listed offerings, you may find that a beer from your favorite brewery has been left out. In reviewing more than a thousand beers from several hundred breweries, be sure to understand that this is not necessarily a reflection on the quality of breweries that don't find their way into these pages. The reviews remain a snapshot of several excellent beers in a style, not the final word on the only acceptable options.

Several great brand ambassadors for the respective beer styles profiled are listed here for your review and choosing. The beers are described in straightforward and plain language designed to preview the experience that awaits you, including the appearance, aroma, flavor, and finish. The reviews start with the selected beer's name, the brewery that produces it, along with relevant contact information. Each beer's alcohol content is listed by volume to give you an idea of the relative strength of the offerings. As beers from various styles can benefit greatly from different glassware, the reviews suggest a glass or two that will help complement each style. If you want to learn more about the particular glassware noted in the reviews, feel free to skip ahead to the *Picking The Right Glass For The Right Moment* on page 254. Each review also lets you know whether the beer is a product the brewery makes year-round or only during certain seasons or times during the year. For those offerings listed as "Limited Release," the beers may only be sold to the public at very infrequent times of the year and may sometimes be difficult to procure. As it can be frustrating to read about an unattainable beer, I've tried to restrict the number of beers that are harder to find than Sasquatch. I've also tried to create a balance between the beers produced by production breweries, whose products are primarily purchased and enjoyed off-premise, and brewpubs, whose beers are generally enjoyed in-house. As brewpub beers rarely get distributed too far from their central base of operations, beers from production breweries tend to outnumber those from brewpubs in the following pages. While a great deal of work went into crafting a balanced list of beers—with some consideration given to geographic diversity and product availability—it's important to keep in mind that breweries frequently change their lineups and some beers may occasionally get dropped from portfolios, while others may transition from seasonal to year-round release. If your heart is set on trying a particular beer that you can't quite seem to find, feel free to give the brewery a call for some assistance.

If you're ready to take the leap into the deep end of the craft beer pool, feel free to skip ahead to the section that best fits your mood. Do you want something Cool and Refreshing? Let me suggest a hazy, luminous Hefeweizen filled with fruit and banana flavors and served in a long, tall, and shapely weizen glass. Or perhaps something a touch hoppier in the Heavenly Hoppy section, such as a zesty, clean, and pleasingly bitter German Pilsener. If you are in the mood for a slightly sweeter beer packed with cherry flavors, try the Lush and Fruity section. Or maybe you prefer to live on the edge and want a high octane, bourbon barrel-aged behemoth listed in the Extreme Tastes section. Whatever mood you are in and whatever flavor you desire, you can find it here. Because when it comes to making your selection, it is all about finding the right beer for the right moment. Cheers.

EASY DRINKERS

Don't you dare use the "L" word to describe this group of approachable and thirst quenching beers. While they might hit the spot after an hour mowing the grass, they are far from your typical lawnmower beers. Beyond mere extensions of the ubiquitous American-style lager, these lighter bodied styles are distinctive, wonderfully expressive beers with independent and valuable characteristics that deserve to be appreciated. Generally lower in alcohol, Easy Drinkers offer the session drinker an opportunity to sample a few in a sitting, all without palate or alcohol fatigue. Striking in appearance, the beers are uniformly bright and brilliantly hued, often beaming in yellow and golden colors from clean glassware, hopefully with sizable, sustained foamy white heads.

Often overlooked by hard-core beer geeks, Easy Drinkers represent focused offerings with clean malt and hop flavors, whose subtlety is a thing of beauty too often lost in the sea of palate-bruising bigger beers. Their flavors range from soft and gentle hop grassiness to bready and light malt toastiness, depending upon the style, all while remaining accessible for novice drinkers looking to go beyond their usual macro-produced favorites.

Beers in the Easy Drinkers category also serve as a useful means for judging the overall quality of a brewery. If a brewery's lighter, more delicate ales and lagers are clean, crisp, and flavorful, it's a good sign that the brewer knows his trade. With the absence of prodigious hop and malt additions, there is simply nowhere to hide flaws in these lighter styles.

BLONDE ALE/GOLDEN ALE

As with many styles, the Blonde Ale style is a twist on another classic style, this time the German Kolsch. Very light in color, usually pale gold or straw, the best examples are crisp and dry, well-attenuated, with a mild maltiness for balance. A popular entry-level take on the prototypical American lager, craft brewers often use the beer to transition macro drinkers to a more flavorful alternative. Sometimes called golden ales, different versions of this beer may weigh heavier on the bready or toasted malt side or even exhibit some mild bitterness and a light fruitiness.

Golden Ale

ST. GEORGE BREWING COMPANY
HAMPTON, VIRGINIA
WWW.STGEORGEBREWINGCO.COM
ALCOHOL CONTENT: 5.5% ABV
GLASSWARE: PINT
AVAILABILITY: YEAR-ROUND

So hard to define is the Golden Ale style within the craft beer industry that many of the best examples quietly masquerade as different styles. This offering from the St. George Brewing Company skirts the line between a typical Golden Ale and something a touch hoppier. Despite its name, the beer cascades with a straightforward amber hue with tinges of light orange and gold and an off-white head. This beer favors a slightly European maltier side, with preferences towards mild toasted and caramel notes, all mixed together with a touch of citrus and a fruit base. The hops impart a light grassy and spicy quality alongside a moderate level of bitterness that rounds out the long, dry finish.

Bombshell Blonde

SOUTHERN STAR BREWING COMPANY
CONROE, TEXAS
WWW.SOUTHERNSTARBREWERY.COM
ALCOHOL CONTENT: 5.25% ABV
GLASSWARE: PINT
AVAILABILITY: YEAR-ROUND

A canned offering from this classic Texas brewery, the Bombshell is not nearly as robust as its name suggests. The gold colored beer with hints of amber pours with a fluffy white head and a tight level of carbonation. The aroma is filled with hints of fresh baked bread, touches of wheat and an overall malty disposition. The flavor follows suit, with the additions of a light fruit hint and some noble hop earthiness, and finishes up clean, crisp, and refreshing.

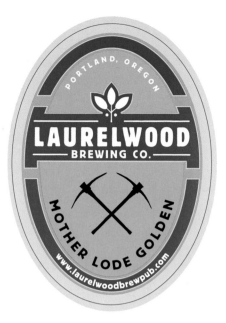

Bailey's Ale

CISCO BREWERS
NANTUCKET, MASSACHUSETTS
WWW.CISCOBREWERS.COM
ALCOHOL CONTENT: 7.5% ABV
GLASSWARE: PINT
AVAILABILITY: YEAR-ROUND

From the brewer tucked away on the island of Nantucket, off Cape Cod's southern coast, this full-bodied golden ale is a touch stronger in terms of alcohol and flavor than most traditional versions of the style. Often served in a 750-milliliter bottle, Bailey's pours a deep gold color with orange hints and substantial lacing. The nose boasts an eclectic array of grassy, fruity, and lightly malty aromas, clean and encouraging, with a touch of carbonation bite and zest. The medium body offers another round of light pale maltiness mixed with an earthy hop character and a solid, present bitterness that continues through to a mildly fruity finish. A definite step up from more tepid Blonde Ale offerings.

Mother Lode Golden Ale

LAURELWOOD BREWING COMPANY
PORTLAND, OREGON
WWW.LAURELWOODBREWPUB.COM
ALCOHOL CONTENT: 5.1% ABV
GLASSWARE: PINT
AVAILABILITY: YEAR-ROUND

This award-winning gem from Portland's popular Laurelwood group of brewpubs pours with a slightly dull golden yellow color and slight lacey head. The somewhat hoppy aroma is laced with equal parts earth and citrus, with an herbal quality that floats through from time to time. As balance is key with this style, the countervailing toasted malt flavors offer a bready contrast to the earthy hop flavors, which gives it a slightly Germanic touch. Smooth, accessible, and mellow without being boring, Laurelwood's Golden Ale remains a great session offering.

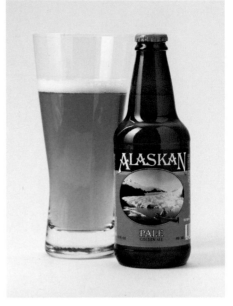

Aud Blonde
RUSSIAN RIVER BREWING COMPANY
SANTA ROSA, CALIFORNIA
WWW.RUSSIANRIVERBREWING.COM
ALCOHOL CONTENT: 4.5% ABV
GLASSWARE: PINT
AVAILABILITY: YEAR-ROUND

Russian River is best known for its eclectic work with sour and barrel-aged beers, having turned out some of the most interesting craft beers available. The brewery's Aud Blonde is easily its most overlooked treasure. Pouring light pale gold in color with a wispy, soft white head that quickly retreats, this surprisingly character-rich blonde ale boasts a mild grainy pilsner malt note of European origin with a touch of citrus. The beer deftly presents with a light body that still manages to pack in some well-trained earthiness, a light bitterness, and a citric zing, all resulting in a very drinkable and quenching beer. Crisp and clean from start to finish, the occasional peaks of bitterness and fruit punctuate an otherwise sturdy and reliably soft golden ale. This ale goes to show that tending towards a brewery's biggest and baddest beers is not always the way to go.

Alaskan Pale
ALASKAN BREWING COMPANY
JUNEAU, ALASKA
WWW.ALASKANBEER.COM
ALCOHOL CONTENT: 5.2% ABV
GLASSWARE: PINT
AVAILABILITY: YEAR-ROUND

Another one of those style-bending beers if you simply go by the name, the "Pale" in this Alaskan's name refers to its color not to its categorization as a Pale Ale family member. Pouring a bright off-golden color with a substantial creamy white head, the nose zips with a creative mixture of citrus and earth, a blend of the European and Pacific Northwest hops employed in this beer. A sustained level of crispness defines this drinkable beer, starting with a soft, biscuity malt body that gives way to playful tinges of floral fruit, touches of earth, and a hint of hop spiciness throughout for good measure. The beer finishes dry and its moderate to low bitterness cleans up for a smooth finish.

CREAM ALE

One of a handful of truly American styles of beer to pre-date the craft beer movement, Cream Ale is often described as a hybrid-style, bridging the gap between ales and lagers. Brewed with either an ale or lager yeast (and occasionally both) sometimes warm fermented and cold conditioned, the style was created to compete with the developing American light lager category. Larger brewers will sometimes use adjuncts, such as rice or corn, to help lighten the beer's body, while craft brewers often choose to produce fuller all-malt varieties. Cream Ales and Lagers are pale in color, light in body, with very little bitterness, a mild fruit ester aroma, and a gentle pale malt flavor that is smoothed out when lagered.

Coon Rock Cream Ale

LAKE LOUIE BREWING COMPANY
ARENA, WISCONSIN
WWW.LAKELOUIE.COM
ALCOHOL CONTENT: 5.0% ABV
GLASSWARE: PINT
AVAILABILITY: YEAR-ROUND

The tiny Lake Louie Brewing Company makes some surprisingly big and bold beers, but Coon Rock Cream Ale is not one of them. Instead, the brewers set out to brew a Midwestern classic, a throwback to a different era of drinking. The beer possesses a hazy amber-golden color, almost almond in nature, with honey highlights. The aroma is crisp and full of a pleasant, mildly sweet corn character that comes from the ingredient's use in the mash. Spot on for its style, Coon Rock showcases a mildly sweet pale malt that gives way into a quickly changing bevy of flavors, from butter to honey with touches of citrus, eventually finishing with a clean, crisp, and lightly fruity bow.

Sirius Ale

LAGUNITAS BREWING COMPANY
PETALUMA, CALIFORNIA
WWW.LAGUNITAS.COM
ALCOHOL CONTENT: 7.0% ABV
GLASSWARE: PINT
AVAILABILITY: SUMMER

This bigger offering from Lagunitas starts with a translucent orange hue and a craggy off-white head. The aroma is filled with fresh candy malt notes, wrapped in thin blankets of herbal, grassy, and slightly fruity hop notes. Upping the alcohol level here results in some rather unusual complexity, bounding from the honey-like malt notes to an array of fruits, including orange and apple, and topped off with a mild earthy backbone. The finish remains dry, with fruity and bitter hop accents, and the cold-conditioning that often mellows the Cream Ale style occasionally peeks its head through the layered mixture of flavors. A step up in terms of flavor from many more traditional Cream Ales.

Kiwanda Cream Ale

PELICAN PUB AND BREWERY
PACIFIC CITY, OREGON
WWW.PELICANBREWERY.COM
ALCOHOL CONTENT: 5.1% ABV
GLASSWARE: PINT
AVAILABILITY: YEAR-ROUND

This multiple award-winning beer starts with a brilliant and bright golden color and a moderate head. The Kiwanda's nose is filled with light fruity notes of orange, passion fruit, and the slightest bit of lemon. Benefiting from the mellowing effects of cold-conditioning, the resulting flavor is very light and smooth, mainly dotted by citrus fruit notes and a reserved maltiness, all bound together with an effervescent carbonation. The initial burst of light fruity flavors, followed by the smooth, simple malty backbone, makes for a soft but character-rich drinking experience.

Cream Ale

LAUGHING DOG BREWING COMPANY
PONDERAY, IDAHO
WWW.LAUGHINGDOGBREWING.COM
ALCOHOL CONTENT: 5.0% ABV
GLASSWARE: PINT
AVAILABILITY: YEAR-ROUND

Laughing Dog's Cream Ale presents with a mild golden-straw color and a loose white head that quickly fades. The aroma is very reminiscent of a bakery, filled with fresh bready aromas and touches of caramel and toasted malt, with a lingering spiciness deep in its core. The mild-mannered flavor exhibits the benefits of lagering this style, with hints of bready, toasted malts, sweet corn additions, and a mildly hop zest and resin to balance the whole package out.

Designed for the discerning, modern palate HaverAle is fermented warm for a fruity nose, lagered for a crisp, dry finish, and then filtered to sparkling perfection with a hint of herbal hops.

Haverhill, the "Queen Slipper City", was once home to over 100 shoe factories.

Haverhill Brewery dedicates this light but substantial cream ale for those who need to kick back after clocking out from a hard day's work.

WWW.HAVERHILLBREWERY.COM

HaverAle

THE TAP BREWPUB
HAVERHILL, MASSACHUSETTS
WWW.TAPBREWPUB.COM
ALCOHOL CONTENT: 4.5% ABV
GLASSWARE: PINT
AVAILABILITY: YEAR-ROUND

This brewpub, located in an historic building in the northern Massachusetts town of Haverhill, uses its Cream Ale as an entry-level beer for its beer-wary customers. As a tool towards this end, the HaverAle boasts a deep golden color with a moderate off-white head that leaves some lacing on the glass. Full of caramel and toasted malt notes, with hints of fruit and a touch of earthy hops, the aroma well-characterizes this classic American style's balance between ale and lager characteristics. The ensuing flavor tends towards the maltier side, with caramel taking the lead, followed by a mellow fruity finish.

Angry Angel

BIG BOSS BREWING COMPANY
RALEIGH, NORTH CAROLINA
WWW.BIGBOSSBREWING.COM
ALCOHOL CONTENT: 4.5% ABV
GLASSWARE: PINT
AVAILABILITY: YEAR-ROUND

Listed as a Kolsch style beer by the brewery, I think the Angry Angel also does well under the Cream Ale heading due to its extended period of cold fermentation and conditioning. This heavenly delight pours with a deep and hazy golden amber color and loose carbonation level. The aroma delightfully balances a blend of biscuit and toasted malt notes with well-composed, floral fruit hop flairs to tempt the first sip. With a relatively low alcohol level, this beer provides the equilibrium you hope for when weighing the ingredients in this style.

KÖLSCH

The classic and popular Kölsch style hails from the brewing city of Cologne ('Köln' in German), on the Rhine River in Germany's northwest corner. Still brewed at several locations in the city, the Kölsch (pronounced 'kull-shh' or 'cool-shh') style was eagerly adopted in the early days by craft brewers seeking to make an inviting crossover beer for flavor-wary customers. Most American varieties claiming to be of this delicate yet impressive style are lighter and less flavorful than those found in its home city. Possessing a light, radiant golden color and a sizable, well-sustained white head, true Kölsch beers maintain a subtle balance between dryness and sweetness, soft but not cloying malts, and a touch of fruitiness that makes for one of the world's most drinkable and refreshing styles.

Copper Hill Kölsch

THE CAMBRIDGE HOUSE BREW PUB
GRANBY, CONNECTICUT
WWW.CBHBREW.COM
ALCOHOL CONTENT: 5.1% ABV
GLASSWARE: PINT
AVAILABILITY: YEAR-ROUND

A two location brew pub operation, Cambridge House seeks to bring top-notch ales to the otherwise beer desert of northern Connecticut. For new entrants to craft beer, Cambridge House suggests a bit of a bait-and-switch with its deceptively complex Kölsch. With a pale straw color, a moderate white head, and clean and balanced aroma, Copper Hill looks innocuous enough. The flavor, however, distinguishes this beer from other attempts at the style. A light pale malt sweetness parades forward, followed by a lightly fruity hop charge and finally a crisp crack of spicy hop bitterness, managing the rare achievement of accessibility and flavor-forward power all at once.

Kölsch

BREWERS ALLEY BREWING COMPANY
FREDERICK, MARYLAND
WWW.BREWERS-ALLEY.COM
ALCOHOL CONTENT: 5.0% ABV
GLASSWARE: PINT
AVAILABILITY: YEAR-ROUND

This Maryland brewpub produces an excellent Kölsch that mimics some of the slightly sweeter versions found in the Cologne region of Germany. Its honey-yellow gold color displays a soft crown of craggy foam and floral and bready aromas that lift you back to the Old Country. The bouquet of floral hops mixes in with a sweeter, lightly toasted malt flavor and finishes with a kiss of hops for a crisp and rounding bitterness. A very respectable version of this classic German ale style.

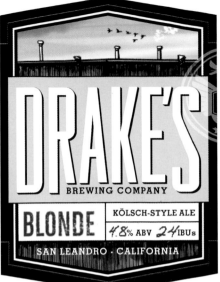

Summer Beer

HARPOON BREWERY
BOSTON, MASSACHUSETTS
WWW.HARPOONBREWERY.COM
ALCOHOL CONTENT: 5.0% ABV
GLASSWARE: PINT
AVAILABILITY: SUMMER

Presenting with a dull straw color and a waifish off-white head, this Kölsch smells and tastes firmly of clean malt and a touch of grassy earth. The nose starts with a partially grainy blend of wheat and a floral and mildly spicy hop earthiness with a fleeting touch of lemon. The appropriately named Summer Beer's taste is surprisingly hoppy at times, but never overpowering, considering the style. An untoasted grain flavor melds with a slightly sweet hint but continues dry through to a drawn-out and pleasantly zesty and bitter finish.

Blonde Ale

DRAKE'S BREWING COMPANY
SAN LEANDRO, CALIFORNIA
WWW.DRINKDRAKES.COM
ALCOHOL CONTENT: 4.8% ABV
GLASSWARE: PINT
AVAILABILITY: YEAR-ROUND

With a shimmering yellow golden color and a prodigious white cap of foam, Drake's Blonde Ale makes quite an impression at first glimpse. The beer's nose is punctuated with an airy quality that dances between pilsner-style hoppiness and a softer, gentler maltiness. The malts cascade across the palate in a well-orchestrated entrance, leading towards a lovely and smooth finish of herby and zesty hop flavors. The beer's mellow quality derives from its extended period of cold-conditioning.

Schlafly Kölsch

THE SAINT LOUIS BREWERY
SAINT LOUIS, MISSOURI
WWW.SCHLAFLY.COM
ALCOHOL CONTENT: 4.8% ABV
GLASSWARE: PINT
AVAILABILITY: YEAR-ROUND

A lovely marigold yellow color with a continual rush of carbonated bubbles, the aroma jumps out with handshakes of floral hops and bready malts. Filled with grassy and earthy notes mixed with slight fruit hints, Kolsch's aroma remains engaging, especially for hopheads. While it certainly contains a strong noble hop level, resulting in some lemon and earthy notes, the balancing cereal grain malt flavors serve to equalize the scales for malt lovers. Offering more than a refreshing break from the summer heat, Schlafly Kolsch remains a great session beer for year-round drinking.

Fancy Lawnmower Beer

SAINT ARNOLD BREWING COMPANY
HOUSTON, TEXAS
WWW.SAINTARNOLD.COM
ALCOHOL CONTENT: 4.9% ABV
GLASSWARE: PINT
AVAILABILITY: YEAR-ROUND

This creatively named beer from Texas's oldest craft brewery exhibits a playful quality, both in temperament and substance, which brings an additional touch of fun to drinking. Great for tailgating at college football games or as a refreshment after yard work, this mildly cloudy (with yeast added) yellow-gold colored beer gives off a straightforward yet absorbing aroma of herbal, grassy, and spicy hops, mingled with pale malt and a smidge of wheat. Clean and crisp from start to finish, the mild hop bitterness and flavor shine through, resulting in a highly drinkable summer beer.

DORTMUNDER

Things tend to get a bit hazy when contemplating the distinctions between certain European lager styles, but it is slight differences that make these beers classics. Take the Dortmunder style for example, a nineteenth-century development of the German town of the same name. Dortmunder beers, occasionally referred to as Export due to an old German tax system designation, offer the best of both beer worlds; a sweet and sometimes bready European malt flavor, similar to the Helles style, mixed with a pronounced mid-level bitterness and noble hoppiness, reminiscent of the German Pilsener branch of lager brewing. Though it is a style that is having great difficulty retaining interest in its home country, Americans still produce a handful of excellent versions of this classic style.

Dominion Lager

OLD DOMINION BREWING COMPANY
DOVER, DELAWARE
WWW.OLDDOMINION.COM
ALCOHOL CONTENT: 5.6% ABV
GLASSWARE: PINT
AVAILABILITY: YEAR-ROUND

Once the pride of the Virginia craft beer scene, the Old Dominion brewery was sold in 2007 to a joint venture between the Fordham Brewing Company and Anheuser-Busch. Now brewed in Delaware, the golden amber colored beer offers a strong white cap of sticky foam. The nose suggests a balance of lightly sweet and toasted malt curbed by soft, herbal noble hops. A lightly buttery quality balances against the substantial maltiness and finishes with a lingering earthy quality that remains eminently drinkable.

Hoster Gold Top

HOSTER BREWING COMPANY
COLUMBUS, OHIO
WWW.HOSTERBEER.COM
ALCOHOL CONTENT: 5.0% ABV
GLASSWARE: PINT
AVAILABILITY: YEAR-ROUND

It is far from intentional that many of the Dortmunder style beers profiled in this section hail from the Midwest. While craft lager beer has not yet taken off in all parts of the country, states such as Ohio have embraced the Old World German classic styles. This flagship brand pours with a deep golden color and a moderate foamy white head. The aroma extends swirls of bready malt and a touch of earthy hops. The Gold Top's flavor continues with additions of toasted and bready malts, a mild grainy hoppiness, and minute citrus notes that dash across the palate.

Summer of Lager

CISCO BREWERS
NANTUCKET, MASSACHUSETTS
WWW.CISCOBREWERS.COM
ALCOHOL CONTENT: 6.2% ABV
GLASSWARE: PINT
AVAILABILITY: SUMMER

Brewed at a farm brewery on Nantucket Island, not far from the relaxed glitz of the place, the Summer of Lager shares its home with the same family that also runs a winery and distillery. It pours a deep gold and slightly hazed color with substantial light foam and aroma that is clean and slightly corny at times, with European malt notes and a whiff of fruit esters with an added touch of wheat. As the bright beer warms, its clean, bready malt flavors come to rest on top of a reserved but earthy and even spicy noble hop bitterness. The toasted malt and herbal hop bitterness mix for a dry and refreshing finish.

Dortmunder Gold

GREAT LAKES BREWING COMPANY
CLEVELAND, OHIO
WWW.GREATLAKESBREWING.COM
ALCOHOL CONTENT: 5.8% ABV
GLASSWARE: PINT
AVAILABILITY: YEAR-ROUND

The pride of a particularly deep portfolio at this Midwestern brewing powerhouse, the Dortmunder Gold is perhaps America's best version of the style and remains a classic beer for transitioning hesitant macro drinkers to the glories of craft beer. Pouring a deep golden color with amber flecks and a sizable sustained off-white head, the clean aroma ignites with subtle, yet passionate hints of European malt with touches of wheat and bready, toasted malt. The flavor-forward, accessible body presents a short bolt of light fruity notes that quickly gives way to a well-structured, mildly toasted malt base, and a clean, crisp, and sometimes flinty finish.

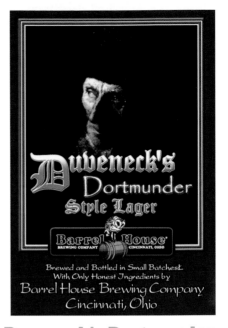

Dog Days Dortmunder

TWO BROTHERS BREWING COMPANY
WARRENVILLE, ILLINOIS
WWW.TWOBROSBREW.COM
ALCOHOL CONTENT: 4.9% ABV
GLASSWARE: PINT
AVAILABILITY: SPRING

This seasonal offering helps folks in the Chicago metro area and beyond deal with the brutally hot days of summer. Filling the glass with a rich, bright golden yellow color and a substantial head, Dog Days is a good looking beer. The aroma fuses gentle toasted and caramel malt notes with waves of fresh, herbal, noble hops for a clean, drinkable lager. The dominating malt flavors give way to a moderate but pleasant earthy bitterness that keeps the structure sound.

Duveneck's Dortmunder

BARREL HOUSE BREWING COMPANY
CINCINNATI, OHIO
WWW.BARRELHOUSE.COM
ALCOHOL CONTENT: 4.5% ABV
GLASSWARE: PINT
AVAILABILITY: YEAR-ROUND

Named after a local painter whose father owned a brewery, this striking, vibrant golden colored beer offers a frothy white cap of foam. This Dortmunder's nose is deep with rich Munich malt, offering a mild earthy character that gives way to the floral and grainy character derived from substantial additions of German noble hops. Dortmunders don't always like to play nice, and Duveneck's has some kick from earthy, grainier edges mixed in with a gentler, even fruity and sweet malt base. This refreshingly complex take on the Dortmunder style has something to offer for malt and hop lovers alike.

HELLES

If you've spent any time in Germany, especially near Munich, you've likely tried this style of beer (pronounced 'hell-us'), perhaps at Oktoberfest without even knowing it. Developed in the late nineteenth century by Bavarian brewers to compete with their Czech Pilsener rivals, this classic lager focuses on a mild yet grainy malt flavor and possesses a light and sometimes spicy hop bitterness. While a bit hoppy, the smooth-drinking bready Munich malt flavor is key to the popularity of the Helles style, which is often sold under the generic Lager designation in southern Germany. With a sustainable, tight white head of foam and striking golden color, a glass of the clean, medium-bodied Helles is sure to catch your eye and convince you to order another round.

Munich-Style Golden Lager

THOMAS HOOKER BREWING COMPANY
BLOOMFIELD, CONNECTICUT
WWW.HOOKERBEER.COM
ALCOHOL CONTENT: 4.6% ABV
GLASSWARE: PINT
AVAILABILITY: YEAR-ROUND

Bright golden with yellow-amber flecks and a small top of tacky white foam, this Helles maintains an even keel between the competing elements of malt and hops. The former dominates the aroma with a mixture of Moravian and German varieties that give off cereal, buttery, and lightly toasted notes, while the bittering German and Czech noble hops throw off delicate teems of earthy, herbal bites. Balance is key here, and it stays solid from start to finish in this well-constructed lager.

Penn Gold

PENNSYLVANIA BREWING COMPANY
PITTSBURGH, PENNSYLVANIA
WWW.PENNBREW.COM
ALCOHOL CONTENT: 4.0% ABV
GLASSWARE: PINT
AVAILABILITY: YEAR-ROUND

A top-notch lager, Penn Gold is often considered one of the leading examples of the Helles style produced in America. A deep dusty golden color with small tufts of foam, Penn Gold offers a particularly malty nose balanced by a mere touch of some herbal German noble hops. A cereal grain sweetness pervades the beer, with bready malt diversions, followed by a flavor rounding Hallertau spiciness. Well rounded on all accounts, the Penn Gold typifies the drinkability of the Helles style.

Victory Lager

VICTORY BREWING COMPANY
DOWNINGTOWN, PENNSYLVANIA
WWW.VICTORYBEER.COM
ALCOHOL CONTENT: 4.8% ABV
GLASSWARE: PINT
AVAILABILITY: YEAR-ROUND

Yet another terrific lager beer from Pennsylvania, Victory's Helles offering pours with a brilliant and striking gold color and a prodigious, fluffy white head. The Lager's aroma boasts bready Munich malts, fresh, clean, and zesty hop notes, and an airy grassy quality that attracts you for another pass at the nose. The beer's flavor is much fuller than the nose suggests, with a pleasant and clean texture, light toasted malt notes, a touch of fruit esters, some hop earthiness, and a carbonation and hop bite that rounds out the maltier edges. Clean and fresh from start to finish, Lager's crispness is remarkable and irresistible at times.

Flywheel Bright Lager

METROPOLITAN BREWING COMPANY
CHICAGO, ILLINOIS
WWW.METROBREWING.COM
ALCOHOL CONTENT: 5.0% ABV
GLASSWARE: PINT
AVAILABILITY: YEAR-ROUND

With its strong and sustained white foamy head, this attractive gold colored lager certainly makes an impression upon first view. Fueled by deep Munich malts, the aroma balances a reserved sweetness with grassy, earthy noble hops to form a clean, focused offering. The clarity of Flywheel's flavor profile is striking, even compared to other great examples of the Helles style. With a medium- to full-bodied base, the flavor is deeply filled with bready Munich notes, a touch of corn, and a light grassy and at times fruity hop undercurrent that finishes sharp on the tongue for a final zip of flavor.

Bavarian Lager

CAPITAL BREWERY
MADISON, WISCONSIN
WWW.CAPITAL-BREWERY.COM
ALCOHOL CONTENT: 4.9% ABV
GLASSWARE: PINT
AVAILABILITY: YEAR-ROUND

A powerhouse in the world of American craft lager brewing, this small regional brewery produces a solid Helles style lager that will appeal to all lovers of German lager beer. A golden amber colored beer, Bavarian Lager is moderately carbonated with an ivory top of foam. The aroma imparts a wave of cereal grain, at times bready and even nutty, capped by some zesty, zippy noble hop beats that play nicely with one another. On par with the classic style, this clean and drinkable beer focuses its crisp approach on a grainy malt flavor and mildly spicy hop bitterness.

Gold Lager

STOUDT'S BREWING COMPANY
ADAMSTOWN, PENNSYLVANIA
WWW.STOUDTSBEER.COM
ALCOHOL CONTENT: 4.7% ABV
GLASSWARE: PINT
AVAILABILITY: YEAR-ROUND

The Gold Lager, from a brewery that prides itself on its wide selection of lager beers, pours a pleasant light golden color with a slight head and moderate carbonation level. The aroma is slightly grassy at times with minute wheat and corny hints. The medium-body provides a quick splash of diverse yet clean malt flavors, ranging from bready to slightly nutty, and the tight carbonation dishes out a brief yet sharp bitterness that corrals all of the flavors into a tightly contained package. Despite its sharper notes, the underlying maltiness results in a smooth, eminently drinkable helles.

CALIFORNIA COMMON AND STEAM BEER

Perhaps no American beer style is so-defined by a single selection as the California Common style. First brewed in 1896, Anchor Steam is a deep amber colored beer with a solid creamy head that balances smooth malt character with a mild fruitiness and a touch of hop bitterness. The Anchor Brewing Company's iconic flagship brand derives its name, it is believed, from a time when West Coast brewers produced beer using some unusual refrigeration methods. The hybrid modern version involves using a special lager strain that is capable of maintaining its form when subjected to warmer fermentation temperatures. Today, the Anchor Brewing Company has trademarked the "Steam" name, and most similarly styled craft brands go by the associated California Common name. These beers share Anchor Steam's penchant for light amber colors, medium and toasted or caramel malt body, and smooth yet fruity and hoppy qualities.

In Durango, Colorado, the fittingly named Steamworks Brewing Company produces what it considers to be the finest steam beer in America, a tall statement to be sure. Bright copper in color with mild bready hints and light sweet toasted malt notes, the brewery's Steam Engine Lager exemplifies the clean, easy drinking but flavor forward nature of the California Common style. Light toasted notes wash across the palate with no distractions, finishing clean and smooth.

Moving from Aspen to Denver and finally Maryland, the Flying Dog Brewery has experienced quite a journey. The brewery's near-flagship Old Scratch Amber Lager also bridges a wide divide between ale and lager qualities. Fermented at lower temperatures, the beer develops a mellow caramel and toasted malt character that is balanced in flavor by the use of noble German hops, resulting in a hoppy counterbalance.

Minnesota's Flat Earth Brewing Company produces the unusually named Element 115, named for the late discovered element Ununpentium, given the corresponding atomic number. The copper colored beer possesses a sweet caramel malt aroma with slight fruit hints. Element 115's clean, malty flavor is occasionally interrupted by a quick hint of spicy hop notes. It is a pleasant if aggressive version of this highly drinkable and uniquely American style.

COOL AND REFRESHING

A little cloudy, a bit off-centered, and a touch mysterious, these beers are unquestionably chill, both in terms of temperature and style. From the bright beers of the Easy Drinkers, things take a decidedly hazy turn when it comes to Cool and Refreshing beers. Luminous golden hues give rise to immense white crests of foam, all poured in tall, curving glasses or inviting, rotund tumblers. With their light and refreshing character, these beers define summer drinking in many parts of the world. Beers in the classic German Hefeweizen style cast some of the most impressive and iconic figures in the world of beer, turning heads when served everywhere from the beer gardens of Munich to the beer halls of Tokyo. Across the German border, the Belgian Witbier style rests resplendent in its wide tumbler glass, framed in luminous wheat yellow hues and crisp, white crowns.

Expanding in a funkier direction than those in the Easy Drinkers category, these beers prefer to be a touch more experimental, all while remaining invigorating, approachable, and delicious. Full of exotic fruit flavors, ranging from banana to coconut and passion fruit, mixed together with chalky wheat notes and zesty, phenolic spiciness, they quench thirst with the best of them. For the adventurous, dunkelweizens and weizenbocks playfully twist and bend style conceptions to fuse the best of both ales and lagers. As their unusually complex and juicy, fruity elements mingle with rich, deep malt notes, the palate is at once cleansed and awash in silky flavors, all with an ethereal lightness of body. While guaranteed to remain palatable and of interest to your lager drinking friends, beers of the Cool and Refreshing stripe boast substantial nuance and possess great stories to tell.

AMERICAN WHEAT ALE

The American craft beer scene is split on the topic of wheat beers. Some purists adamantly prefer the traditional German-style Hefeweizen, while many craft breweries prefer to strike their own path, resulting in the American Wheat Ale. A bit of a hybrid, beers in this style range from pale to gold in color, and often remain hazy and unfiltered but sometimes pour bright. Depending upon how much the brewer borrows from Germany, aromatics can range from mild Hefeweizen-esque bananas and cloves, but the American Wheat Ale is more likely to possess subtle, wheat notes with some papery yeast hints. Hop bitterness and flavor are generally low and the flavor in better versions is a touch grainy and mildly wheaty, possibly with some citrus notes, all with a smooth, clean, and crisp flavor profile. The often offered lemon wedge is optional, but may overpower the beer's subtle flavor and aroma.

312 Urban Wheat Ale

GOOSE ISLAND BREWING COMPANY
CHICAGO, ILLINOIS
WWW.GOOSEISLAND.COM
ALCOHOL CONTENT: 4.2% ABV
GLASSWARE: PINT OR TUMBLER
AVAILABILITY: YEAR-ROUND

Named after the city's main area code, this Goose Island standard starts with a pale gold color, some residual haziness, and a slight off-white head that showcases a deep wheat aroma similar to breathing in whole grain cereal. Modest tart flecks zing with acidity in the nose, which previews the light bodied and refreshing drink to follow. A lemony citrus fruit flavor starts things off, trailed by zesty and dry wheat notes, and a touch of malt character that leaves 312 very drinkable and far above average for beers of this style.

Circus Boy

MAGIC HAT BREWING COMPANY
BURLINGTON, VERMONT
WWW.MAGICHAT.NET
ALCOHOL CONTENT: 4.4% ABV
GLASSWARE: PINT OR TUMBLER
AVAILABILITY: YEAR-ROUND

A bit of a late entrant to Magic Hat's portfolio of beers, Circus Boy quickly grew to become one of the brewery's most popular brands. Tipping more towards pale yellow than orange and with a frothy white cap of foam, the clean aroma boasts an herbal mixture of lemon, dry wheat, and earthy hops. Almost tending towards lemongrass in nature, the residual fruitiness plays against the grainier elements of the wheat malt and the herbal, grassy hop qualities to spark a tartness that reels in any overreaching in this medium bodied offering.

Gumballhead

THREE FLOYDS BREWING COMPANY
MUNSTER, INDIANA
WWW.THREEFLOYDS.COM
ALCOHOL CONTENT: 4.5% ABV
GLASSWARE: PINT OR TUMBLER
AVAILABILITY: YEAR-ROUND

Despite its playful name, Three Floyd's popular Gumballhead is serious about providing flavor in a category of beers often derided for their absence of character. With its pale golden-amber color and modest but well-sustained head, Gumballhead looks the part of an American Wheat Ale, but the nose is where everything changes. Filled to the brim with juicy, fresh American hops, robust yet subtle tropical fruit esters pour blended pineapple and pine notes over a base of mildly sweet wheat malt. In the flavor, the beer pulls back a touch from its hoppy opening gambit, slyly relying upon its Champagne-like effervescence to provide stability for its layers of wheat-accented malts mixed with fruits and a very modest amount of bitterness.

Dreamweaver

TRÖEGS BREWING COMPANY
HARRISBURG, PENNSYLVANIA
WWW.TROEGS.COM
ALCOHOL CONTENT: 4.8% ABV
GLASSWARE: PINT OR TUMBLER
AVAILABILITY: YEAR-ROUND

Opening with a gentle straw golden base coat over a bright, shiny white foam crest, the regal looking Dreamweaver treats its guests to a nuanced performance of clove, banana, and even baked Rice Krispy-like wheat quality in the aroma. After a few swirls, the initial flavor continues with a modest but dry wheat base that lays the groundwork for the interplay of light fruits, including banana, all with a snappy phenolic quality that neatly ends each round. A bit of a hybrid between the American Wheat Ale and Hefeweizen styles, Dreamweaver remains decidedly in the former's camp, while showing that it learned a few tricks from its Bavarian relative.

Unfiltered Wheat

BOULEVARD BREWING COMPANY
KANSAS CITY, MISSOURI
WWW.BLVDBEER.COM
ALCOHOL CONTENT: 3.5% ABV
GLASSWARE: PINT OR TUMBLER
AVAILABILITY: YEAR-ROUND

The flagship brand from this Midwestern brewery unveils a pale, hazy yellow lemon color with a respectable boost of off-white foam, all encapsulating a grainy wheat malt aroma that mixes in acidic citrus touches. Clean in its flavor profile as the style should be, Unfiltered Wheat gains points in terms of complexity from its adherence to a strict regiment of balancing grainy wheat malts with a mildly tangy fruit tartness that leaves a crisp and clean impression throughout the highly drinkable and quenching beer.

Sweaty Betty Blonde

BOULDER BEER COMPANY
BOULDER, COLORADO
WWW.BOULDERBEER.COM
ALCOHOL CONTENT: 5.9% ABV
GLASSWARE: PINT OR TUMBLER
AVAILABILITY: YEAR-ROUND

Getting past its rather unappealing name, this Boulder offering presents with a hazy, unfiltered blond amber appearance and simple, soft white head, giving way to notes of citrus, coriander, and a lightly sour and tart quality. In its medium body, a granular malt quality meshes with the yeast to create a touch of tart tanginess that nicely accents the modest nimble clove and banana traces. Well balanced and very drinkable, this American Wheat Ale steps up the flavor while managing a measured approach to the style.

HEFEWEIZEN

The ultimate embodiment of Cool and Refreshing, German-style Hefeweizen casts one of the most striking figures in the beer world. Best served in tall, shapely, and sloping weizen glasses, topped by a thick dollop of sustained white foam, and boasting a brilliant mixture of cloudy yellow mixture hues, hefeweizens rule the warmer months and call for outdoor enjoyment. Made with a healthy dose of wheat malt, often 50 percent of the mash, they achieve a rare lightness of body without relinquishing character. A classic Hefeweizen's aroma is a distinctive calculus of banana, bubble gum, and spicy clove phenols, dry wheat hints, and a distant and balancing tartness. Flavors generally mimic the aroma, often with subtler results. Banana flavors rarely play through, with light fruit traces, and often a drier quenching character. Hop levels are low throughout and the beer exudes drinkability.

Hefeweizen

YAZOO BREWING COMPANY
NASHVILLE, TENNESSEE
WWW.YAZOOBREW.COM
ALCOHOL CONTENT: 5.0% ABV
GLASSWARE: WEIZEN
AVAILABILITY: YEAR-ROUND

A classically designed German Hefeweizen, the layers of pale gold match with a camp of fluffy white foam that craters into a light yet impactful aroma of clove, light fruit, and a bubble gum quality. Clean and to the point, Yazoo's version sticks to the light fruit flavors, with long portraits of banana and a slight wheat bite that, along with the carbonation level, helps maximize drinkability. A touch of cracked black pepper offers a tart balance to the occasional bready malt flavors.

Crop Circle Wheat

GREAT DANE PUB AND BREWING COMPANY
MADISON, WISCONSIN
WWW.GREATDANEPUB.COM
ALCOHOL CONTENT: 5.0% ABV
GLASSWARE: WEIZEN
AVAILABILITY: YEAR-ROUND

Made with over 60 percent wheat malt and imported German yeast and hops, the Crop Circle Wheat pours with a dull yet luminous hazy yellow-orange color and a substantial off-white head, with an aroma that is filled with pronounced wheat bursts and the characteristic mixture of banana and clove, with a touch of black pepper. The surprise in the flavor is a light sour tartness that pervades the beer, which helps cut through the playful banana, tropical fruit, and clove flavors, which results in a remarkably drinkable Hefeweizen.

Winnebago Wheat

FOX RIVER BREWING COMPANY
APPLETON, WISCONSIN
WWW.FOODSPOT.COM/FOXRIVER-
BREWINGAPPLETON/
ALCOHOL CONTENT: 5.0% ABV
GLASSWARE: WEIZEN
AVAILABILITY: YEAR-ROUND

Located in an airy pub on the banks of the Fox River, this brewpub produces an excellent Hefeweizen named in honor of a local Native American tribe. The beer pours with a beautiful, hazy, and layered orange-yellow hue, a sizable, fluffy white head, and a tight level of carbonation. The aroma is filled with big juicy fruits, including bananas and a light chalkiness. The flavor follows the aroma closely with big banana and clove flavors, touches of coconut and cocoa butter, and with the carbonation level providing a solid structure to this flavorful style. A very drinkable Hefeweizen and great for warm summer days by the river.

Hinterland Hefe Weizen

APPALACHIAN BREWING COMPANY
HARRISBURG, PENNSYLVANIA
WWW.ABCBREW.COM
ALCOHOL CONTENT: 5.3% ABV
GLASSWARE: WEIZEN
AVAILABILITY: YEAR-ROUND

Through the hazy walls of this yellow-amber colored beer, you can see three-fingers of crusty foam lingering, and a deep breath takes in the classic German esters of banana and clove phenolics, mixed with a touch of dry wheat malt. A well-balanced array of fruit flavors dart out from the hazy shadows, with a parade of banana, tropical fruit, and then a tartness of clove and wheat malt cleaning up for a dry and yeasty finish. Appalachian has brewed a highly drinkable Hefeweizen that is both flavorful and approachable.

Hoffman Weiss

**MOAT MOUNTAIN SMOKEHOUSE
& BREWING COMPANY
NORTH CONWAY, NEW HAMPSHIRE
WWW.MOATMOUNTAIN.COM**
ALCOHOL CONTENT: 5.7% ABV
GLASSWARE: PINT OR WEISS
AVAILABILITY: YEAR-ROUND

While the picturesque Moat Mountain brewpub is perhaps best known for its lagers, its German-style Hefeweizen beer pays tribute to the traditions of southern Deutschland as well. Named after a restaurant formerly occupying its space, this wheat beer commences with a robust and gloriously hazy golden-orange color and its nose peaks with the customary traces of banana, phenolic clove spiciness, and a slight dry bite from yeast and wheat malt. In the glass, the first sip is mildly spicy, leading the way to some dry wheat notes, and followed by a quiet play of banana and tropical fruit flavors.

HefeWeizen

**LIVE OAK BREWING COMPANY
AUSTIN, TEXAS
WWW.LIVEOAKBREWING.COM**
ALCOHOL CONTENT: 4.1% ABV
GLASSWARE: WEIZEN
AVAILABILITY: YEAR-ROUND

With its dull and luminous yellowy-orange color and sizable and tightly carbonated white head, Live Oak's HefeWeizen is a looker. This Texas original booms with a massive aroma of bananas, phenolic pepperiness, light creamy qualities, and mimics the German style. The medium-bodied beer starts with a burst of Juicy Fruit gum-like banana qualities, aided by a tight carbonation bite, light wheat notes, a touch of bubble gum, and a mild toasted malt balance. Far from a thin or artificial tasting Hefeweizen, it appears to derive a lot of its character from the ingredients and not just from the yeast. A slight acidic tang in the finish is refreshing in this very pleasant offering, which is reminiscent of the classic German style.

WITBIER

Hardly content to let southern Germany hog all the attention, the Belgian-style Witbier is another global contender for the Cool and Refreshing crown. Hauntingly luminous and pale yellow in appearance, topped with a frothy, clean white foam, witbiers are eye-catching and attention grabbing in nature. Brewed using high proportions of unmalted wheat, brewers employ a range of spices, coriander, and orange peel to achieve unusual and intricate aromas. Backed by a lively carbonation, resulting in a sustained head, the aroma is a mixture of dry, grainy wheat and citrusy, piquant touches. Witbiers start crisp and dry from the wheat, followed by interplay of the various spices, leaving the palate with faint dashes of fruit and even the occasional light acidic tang.

Celis White

MICHIGAN BREWING COMPANY
WEBBERVILLE, MICHIGAN
WWW.MICHIGANBREWING.COM
ALCOHOL CONTENT: 3.9% ABV
GLASSWARE: TUMBLER
AVAILABILITY: YEAR-ROUND

The original Witbier style was resurrected in the beer called Hoegaarden, made by Belgian brewer Pierre Celis, who, after toiling with corporate brewers, later moved to Texas and opened his own brewery. After selling his American brewery to another corporate giant, who later closed it, the labels were transferred to Michigan Brewing, where the brand is now lovingly cared for in its slightly altered form. In the round tumbler, we find a pale straw color with a wavering white cap head, and a nose full of the fruit end of a spice drawer, including clove, orange zest, lemon, coriander, and a slight yeast funk. The dry wheat malt base provides a touch of sweetness along with structure to this medium bodied beer, with sidenotes of clove and citrus fruit. The new Celis White is a commendable testament to the beer that kicked off this style's resurgence.

Calabaza Blanca

JOLLY PUMPKIN ARTISAN ALES
DEXTER, MICHIGAN
WWW.JOLLYPUMPKIN.COM
ALCOHOL CONTENT: 4.8% ABV
GLASSWARE: TUMBLER
AVAILABILITY: YEAR-ROUND

This unconventional Witbier entry showcases a cloudy yellow-apricot color with a tight carbonation level and a doughy white cloud of foam, with an aroma that masterfully mixed tart and sour notes, with some mild Belgian funk, light tropical fruit and clove spice notes, and a dry wheat component. The resulting flavor is light on the palate, alternating between clove spiciness, dry wheat, and a substantial yet soothing acidic tang that hits you in the cheeks towards the end. The substantial carbonation's scrubbing bubbles clean your palate, leaving a bone dry impression in their wake.

Allagash White

ALLAGASH BREWING COMPANY
PORTLAND, MAINE
WWW.ALLAGASH.COM
ALCOHOL CONTENT: 5.0% ABV
GLASSWARE: TUMBLER
AVAILABILITY: YEAR-ROUND

An early entry in the pantheon of Belgian-influenced craft beers, Allagash White helps define the Witbier style for many brewers in this country. Incredibly easy on the eyes, the White pours with a delightfully hazy golden blonde color and a substantial band of white foam. The aroma brightens your day with a pleasurable mixture of spices, including orange peel and coriander, with touches of lemon and a slight biting yeast note. Refreshing from the start, an effervescent carbonation ping helps bring structure to the softly spicy coriander and wheat elements, ending with a careful balance of sweeter malt. The Allagash White is easily one of the best witbiers produced today and serves as one of the great beers of New England.

Wheat Ale

UPLAND BREWING COMPANY
BLOOMINGTON, INDIANA
WWW.UPLANDBEER.COM
ALCOHOL CONTENT: 4.5% ABV
GLASSWARE: TUMBLER
AVAILABILITY: YEAR-ROUND

This faint pale lemon colored beer pours as near translucent yellow as one can get without turning white, with a very mild white head, and the aroma presents one of the cleanest expressions of coriander you will ever find. The pale color translates into a light bodied flavor, with a crisp and winning coriander flavor mixed with a dry wheat flavor and finishing with a mild tang of sourness. Upland's Wheat Ale is dry throughout and very drinkable, especially if you're a fan of coriander and its mild spicing and fruit qualities.

Orchard White

THE BRUERY
PLACENTIA, CALIFORNIA
WWW.THEBRUERY.COM
ALCOHOL CONTENT: 5.7% ABV
GLASSWARE: TUMBLER
AVAILABILITY: YEAR-ROUND

The flagship beer from the upstart Bruery exhibits a timidly hazy light golden cast with tinges of amber in the right light and capped by a well-sustained house of fluffy white foam. The aroma swirls with a complicated floral cabaret of lemon zest and grapefruit mixed with earthy and mineral yeast, a little farmhouse funk, and even a touch of European malt character that tastes a bit like artificial purple candy. The concentrated yet smooth flavors range from the aforementioned earth and minerals to lavender, wheat, and a mild Band-Aid character, all coming to a dry, tight finish. Orchard White is a supremely complex Witbier that remains drinkable.

Double White Ale

SOUTHAMPTON BREWING COMPANY
SOUTHAMPTON, NEW YORK
WWW.SOUTHAMPTONPUBLICKHOUSE.COM
ALCOHOL CONTENT: 6.6% ABV
GLASSWARE: TUMBLER
AVAILABILITY: YEAR-ROUND

Tumbling into the glass with deep, bright, and luminous golden yellow radiant hues and a pure white foam swirl, the tight carbonation levels suggest a clean and refreshing experience to follow. The unconventional aroma catches you off guard with lactic sour notes and a touch of funk mixing with the more typical dry wheat notes and citrus esters. Labeled as a double Witbier, it shouldn't surprise you to find that the body boasts an elevated taste character, with strong malt and wheat flavors competing with citrus flairs, all wrapped up with a light citric and wheat tang that cleanses the palate. Escaping the dangers of imperialization, the mouthfeel possesses a medium-body and the Double White Ale remains eminently drinkable, true to the style.

DUNKELWEIZEN

A cross between the classic German Hefeweizen and Dunkel styles, dunkelweizens confound on multiple levels. From their deceptively dark appearance to the unexpected and pronounced banana, vanilla, and spice aromas, these deliciously intricate beers burst with concentrated and eccentric flavors. Typically dark brown in color from the addition of roasted malts, with an often murky yeast haze, the aromas pack powerful banana, fruit, spicy clove, and bready malt notes. The Dunkelweizen's flavor closely resembles its unusual nose, with toasted or caramel malts balancing juicy, fruity, and spicy hints. While some equate dunkelweizens with liquid banana bread, the best examples do not overwhelm the palate, but maintain a pleasant and refreshing balance that is perfect for warm summer nights and cool winter afternoons alike.

Bonfire Dunkel Weiss

TWO BROTHERS BREWING COMPANY
WARRENVILLE, ILLINOIS
WWW.TWOBROSBREW.COM
ALCOHOL CONTENT: 6.2% ABV
GLASSWARE: WEIZEN
AVAILABILITY: LIMITED RELEASE

Pouring a deep russet brown with amber and rouge highlights in the light, an off-tan head gently floats above the fold, giving off a charming display of aromatic tones, including bananas, phenolic spiciness, dark roasted malts, treacle, caramel, toffee, and a touch of bubble gum. Smooth and reassuring upon first sip, the medium-bodied Dunkelweizen starts with a kick into phenolic tanginess before introducing caramel sweetness and some welcomed roasted malt to smooth the equilibrium.

Dunkle Witte

FRENCH BROAD BREWING COMPANY
ASHEVILLE, NORTH CAROLINA
WWW.FRENCHBROADBREWERY.COM
ALCOHOL CONTENT: 7.5% ABV
GLASSWARE: WEIZEN OR TUMBLER
AVAILABILITY: YEAR-ROUND

Taking the cross-dressing Dunkelweizen style to its extreme, French Broad aims to brew a deceptively dark version that demands attention with its deep, foreboding dark brown color and its creamy foam tower. Once you find your opening, deep waves of caramel malt wash over the rim of the glass, calling you to enjoy its unusual pleasures. Employing a much more measured approach when it comes to the fruit and phenolic flavors, this version actually tends more towards a Witbier, with occasional coriander and orange peel notes complementing the deep roasted caramel malt qualities, finished off with a peppery spiciness.

Dark n' Curvy Dunkelweizen

PIECE BREWERY & PIZZERIA
CHICAGO, ILLINOIS
WWW.PIECECHICAGO.COM
ALCOHOL CONTENT: 5.5% ABV
GLASSWARE: WEIZEN
AVAILABILITY: YEAR-ROUND

This well-named beer is deeply soulful and multi-hued, with dark brown cascading from the top into lighter reddish tones at the base and with a fluffy cloud of light tan foam. The aroma sparkles with fruity banana esters with a touch of clove, all atop a mild wheat malt base. The swirling banana aromas nearly disappear in the beer's medium body, giving way to tangy wheat bites, slight caramel malt hints, and mild fruit tones, all wrapped up in a surprisingly bitter finish. Despite its disappearance, banana ends up being a player in the beer's finish, where hints of the fruit linger long on the palate.

Ramstein Classic

HIGH POINT BREWING COMPANY
BUTLER, NEW JERSEY
WWW.RAMSTEINBEER.COM
ALCOHOL CONTENT: 5.5% ABV
GLASSWARE: WEIZEN OR TUMBLER
AVAILABILITY: YEAR-ROUND

The Classic is an accurate name when it comes to this excellent American version of the little understood Dunkelweizen category. Boasting a deep auburn tone with darker hues sneaking by, the creamy head teems with a craterous mousse and a complex melody of candy caramel, darker roasted notes, and light, playful fruit notes ranging from pear to clove. Richly filled with mellow caramel malt that dances with a bubble gum phenolic partner, the Classic also celebrates its dark, roasted heritage as a dunkel. Dry in the finish, this High Point offering remains refreshing and drinkable even while stage managing the fussy fruit and roasted malt star players.

Black Wheat

NEW GLARUS BREWING COMPANY
NEW GLARUS, WISCONSIN
WWW.NEWGLARUSBREWING.COM
ALCOHOL CONTENT: 5.7% ABV
GLASSWARE: WEIZEN
AVAILABILITY: SPRING

With a gloriously cloudy brown hue and a dark tan head full of wondrous, inviting chocolate, caramel, and clove aromas, this lesser well-known New Glarus offering replenishes the spirit while refreshing the body. Complementing the aromas of clove and cinnamon, the Black Wheat possesses a rich stable of chewy caramel and toffee malt flavors that mix through a moderate, cleansing carbonation level with the Hefeweizen-style banana and bubble gum characters. Welcoming the spring after a long winter season, the combination of malt and fruit elements is both restorative and complex without being overbearing.

Leavenworth Dunkelweizen

FISH BREWING COMPANY
OLYMPIA, WASHINGTON
WWW.FISHBREWING.COM
ALCOHOL CONTENT: 4.7% ABV
GLASSWARE: WEIZEN OR TUMBLER
AVAILABILITY: YEAR-ROUND

Popping with active carbonation, deep brown liquid issues forth with a satisfyingly tacky off-white foam head, which is met with several rounds of dark, roasted caramel malt and faint clove and fruit hints. The yeast plays a prominent role in the nose but stays out of the way in the body, where the darker caramel flavors mesh with quick flits of banana, clove, and light tropical fruit. The impression left by this Dunkelweizen is one of fulfillment and thoughts of another round.

WEIZENBOCK

Consider this style an amped up version of the Dunkelweizen, with a dark lager history lurking deep within its body. Weizenbocks usually pour amber ruby to dark brown in color and with a hazy appearance and impressive foamy head. While offering the usual fruit and clove dashes, a Weizenbock's aroma possesses noticeably more alcohol and malt warmth than standard issue Hefeweizen and Dunkel beers, and is more in line with the classic German Bock style. Beers of the style maintain a difficult to achieve equilibrium, with matching parts dark, zesty fruit and toasted, bready malts, all resulting in a smooth, drinkable, if potent, offering.

Slam Dunkel

WEYERBACHER BREWING COMPANY
EASTON, PENNSYLVANIA
WWW.WEYERBACHER.COM
ALCOHOL CONTENT: 7.0% ABV
GLASSWARE: WEIZEN
AVAILABILITY: SPRING

With its deep chestnut color, hazy ruby hues, and mild-mannered boost of foam, the creatively named Weizenbock from this Pennsylvania craft brewer offers wave after gentle wave of neatly folded caramel malt alongside accompaniments of classic Bavarian Hefeweizen yeast notes, including banana and clove. Translated into the tall, slender weizen glass, the Slam Dunkel indeed shuts the door on many other versions of the style, carefully meshing the complex worlds of sweet caramel and chocolate malts and banana and spicy clove phenolics. A touch light on the palate, the beer sneaks up on you with a developing mouthfeel that ends with a velvety wash of caramel fruits.

Volks Weizenbock

APPALACHIAN BREWING COMPANY
HARRISBURG, PENNSYLVANIA
WWW.ABCBREW.COM
ALCOHOL CONTENT: 7.2% ABV
GLASSWARE: WEIZEN OR TUMBLER
AVAILABILITY: WINTER

Appalachian's Brewing Company successfully married its Hefeweizen and Bock beers to create the People's Beer. A dark auburn, Sherry color with a lean tan head of foam, the Volks breathes of fruit, with smashed bananas shaking hands with a nutmeg and clove spiciness, all while a caramel and bready maltiness stands by smiling on the affair. Full of banana and mild tropical fruits, a defined spicy quality, including cinnamon and allspice, appear in the medium bodied beer, with touches of sweet, caramel malt providing a strong backbone. Surprisingly refreshing considering its robust character, the Volks Weizenbock is a fine example of this style.

Moonglow Weizenbock

VICTORY BREWING COMPANY
DOWNINGTOWN, PENNSYLVANIA
WWW.VICTORYBEER.COM
ALCOHOL CONTENT: 8.7% ABV
GLASSWARE: WEIZEN
AVAILABILITY: FALL

As a master of German styles, it comes as no surprise that Victory's Moonglow is a fantastic Weizenbock. With its mildly hazy rouge-apricot tone and pronounced and pillowy soft beige colored peak, the aroma blends restrained doses of spiced fruit, including cinnamon coated apple pie, with touches of peppery clove, all tucked into a glove of tangy and sweet bready malt. In the glass, the beer transforms into a drinking marvel, with luxuriant toasted malt swirls mixed with touches of cocoa and dry wheat, all surrounded in a cocoon of spicy clove and mild banana fruits. A mild tanginess pervades the heavenly mixture, bringing order where needed to keep this medium-bodied beer in proper order.

Glockenspiel Weizenbock

GREAT LAKES BREWING COMPANY
CLEVELAND, OHIO
WWW.GREATLAKESBREWING.COM
ALCOHOL CONTENT: 8.0% ABV
GLASSWARE: WEIZEN OR GOBLET
AVAILABILITY: SPRING

From the time the cap is loosened from its resting place atop a bottle of Glockenspiel, you know you're in the presence of greatness. It's a beautiful beer to be sure, with deep auburn and ruby swirl and a fat chunk of beige foam. But it's the aroma that will hook you, with its expertly arranged symphony of toasted and caramel malts, wondrous clove balance, and delightful spray of banana fruitiness. And it's a pleasant surprise when the flavor achieves greater heights than even the fantastic aroma would suggest, with roasted toffee providing the dark counterbalance to the plush offerings of banana and tropical fruits, all with a spicy clove balance and a gentle but absorbing alcohol base.

Ramstein Winter Wheat

HIGH POINT BREWING COMPANY
BUTLER, NEW JERSEY
WWW.RAMSTEINBEER.COM
ALCOHOL CONTENT: 9.5% ABV
GLASSWARE: WEIZEN
AVAILABILITY: WINTER

The Winter Wheat is another offering from a brewery that knows how to brew flavor-forward wheat beers. Garnering a cloudiness from its unfiltered nature, this ruddy brown beer with its wide-eyed beige foam crown offers a playful smattering of sweet dried fruits mixed with decidedly caramelized toffee malt sweetness, with dashes of phenolic bubble gum and a shot of alcohol to jolt the gathering. Medium bodied and creamy in texture, the roasted malt dextrins offer a caramel sweet counterbalance to occasional dark malt touches, all mixed together with waves of phenolic fruit and spices. A light tang from the wheat keeps the peace here, leaving a mild sourness that substantially dries out the finish.

Hang Ten Weizen Doppelbock

HEAVY SEAS BEER
BALTIMORE, MARYLAND
WWW.CCBEER.COM
ALCOHOL CONTENT: 10.0% ABV
GLASSWARE: WEIZEN OR GOBLET
AVAILABILITY: SUMMER

A classic looking Weizenbock with a tawny copper base coat accented by a serious cocoa wheat plume of foam, the nose greets you with subtle layers of caramel malt wrapped around a partially phenolic clove and modest banana dusting. A slow starter, the Hang Ten starts to build momentum as it warms, with additional sheets of toasted malt peeling back to reveal new layers of caramelized fruit, chocolate malt, and a warming alcohol base. Silky smooth in body into the finish, Heavy Sea's offering is a welcome addition to the stable of great weizenbocks.

BERLINER WEISS

A real outlier in the beer world, one that celebrates both sourness and low alcohol levels, Berliner Weiss is a style whose representations in its region of origin have all but disappeared. As the style is understood today, these beers define themselves by painting with tart, sour, and acidic strokes. Slightly hazy and luminous in appearance, foreboding in the polar opposite manner of an Imperial Stout, with a pale straw color and a simple, quickly evaporating head, this rare style delivers with its tart, sharp aroma and distinctly and pleasantly sour flavor. Similar to the thirst-quenching qualities of lemonade, Berliner Weiss delivers a refreshing blend of tartness derived from a lactic acid bacteria addition. Light bodied and very low in alcohol, often around 3 percent by volume, some brewers offer a lightly sweet raspberry or woodruff syrup that dyes the beers either bright red or green and mellows their acidity. Traditional brewers often blend batches of various ages to achieve their preferred level of sourness, a practice less often employed in modern recreations of the style.

Dogfish Head's Festina Peche is perhaps the most widely available version of what it calls the neo-Berliner Weiss style. Brewed to 4.5 percent alcohol, Festina Peche's light interplay of tart and sour notes is achieved in part through the use of peach concentrate and lactic acid cultures. The resulting unfiltered beer is a deep, luminous hazy orange with sharp, piquant, and lightly fruity aromas. But it is the beer's mouthpuckeringly sour body that helps separate it from tamer summer seasonals.

In Haverhill, Massachusetts, a small brewpub called The Tap produces a classic Berliner Weiss. With a dull, hazy yellowish orange hue and a light tart aroma, the beer is mildly effervescent and mixes sour, tart, and gentle fruit flavors for a very dry and drinkable beer.

The Bruery of California's Hottenroth Berliner Weisse uses lactobacillus and a touch of brettanomyces to sour its very low alcohol wheat beer. The result is a dull straw colored beer with a mild tartness and an airy lightness of body.

Adding to its collection of fruit beers, the New Glarus Brewing Company of Wisconsin produces a Berliner Weiss it calls "the Champagne of the North," in a play on how Napoleon referred to this tart style. Using a mixture of Pinot Grigio and Riesling grapes, this hard-to-find version balances tartness with stronger fruity notes in a well-carbonated beer that is at times reminiscent of cider.

MELLOW AND MALTY

Smooth, balanced, restorative, and subtle capture the essence of Mellow and Malty beers. These well-structured and accessible beers assert their proud character, displaying a rich mixture of playful sweetness against a solid, drinkable, and well-structured background of flavors. The best offerings fill your mind with thoughts of English toffee, fresh baked bread, and caramel sugars, adding deep layers of character to their respective beer styles. These smooth operators, with their inoffensive and familiar flavors, remain the gateway to better beer for many drinkers.

With hops tending to capture a lot of the attention when it comes to flavors and aromas in beer, the attendant beauties of malt often get brushed aside as just another ingredient, the lowly fuel necessary for the fermentation process. While deep amber fields of gently flowing barley remain an enduring American symbol, having been enshrined in diverse forms such as *America the Beautiful* and countless mass-market beer commercials, the contributions of malt to the pint in front of you remain elusive for most drinkers. Too often dismissed by self-professed craft beer experts as simple and unrefined, flavor-friendly, malt-centric beer celebrates an equally complex and sophisticated flavor palate.

Whether used as a sweet, balancing backbone in otherwise crisp, hoppy German-style pilseners, or as the focal point in Vienna-style lagers and Scottish-style ales, malt brings far more than sugar for alcohol conversion to the world's great beers. Never overpowering, sweet and light on the palate, and always exuding a noble subtlety, Mellow and Malty beers define drinkability. Rejecting ostentation and flash, these charmers expertly use hops to balance their sweeter sides, resulting in soothing, rich session beers.

AMERICAN AMBER

It seems as if every American craft brewer sells an Amber beer. Often treated by brewers as a catchall class of beers, encompassing everything from smooth, malty lagers to bitter, hoppy ales, the American Amber style described here focuses on balanced malt sweetness. These beers are differentiated from the Irish-style Red Ale and Vienna-style Lager styles by their use of American hops and less focus on continental European malt varieties. They can be ales or lagers, range in color from light orange-amber to deep red in hue, have medium bodies, and low to medium bitterness. The defining characteristic of the American Amber style is its dedication to toasted, caramel malt flavors. Some might posses light fruit hints, depending upon the hops used, but the sweet, biscuity malt flavor should predominate in a pleasant, smooth experience.

Prohibition Ale

SPEAKEASY BREWING COMPANY
SAN FRANCISCO, CALIFORNIA
WWW.GOODBEER.COM
ALCOHOL CONTENT: 6.1% ABV
GLASSWARE: PINT
AVAILABILITY: YEAR-ROUND

Prohibition bestows a hazy brown toned pint with mild auburn hues at the far reaches, a khaki colored soft layer of pillowy foam, and a cracking mélange of sweet, biscuity, and creamy malt mixed with a mild piney hop ester. The first sip starts creamy, with light citrus hop flavors making a quick appearance before deferring to a medium-bodied malt sweetness comprised of bready, biscuity, and caramel sugar notes. A smartly crafted American Amber, the Prohibition effectively balances the American hops with the level of malt sweetness necessary to maximize drinkability.

Old Yankee Ale

COTTRELL BREWING COMPANY
PAWCATUCK, CONNECTICUT
WWW.COTTRELLBREWING.COM
ALCOHOL CONTENT: 5.0% ABV
GLASSWARE: PINT OR MUG
AVAILABILITY: YEAR-ROUND

Long the brewery's only beer, Cottrell's Old Yankee Ale is brewed in a nineteenth century warehouse that once housed a manufacturing plant owned by the owner's ancestors. Meting out a bold and clean copper color with a moderate off-white head, the complex aroma teems with pleasant biscuity and toasted malt flavors that gel effectively with its earthy, citrusy hop esters. Starting with a toffee and caramelized sugar malt sweetness, Old Yankee Ale transitions to a light fruity and earthy flavor before returning to the true bready malt elements that define its character.

Ambergeddon

ALE ASYLUM
MADISON, WISCONSIN
WWW.ALEASYLUM.COM
ALCOHOL CONTENT: 6.8% ABV
GLASSWARE: PINT
AVAILABILITY: YEAR-ROUND

The cleverly named flagship from the capital city's curious brewpub pours with a deep copper amber color, a poof of wheat foam, and demands your attention with its toasted malt esters mixed with a sharp edged earthy hop quality. Essentially a mash-up of an English Pale Ale and an American Amber, the biscuity malt flavors take over from the earthy and grassy hop notes as the beer warms. Light caramel and creamy flavors come to dominate before relinquishing control to a long, earthy, and mildly bitter finish that never oversteps its welcome.

Coney Island Lager

SHMALTZ BREWING COMPANY
SAN FRANCISCO, CALIFORNIA
WWW.SHMALTZ.COM
ALCOHOL CONTENT: 5.5% ABV
GLASSWARE: PINT
AVAILABILITY: YEAR-ROUND

With a copper-amber color and modest off-white head, this lager offering shows a mellower side of the sometimes fruity and hoppy American Amber category. The aroma fills with toasted caramel and bready malts mixed with the lightest fruit and apple notes, with a nutty touch added. The flavor suggests toasted bread, with sweeter grain elements playing against a caramel coating, all mixed with a slight creamy quality and a moderate carbonation level that helps smooth out any rougher edges.

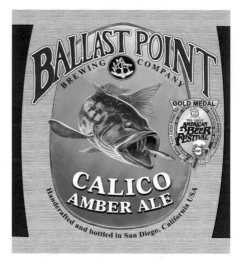

Copper Ale

OTTER CREEK BREWING COMPANY
MIDDLEBURY, VERMONT
WWW.OTTERCREEKBREWING.COM
ALCOHOL CONTENT: 5.4% ABV
GLASSWARE: PINT
AVAILABILITY: YEAR-ROUND

A style bending beer from a stalwart New England brewery, Copper Ale presents with a glowing golden amber color and a sustained cap of white foam with tight carbonation. The aroma tends decisively towards a nuttier malt quality, with touches of caramel and toasted malt playing against predominating nutty tones. Despite its reliance upon caramel malt additions, the flavor is dry throughout and finishes long and dry on the palate. Sometimes advertised as an Altbier, Copper Ale is a bit of a style hybrid that bridges several gaps but properly finds its home in the American Amber style.

Calico Amber Ale

BALLAST POINT BREWING COMPANY
SAN DIEGO, CALIFORNIA
WWW.BALLASTPOINT.COM
ALCOHOL CONTENT: 5.0% ABV
GLASSWARE: PINT OR MUG
AVAILABILITY: YEAR-ROUND

Amber ales from the West Coast generally tend to offer a fast head fake towards the malty side before quickly defecting for hoppier pastures. Ballast Point's offering chooses to showcase some American hops but not before giving long attention to its sweeter, maltier roots. Pouring with a radiant, deep reddish amber color and sustained off-white head, light citric notes mix with pale caramel malt tones, creating a playful toasted cotton candy sensation, rounded out by a light acidic tang. Fluent in both hop and malt dialects, Ballast Point's brewers translate the aroma into a blend of toasted caramel malt sweetness with an overlap of subtle earthy bitterness for a quixotic and highly drinkable amber ale.

BROWN ALE

Another expansive category, Brown Ales encompass the classic English variety, which focuses on toffee, nutty, and dark caramel malt flavors, and its slightly hoppier American descendent. The English variety dominated the early days of the craft beer movement before giving way to the stronger, maltier, and hoppier American version. Brown Ales range in color from dark copper to deep brown with ruby hues, all with a normal level of head retention. The aroma is strongly of sweet, bready malts, with hints of chocolate, toasted malts, and caramel. The Brown Ale's classic silky flavor focuses entirely on the beauty of malt, from mild, sweet caramel to modest roasted hints, with color imparted by darker malts. American versions may veer into hoppier grounds but generally stay close to this tried-and-true formula.

Ad Astra Ale

FREE STATE BREWING COMPANY
LAWRENCE, KANSAS
WWW.FREESTATEBREWING.COM
ALCOHOL CONTENT: 5.0% ABV
GLASSWARE: PINT
AVAILABILITY: YEAR-ROUND

Taking its name from the Kansas state motto of *Ad Astra per Aspera*, Latin for "To the stars through difficulties," this Brown Ale offers drinkers no troubles on the way to its easy drinking finish. A deep brown hued liquid with ruby hues presents itself with a mild-mannered, off-tan head before filling your nose with a robust blend of caramel malts, dried fruit tones, and a steadying dose of earthy hops. The taste kicks forth with a wave of toasted and caramel malts, some European in flavor, followed by a slight hop bite, light salt on a sugary dessert, and finishing a touch sweet on the palate.

Pullman Nut Brown Ale

FLOSSMOOR STATION RESTAURANT AND BREWERY
FLOSSMOOR, ILLINOIS
WWW.FLOSSMOORSTATION.COM
ALCOHOL CONTENT: 6.0% ABV
GLASSWARE: PINT OR TULIP
AVAILABILITY: YEAR-ROUND

Pouring with a deep ruby brown appearance and tight off-tan head, this Flossmoor Station offering is a simple yet stately looking beer. The aroma showcases a complex arrangement of sweet molasses and creamy notes, alongside touches of vanilla and oak, tethered to mild roasted malts. With its medium body, the Pullman displays a very creamy texture without becoming syrupy, a mixture of playful toasted malt sweetness, toffee cream candy and chocolate, and closely guarded by a decidedly bitter roasted malt finish. Using a mixture of eight malts and blackstrap molasses, the nuanced beer swings between several styles before settling in the Brown Ale family.

Maduro

CIGAR CITY BREWING COMPANY
TAMPA, FLORIDA
WWW.CIGARCITYBEER.COM
ALCOHOL CONTENT: 5.5% ABV
GLASSWARE: PINT
AVAILABILITY: YEAR-ROUND

The flagship brand for the upstart Cigar City Brewing Company, which is run by a beer columnist for a Tampa newspaper, Maduro starts with a dull, deep brown color and a light tan head with moderate carbonation. The aroma offers slight toffee malt qualities combined with light fruit esters, including prunes, a touch of dry chalkiness, and the slightest hints of smoke. The flavor follows suit with the addition of an oatmeal component that melds with a light residual sweetness that continues through to the finish. Maduro is a very drinkable addition to the Florida Gulf Coast market.

Turbodog

ABITA BREWING COMPANY
ABITA SPRINGS, LOUISIANA
WWW.ABITA.COM
ALCOHOL CONTENT: 5.6% ABV
GLASSWARE: PINT OR MUG
AVAILABILITY: YEAR-ROUND

With its robust ruby brown frame and wheat, pillowy head, this unusually named Brown Ale emphasizes a touch more dark and roasted malts than your average, flabbier version of the style. Starting with coffee and dark chocolate notes mixed with a cashew nutty quality, a slight residual sweetness hides deep within the dry confines of this beer. Playing off its darker elements, the flavor corresponds to a roasted Stout crossed with a chocolate and caramel candy factory. The dry, nutty quality returns towards the end, smoothing out the edges and ushering in an easy, creamy finish, marked by traces of caramel malt sweetness.

Southern Pecan

LAZY MAGNOLIA BREWING COMPANY
KILN, MISSISSIPPI
WWW.LAZYMAGNOLIA.COM
ALCOHOL CONTENT: 4.5% ABV
GLASSWARE: PINT
AVAILABILITY: YEAR-ROUND

This Magnolia State beer pours with a bright copper garnet color and a light tan head and possesses an unusual nutty malt and zesty hop aroma, akin to earthy and noble hops mixed together with pecans and toasted grains, which strikes the nose as dry and chalky at times. The medium body starts with a lightly sharp hop zip and then quickly fades into a short touch of earthy bitterness before dropping into a nice toasted caramel malt flavor, replete with mild, astringent tartness and a chalky and dry finish. A bit eccentric in its approach, the beer is made with actual pecans, so take care if you have food allergies.

Hazelnut Brown Nectar

ROGUE ALES BREWERY
NEWPORT, OREGON
WWW.ROGUE.COM
ALCOHOL CONTENT: 6.2% ABV
GLASSWARE: PINT
AVAILABILITY: YEAR-ROUND

In a class by its own in terms of aromatics and flavor, Rogue's all-encompassing entrant into the Brown Ale category has a roasted auburn color with a dense, creamy crown of foam. The aroma is where things start to get interesting, with an intriguing mixture of cocoa cream, vanilla, mild almond nuttiness, and caramel toffee. The flavor continues with an amaretto-like nutty quality over a creamy base, all with a light roasted malt character. Complex and curious, Hazelnut Brown keeps you guessing with each sip.

IRISH-STYLE RED ALE

Aside from the classic Irish-style Dry Stout, the Irish-style Red Ale stands as the most popular contribution of the Emerald Isle to the modern world of craft brewing. Introduced to many drinkers in the United States by the George Killian's version produced by the Coors Brewing Company, Irish-style red ales are understandably light or medium red or amber in color, with a soft tan head, and a mid-range alcohol level near 5 percent by volume. Aromas are of sweet, toasted malts, simple but pleasant in nature, with very little to no hop presence. The flavor follows with a straightforward and easygoing caramel sweetness and occasional fruit hints but with a drier finish. Some versions can be a little grainy or a tad hoppier but most stay true to the style's defining mellow malt core. The style is an excellent selection for bitter beer-phobes and developing craft beer fans.

Lavaman Red Ale

KONA BREWING COMPANY
KAILUA-KONA, HAWAII
WWW.KONABREWINGCO.COM
ALCOHOL CONTENT: 5.6% ABV
GLASSWARE: PINT
AVAILABILITY: YEAR-ROUND

A vibrant red tone with a whipped tan caramel froth of foam leads the way for a wonderfully complex array of fruit and malt flavors, starting with bready, caramel, and chocolate malts, dried fruits, including prunes and dates, and finishing with a mildly piney floral implosion that suggests some citrus notes. The first sip starts with a quick flit of citrus from the hops without imparting any real lingering bitterness, along with a wave of dense caramel malt sweetness that washes over the palate. Lavaman is a relatively complex offering in the style but with enough malt sweetness to balance things out.

Irish Red

DIAMOND BEAR BREWING COMPANY
LITTLE ROCK, ARKANSAS
WWW.DIAMONDBEAR.COM
ALCOHOL CONTENT: 4.69% ABV
GLASSWARE: PINT
AVAILABILITY: YEAR-ROUND

Starting off with a ruddy auburn color from the bottle with a lean beige-hued fop of foam, the unusually spicy aroma mixes the usual sweet caramel malts with tea-like spices, an herbal hop touch, chocolate and cocoa, along with a lingering smoky quality. Irish Red's flavor starts out sweet on the palate, rich with caramel, molasses, and toffee, followed by a flourish of earthy and grassy hops, leaving a finish that is mildly sweet. The mild use of hops adds a nice touch and accent to the breadth of malt flavors on display here.

McIlhenney's Irish Red Ale

ALPINE BEER COMPANY
ALPINE, CALIFORNIA
WWW.ALPINEBEERCO.COM
ALCOHOL CONTENT: 6.0% ABV
GLASSWARE: PINT
AVAILABILITY: YEAR-ROUND

With its bright amber-red color and thick finger of off-white foam, the aroma floods with sweet caramel and toasted malt, with bready hints, and a very mild citrus hop profile that accentuates the malt elements. Brewed using a combination of eleven different malts, the easygoing taste mixes the familiar bready and toasted elements with some caramel malt sweetness and another touch of citrus, all playing in balance with one another to create a very enjoyable pint.

Jeremiah Red

BJ'S RESTAURANT AND BREWHOUSE
MULTIPLE LOCATIONS
WWW.BJSRESTAURANTS.COM
ALCOHOL CONTENT: 7.3% ABV
GLASSWARE: PINT OR TULIP
AVAILABILITY: YEAR-ROUND

With outlets brewing and selling beer in more than a dozen states, BJ's is one of the larger brewpub chains in the country. Its popular Jeremiah Red is brewed in each location with the same basic recipe. It starts with lovely ruby-amber color and an off-white head of foam and breathes of toasted malts with some breadier notes and a citrus hop aroma. With its elevated alcohol levels, the resulting flavor tends to get a little fruiter than many Irish-style red ales, tones that balance well with toasted malt sweetness, ending with a light crispness that aids drinkability in this medium-bodied offering.

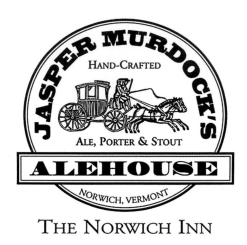

THE NORWICH INN

Amber Ale

STARR HILL BREWERY
CROZET, VIRGINIA
WWW.STARRHILL.COM
ALCOHOL CONTENT: 4.8% ABV
GLASSWARE: PINT
AVAILABILITY: YEAR-ROUND

Unleashing a sharp copper color and robust beige head with tight carbonation levels, Amber Ale showcases sweet pale malts washed in waves of caramel sugar with bready and nutty touches and a hint of English hop character. The flavor provides another swell of sweet caramel malt followed by a faint dusting of chocolate malt and an earthy but not bitter English hop contribution. Lighter in body with a crispness moving throughout, Amber Ale is a highly drinkable session beer.

Whistling Pig Red Ale

JASPER MURDOCK'S ALEHOUSE
NORWICH, VERMONT
WWW.NORWICHINN.COM
ALCOHOL CONTENT: 5.6% ABV
GLASSWARE: PINT OR MUG
AVAILABILITY: YEAR-ROUND

Brewed in a quaint shed structure adjacent to the beautifully restored Norwich Inn near the Dartmouth College campus, Whistling Pig Red Ale pours a deep reddish color and a solid, sustained portion of sticky, khaki-toned head. The aroma is filled with toasted malt, faint citrus and apple fruit notes, a pleasant touch of butter from diacetyl, and a hint of herbal hoppiness. With its moderate body, the flavor kicks off with toasted and caramel grains mixed with a flint of earthy and woody hops, all mixed with another quick dose of rich butter, all highlighted by British and European malt characters.

MÄRZEN

One of the most popular seasonal beers, the Marzen style derives its history from the German brewing center of Munich. A local adaptation of the Vienna style, the amber-hued, full-bodied, toasted malt lager was served during the annual Oktoberfest celebration, from which it takes its other name. Sometimes known as "Fest" beer. Märzens at today's Oktoberfest celebrations are substantially lighter in color and flavor, while American versions tend towards deep gold to copper colors, with strong Vienna or Munich toasted and bready malt aromas, and a slight but present noble hop aroma and bitterness. Oktoberfests are clean lagers, with dedication to classic German and European malts and possess around 6 percent alcohol. Many American brewers produce toasty amber ales with a decided fruit aroma and flavor and call them Märzen or Oktoberfest beers.

Oktoberfest

MILLSTREAM BREWING COMPANY
AMANA, IOWA
WWW.MILLSTREAMBREWING.COM
ALCOHOL CONTENT: 5.4% ABV
GLASSWARE: PINT OR GOBLET
AVAILABILITY: FALL

Appearing with its dark amber-auburn color with a thick dollop of beige foam that craters as it warms, the aroma wafts layers of toasted cereal grain on top of a clean and piquant noble hop sprinkle. The smooth flavored lager relies upon a caramel malt base that rides the flavor wave throughout, occasionally taking on some mild fruit notes mixed with a touch of dark chocolate, before cresting to a clean, crisp, and dry finish that calls for another sip.

Märzen

GORDON BIERSCH BREWERY RESTAURANT
MULTIPLE LOCATIONS
WWW.GORDONBIERSCH.COM
ALCOHOL CONTENT: 5.7% ABV
GLASSWARE: PINT, GOBLET, OR MUG
AVAILABILITY: YEAR-ROUND

Märzen is one of the few examples of the style that is produced throughout the year as part of the offerings from the lager-focused Gordon Biersch chain of brewpubs. Gordon Biersch has also spun off its bottling operation so there may be some variations depending upon whether you have this copper colored beer in a restaurant or from the bottle. The well-sustained beige foam cloud provides ample doses of crisp, clean biscuity malt sweetness, with touches of caramel. The medium body commences a slow-moving journey through malt sweetness, with caramel and toasted notes coating biscuity and bready hints, all wrapped in a light underlying fruitiness, with a dry lilt towards the finish.

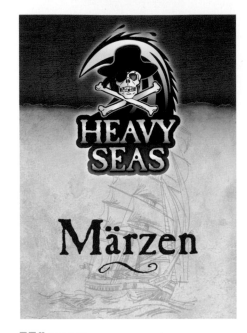

Octoberfest

SUMMIT BREWING COMPANY
SAINT PAUL, MINNESOTA
WWW.SUMMITBREWING.COM
ALCOHOL CONTENT: 7.4% ABV
GLASSWARE: PINT OR GOBLET
AVAILABILITY: FALL

A burnished orange color with some darker amber tones at the fringes and posing a wheat hued pillowy top, Summit's entrant is a classic interpretation of the Märzen category. A moderate and restrained surge of caramel and toasted Munich malts plays with an earthy noble hop character to create a fulfilling first breath. The flavor plays lightly toasted grains against a mildly spicy backdrop of noble hops in a surprisingly complex interplay of flavors. A touch of bitterness is added to the dry finish, making for a tight Märzen production that deserves some applause.

Märzen

HEAVY SEAS BEER
BALTIMORE, MARYLAND
WWW.CCBEER.COM
ALCOHOL CONTENT: 5.2% ABV
GLASSWARE: PINT OR GOBLET
AVAILABILITY: FALL

Playing off the local tradition of calling everyone "hon," this Märzen glows with a brilliant amber-orange body and undulating off-white head, wherein clean and nuanced rows of sweet malt pack together, with bready and toasted malts predominating over lesser notes of caramel, honey, and earthy fruit. Well-balanced from start to dry finish, the well-proportioned malt base glides with nutty and bready sweet notes, which are prodded into form by a residual but mild, earthy bitterness. The Märzen is a well-crafted fall seasonal.

Oktoberfest

STOUDT'S BREWING COMPANY
ADAMSTOWN, PENNSYLVANIA
WWW.STOUDTSBEER.COM
ALCOHOL CONTENT: 5.0% ABV
GLASSWARE: PINT, GOBLET, OR MUG
AVAILABILITY: FALL

A celebration of robust Munich and Vienna malts, Oktoberfest starts with a bright copper hue and a khaki ripple of foam before unleashing a toasted malt nose, replete with bready and caramel notes, all drenched over a reserved earthy noble hop character. In the glass, the aroma transforms into a more moderate experience, with toasted notes predominating in a creamy formation while subtly spicy hops bring a bitter counterbalance to the moderate sweetness level. Clean and crisp to the taste, Oktoberfest draws to a close with a dry, nutty finish.

Oktoberfest

LEGEND BREWING COMPANY
RICHMOND, VIRGINIA
WWW.LEGENDBREWING.COM
ALCOHOL CONTENT: 5.4% ABV
GLASSWARE: PINT OR GOBLET
AVAILABILITY: FALL

With its auburn-orange body and sticky, pale tan foam peak, this southern Märzen smells of toasted grain, sweet caramel and even some roasted malts, all mixed together with a blessing of apple fruity floral hops. Crisp to the taste and dry throughout, a moderate wash of toasted grains predominates, with subtle bready and caramel malt hints, a touch of honey, all rounded out by a slightly earthy noble hop bitterness that holds hands with a grainy and dry finish. A smooth and at times creamy offering, Legend has brewed a very worthy American Märzen.

DUNKEL

Another classic Bavarian beer style that gets overlooked by American consumers and brewers, the Dunkel is an unusually delicate yet complex character. Light to deep brown in color, the darker hues often deceive would-be drinkers into believing the style to be bitter and strongly roasted. In contrast, dunkels are supremely drinkable, balancing rich, layered malt sweetness with touches of chocolate, toffee, and caramel from dark malts, with a light creamy and at times sweet body. Never overpowering, faint hints of noble hops may be present in the aroma, but hops play little other role. The complexity and beauty of the Munich malts combined with the clean flavor and finish renders dunkels an undiscovered challenge for even dedicated beer enthusiasts. These same qualities make dunkels, the perfect meeting grounds for drinkers seeking either comfort or complexity in their half-liter mugs.

Bavarian Dark

MICHIGAN BREWING COMPANY
WEBBERVILLE, MICHIGAN
WWW.MICHIGANBREWING.COM
ALCOHOL CONTENT: 4.0% ABV
GLASSWARE: PINT OR MUG
AVAILABILITY: YEAR-ROUND

With its deep russet amber-brown color and mild off-white foam dollop, Bavarian Dark gives forth a surprisingly strong aroma of roasted malts, ranging from coffee to chocolate, before retreating into a creamier stance. The resulting flavor is a touch malty sweet with hints of smoke punctured by roasted coffee and dark chocolate flutters, with a perceptible level of noble hop bite and flavor underlying the roasted malt cacophony. Surprisingly smooth and drinkable, this sessionable lager demonstrates that oodles of flavor can be packed into smaller alcohol packages.

Franconia Dunkel

FRANCONIA BREWING COMPANY
MCKINNEY, TEXAS
WWW.FRANCONIABREWING.COM
ALCOHOL CONTENT: 5.0% ABV
GLASSWARE: PINT OR MUG
AVAILABILITY: YEAR-ROUND

The upstart Franconia Brewing Company encourages fellow Texans to avoid drinking beer just because they're thirsty. Taking its name from the northern part of Bavaria, this German-inspired brewery offers its deep brown colored Dunkel, with its ruby highlights and solid two fingers of beige foam, as a contemplative replacement for the standard, macro lagers often favored in the Lone Star State. The roasted malt aroma is filled with chocolate, dark bread, and touches of toffee and coffee, with a slight earthy noble hop aroma mixed in for good measure. The similarly situated flavor condenses the aroma into a mélange of dark roasted and chocolate malts, a plum fruit character, and a touch of hop spice in a drinkable and dry finish.

Creamy Dark

JACOB LEINENKUGEL BREWING COMPANY
CHIPPEWA FALLS, WISCONSIN
WWW.LEINIE.COM
ALCOHOL CONTENT: 4.9% ABV
GLASSWARE: PINT OR MUG
AVAILABILITY: YEAR-ROUND

A frequent medalist at the Great American Beer Festival, Leinenkugel's Creamy Dark starts with a robust mahogany color with a creamy, alabaster foam crown and gives off a range of dark roasted malts accented by occasional caramel, burnt brown sugar, and mildly nutty sidenotes. The roasted malt carries over to the flavor, followed indeed by some creamy malt flavors and a touch of brown sugar and molasses, before rounding out with a slight kiss of earthy hops and a whiff of smoke.

Calumet Dark

ROWLANDS CALUMET BREWERY
CHILTON, WISCONSIN
WWW.ROWLANDSBREWERY.COM
ALCOHOL CONTENT: 5.0% ABV
GLASSWARE: PINT OR MUG
AVAILABILITY: YEAR-ROUND

A hit among beer geeks, although a bit hard to find as it is produced by a small town Wisconsin brewery, Calumet Dark pours a deep brown color with touches of ruby at the edges and a quick crown of beige foam. The nose is filled with gentle toasted caramel, darker molasses and treacle, with some harsher roasted elements, and capped by a light blackberry fruit hint. The darker roasted malts flex their muscles in the body, aided by a dry grainy note, some nuttiness, and a touch of fruit accented coffee. A light creamy consistency aids drinkability in this fine Dunkel.

Dunkel Lager

SLY FOX BREWING COMPANY
PHOENIXVILLE, PENNSYLVANIA
WWW.SLYFOXBEER.COM
ALCOHOL CONTENT: 5.3% ABV
GLASSWARE: PINT OR MUG
AVAILABILITY: YEAR-ROUND

With its medium brownish auburn color and solid cream foam set, Dunkel Lager starts with a sweet jolt of European dark malt, with bready and toffee predominating over a mild, zesty hop zing, all with creamy elements mixed in. The smooth, clean flavors tend to favor a bready malt character, with some residual dark grape and plum notes, followed by a slight treacle malt flavor. Aided by an even carbonation level, this Sly Fox offering is rich and flavorful without being too heavy handed.

Doryman's Dark Ale

PELICAN PUB AND BREWERY
PACIFIC CITY, OREGON
WWW.PELICANBREWERY.COM
ALCOHOL CONTENT: 5.8% ABV
GLASSWARE: PINT
AVAILABILITY: YEAR-ROUND

Pouring with a pleasant chestnut brown color and an ivory head of foam, Doryman casts a slightly nutty ester profile, mixed with light touches of alcohol, toasted malt and molasses, but with a decidedly roasted edge for balance. The medium-bodied flavor offers a splash of toasted malt and a nutty, bready quality, before continuing to set a darker, slightly bitter course with a long, drawn-out roasted malt finish that takes a mildly earthy turn towards the finish.

SCOTTISH-STYLE ALE

Centuries ago, Scottish beers were taxed according to their particular alcohol levels. A light Scottish Ale was known as 60 schilling ale, while the more potent Wee Heavy was deemed 90 schilling ale. Four main categories of Scottish-style ales generally exist today, including the mid-range 70 and 80 schilling varieties, offering a wide range of flavors, bodies, and complexities. On the lower side of the flavor spectrum, Scottish-style light ales offer a simple body, low alcohol levels, little bitterness, and mild nutty or caramel malt flavors. Pouring bright and typically amber to brownish-red in color, this style may occasionally possess the faintest touch of smoky or peaty notes, a nod to the country's whisky history. Clean and focused on its signature malt flavors, the overall hop character is low, sporadically floral or herbal, allowing Scottish-style ales to remain very drinkable throughout.

The Duke of Winship

MIDDLE AGES BREWING COMPANY
SYRACUSE, NEW YORK
WWW.MIDDLEAGESBREWING.COM
ALCOHOL CONTENT: 6.5% ABV
GLASSWARE: PINT OR MUG
AVAILABILITY: YEAR-ROUND

Introducing itself with a striking and deep russet auburn color and a wheat hued dollop of robust foam, The Duke continues to impress with its charming nose of toasted malt, slight molasses, and a touch of ashen grain, all mixed with a hint of citrus fruit and butter. A touch darker than many Scottish-style Ales, the flavor continues with a robust display of toffee and roasted malts, but never overwhelming, and a light butterscotch quality atop a creamy medium body.

Kiltlifter Scottish-Style Ale

FOUR PEAKS BREWING COMPANY
TEMPE, ARIZONA
WWW.FOURPEAKS.COM
ALCOHOL CONTENT: 6.0% ABV
GLASSWARE: PINT
AVAILABILITY: YEAR-ROUND

With its amber-orange body and simple cap of beige foam, our second Kiltlifter starts closer to the amber ale side than the Scotch Ale side of the equation, with light caramel notes tied up with a faint, attractive smoky quality. A mild nutty quality pervades the body, followed by dry toasted malt sweetness, a little breadiness, and some wood and earth from the hops. A slightly minty, herbal tang from the hops checks the mild malt sweetness, leaving a clean, creamy, and enjoyable Scottish-Style Ale.

90 Shilling Ale

ODELL BREWING COMPANY
FORT COLLINS, COLORADO
WWW.ODELLS.COM
ALCOHOL CONTENT: 5.3% ABV
GLASSWARE: PINT OR MUG
AVAILABILITY: YEAR-ROUND

Dark amber to ruby in color with a light tan sticky foam head, this excellent Odell's offering starts with a round dose of sweet caramelized malts and a bready component mixed with toffee and light treacle, with a touch of fragrant, fruity hops. The flavor divides its time between light caramel malts and an eccentric toasted bready quality, flanked by a mild fruitiness. Nearing the cross-over point into the more robust Scotch Ale territory, this offering remains slightly more served and highly drinkable.

Pike Kilt Lifter Scotch-Style Ale

PIKE PUB AND BREWERY
SEATTLE, WASHINGTON
WWW.PIKEBREWING.COM
ALCOHOL CONTENT: 6.5% ABV
GLASSWARE: PINT OR GOBLET
AVAILABILITY: YEAR-ROUND

One of many beers similarly named in a tongue-in-cheek manner, Pike's offering starts with a dull amber-orange color, a substantial and sustained off-white deck of foam, and a nose of lightly sticky sweet malt, floral fruit, earthy hops, and a caramel and toffee topping. The flavor involves layers of creamy malt, with occasional heights of toasted grain and sweet caramel, all mixed together with mild fruit notes and a slightly earthy hop and yeast bite over a mildly warming alcohol sensation. The lightly spicy hop dose manages the malt sweetness into a dry finish.

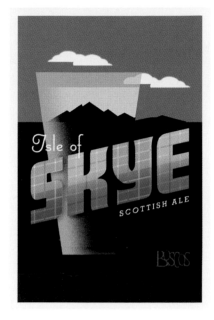

Isle of Skye Scottish Ale

BOSCOS BREWING COMPANY
NASHVILLE, TENNESSEE
WWW.BOSCOSBEER.COM
ALCOHOL CONTENT: 5.5% ABV
GLASSWARE: PINT OR MUG
AVAILABILITY: YEAR-ROUND

A beer commonly brewed at all of the multiple Boscos locations, it pours with a surprisingly dark brown hue with ruby touches and a wheat toned head. With its dark color, the aroma is understandably punctuated by moments of darker, roasted malts, but the lighter toffee and caramel flavors win out over a touch of smoke and fruit. A creamy texture aids the mellowing of the darker malts and a slight alcohol warmth can be felt towards the finish of the pint.

Laughing Lab Scottish-Style Ale

BRISTOL BREWING COMPANY
COLORADO SPRINGS, COLORADO
WWW.BRISTOLBREWING.COM
ALCOHOL CONTENT: 5.3% ABV
GLASSWARE: PINT
AVAILABILITY: YEAR-ROUND

Within its amber colored body, flecks of darker chocolate hints can be seen fleeting at the edges and below the surface of the ample and persistent crest of soft foam. The aroma starts with a curious and intriguing mixture of sweet molasses and caramel malt, followed by a smoky element and an earthy and woody hop note. In the glass, the ale provides a downy balance between its dominant caramel malt bursts and its slightly grainy elements, all with a slight smoke and fruit combination. Bristol provides an interesting interplay of flavors and aromas with its Scottish-Style Ale.

VIENNA-STYLE LAGER

Sometimes it's hard to distinguish the subtle differences between styles, and there is perhaps no closer association, both in terms of flavor and history, than the ties that bind Märzens and Vienna-style lagers. Both derive their origins from the work of enterprising Austrian brewer Anton Dreher, a man some credited with being the father of lager brewing, much to the consternation of the Czech people. Dreher and Gabriel Sedlmayr, Sr. struck up a friendship in Austria and traveled through England together, boldly stealing trade secrets along the way. Often made with a double- or triple-decoction mash, Vienna-style lagers are reddish-orange to copper in color, with a sustained tan head, and full of sweet toasted malt aromas and flavors. A touch of noble hop aroma or flavor can be expected for balance, but as with the Märzen style, the Munich and Vienna malt flavors take center stage.

Fairbanks Lager

SILVER GULCH BREWING AND BOTTLING COMPANY
FAIRBANKS, ALASKA
WWW.SILVERGULCH.COM
ALCOHOL CONTENT: 5.5% ABV
GLASSWARE: PINT OR MUG
AVAILABILITY: YEAR-ROUND

Holed up in frigid central Alaska, Silver Gulch offers local beer drinkers a form of respite with this comforting and hearty lager. With its clear amber body and white cloud of foam, touches of a grainy caramel and toasted malt sweetness meet a bouquet of floral and spicy hops as counterbalance. The flavor tends towards the bready and caramel malt side of the equation, with some grainier notes, and a light yet refreshing earthy hop zest cutting through the sweeter moments. Lighter in body than some ruddy examples, Fairbanks Lager is a welcomed, sweet malt respite.

Snake River Lager

SNAKE RIVER BREWING COMPANY
JACKSON, WYOMING
WWW.SNAKERIVERBREWING.COM
ALCOHOL CONTENT: 4.8% ABV
GLASSWARE: PINT
AVAILABILITY: YEAR-ROUND

A touch hazy from the start, a firm crest of foam hovers above the amber-orange body, giving off hints of sweet caramel malt mixed with a surprisingly fruity floral hop tone. With a slightly over-sized body compared to meeker versions of the style, Snake River Lager blends toasted, grainy malts with sweeter toffee elements and a tinge of orange citrus fruit flavors from the hops. The residual sugars leave a slightly tacky mouthfeel at times that lets you revel in the robust malt flavors.

Toasted Lager

BLUE POINT BREWING COMPANY
PATCHOGUE, NEW YORK
WWW.BLUEPOINTBREWING.COM
ALCOHOL CONTENT: 5.3% ABV
GLASSWARE: PINT OR MUG
AVAILABILITY: YEAR-ROUND

With a deep copper color and creamy beige-white head, Toasted Lager lives up to its name when the clean aroma unveils light caramel and toasted malt notes over a reserved creamy quality and a touch of yeast bite character. With a medium body and moderate carbonation level, the Lager effortlessly shifts between reserved biscuity malt sweetness, a mild creaminess, and a slight minerally yeast bite in the finish, each punctuated by quick bursts of dull, baked apple. The bitterness levels provide balance, and a grainy malt character provides some additional texture in this fine Vienna-style Lager.

Dynamo Copper Lager

METROPOLITAN BREWING COMPANY
CHICAGO, ILLINOIS
WWW.METROBREWING.COM
ALCOHOL CONTENT: 5.6% ABV
GLASSWARE: PINT
AVAILABILITY: YEAR-ROUND

With its golden amber color and big off-white head, Dynamo strikes an attractive first pose, followed by an even more impressive aroma of enticing biscuity and toasted malts mixed with slight nutty touches and a little residual noble hop zest. As clean and crisp as Dynamo's aroma, the flavor spikes with waves of rich malt flavor, swaying from toasted to biscuity with bready, caramel, and nutty touches, all with a mild citrus undertone that somehow accentuates the sweetness of the malt by contrast. A clean, mild, and zesty hop bite in the finish ties this excellent lager into a nice, neat package.

Eliot Ness Vienna Lager

GREAT LAKES BREWING COMPANY
CLEVELAND, OHIO
WWW.GREATLAKESBREWING.COM
ALCOHOL CONTENT: 6.2% ABV
GLASSWARE: PINT OR MUG
AVAILABILITY: YEAR-ROUND

Ask usually lager-phobic beer geeks about their favorite lager and more times than not you'll hear them mention Eliot Ness. With its brilliant amber color and citrus fruit accented off-white head, Eliot Ness brims with a spectacular arrangement of sweet malts, ranging from caramel to toasted cereal and bready, each embraced by a spicy and earthy noble hop quality that snaps the elements into an expertly orchestrated display. In glorious parity with the aroma, the medium body results in a wash of sweet, expressive caramel and toasted malt flavors, all balanced by a touch of citrus and spice from the hops, but without any lingering, distracting bitterness to take away from the malt parade.

Jomo Lager

STARR HILL BREWERY
CROZET, VIRGINIA
WWW.STARRHILL.COM
ALCOHOL CONTENT: 4.6% ABV
GLASSWARE: PINT
AVAILABILITY: YEAR-ROUND

Angling for the fruitier side of the style, perhaps showing some roots in American ales, Starr Hill's Jomo Lager pours with a bright copper color and a huge, well-retained chunk of foam. The nose offers long glimpses of the Munich base malt, with its signature caramel and bready flavors, before introducing its juicy pear and apple friends that do not feel out of place in this style. The flavor is all Vienna, with doses of rich caramel and toasted grain raked over earthy noble hops, leading to a delectable, creamy finish. Jomo Lager is highly drinkable and also a session beer candidate, considering its respectably low alcohol level.

MILD ALE

An often misunderstood and underappreciated entrant into the Mellow and Malty category, England's classic Mild Ale is a curiosity in the modern age of brewing. Near uniformly rejected by young British drinkers and beer snobs alike as a simple, unexciting low-alcohol beer style, these ales confound modern brewers and the populaces that love them. The term "mild" once referred not to a style but a young beer meant to be drunk fresh, with many examples exhibiting a higher hop presence and alcohol content than today's versions. There were mild bitters, stouts, and porters, and the beers sold singularly as "milds" were a far cry from today's brands. Alcohol levels were always in the mid-range as the beer did not require preservation beyond a few days for fast consumer enjoyment. Fast-forward to today and modern Mild often represents a lower alcohol beer, around 4 percent, with sweet, roasted malt flavors, and a low bitterness level. American craft brewers are slowly beginning to embrace the session ale qualities of Mild Ale.

The modern day Mild may be the ultimate Mellow and Malty beer. In Detroit, the Motor City Brewing Works produces the creatively named Ghettoblaster, which despite its in-your-face moniker, actually represents a delicious Mild Ale. Around 5 percent alcohol, the light reddish-brown beer displays the malt-forward profile so crucial to the style, with nutty and toasted malts doing much of the work, while a piney and candy-sweet hop balance brings up the finish.

A few paces from the campus of Yale University in New Haven, Connecticut, students and locals enjoy Raven Haired Beauty at the quixotic Brü Rm @ Bar. With its black amber frame and wispy white head, this Mild weighs in at under 4 percent alcohol and displays aromas and flavors of toffee, treacle, lightly roasted coffee, and a burnished fruitiness that draws you back in for another pint or two.

Better known for its palate-smacking array of Hop Monsters, the Pizza Port brewpub chain in southern California brews a 3.2 percent alcohol beauty called Dawn Patrol Mild. A robust deep amber color, this Mild starts with a soft nose of toffee malts, followed by sprays of chocolate and cocoa, alongside some plum and dried cherry notes. The body adds a touch of fruitier hops, but the exploration of light and dark malts continues in this easy-going yet quite nuanced offering.

ROBUST AND RICH

The ultimate expression of the inner sweet and bold beauty of malt, the soul of beer and perhaps its most complex ingredient, is reflected in the hearty and expressive beers collected here. Breweries have long relied upon malt as the foundational base upon which to paint the colors of their final products. Hardly content to quietly idle with the subtle chamber music of their Mellow and Malty brethren, brewers possessed the need to produce stronger, greatly fortifying beers, whether to last a Lenten period, in preparation for a winter season, or to celebrate other cultural or religious events. The beers in this library possess a fuller body and spirit, all with the centralizing charm that their focus remains dedicated to a balanced malt sweetness. Far from cloyingly sweet sugar bombs, these malt masters require time to age before developing into their complex and striking final forms. With the malt-forward approach to sweetness, Robust and Rich offerings match beautifully with many desserts, including chocolate and fruits, but also hold their own against heavier meat and potato dishes. With their residual sweetness and low levels of bitterness, these rich, stronger beers are also great at breaking down beer stereotypes for those who fear a little color in their pints.

BOCK

Invented in the North German city of Einbeck, from which it may derive a garbled version of its name, bocks have a long history dating back to the fourteenth century, and are associated with goats, an image appearing on many labels. Like a good power hitter, Bock is an exercise in measured strength. Controlled and focused, yet strong, these medium- to full-bodied beers should be a rich ruby color and possess a broad malty aroma. A touch of caramel malt may be present, but the flavor usually focuses on classic Munich and Vienna malt flavors, not quite toasted or bready, but full, rich, and a touch sweet. Hops play little role with bocks, except to provide some structure and balance. Clean and smooth to the taste despite a 6 percent alcohol level or higher, bocks remain drinkable and tempered in the face of a soulful malt experience.

Lakefront Bock Beer

LAKEFRONT BREWERY
MILWAUKEE, WISCONSIN
WWW.LAKEFRONTBREWERY.COM
ALCOHOL CONTENT: 6.7% ABV
GLASSWARE: PINT
AVAILABILITY: SPRING

Makers of many fine ales and lagers, Lakefront pulls out all the stops with its Bock offering, a scarlet-orange colored beer with a wheat brown cap of creamy foam. The aroma exhibits prodigious amounts of sweet and bready Munich malts, mixed with tones of molasses and light earthy noble hop hints. The flavor is dominated by the bready Munich malts, with slight darker touches, all rounded out by molasses sweetness.

Winter Brew

SPRECHER BREWING COMPANY
GLENDALE, WISCONSIN
WWW.SPRECHERBREWERY.COM
ALCOHOL CONTENT: 5.7% ABV
GLASSWARE: PINT OR MUG
AVAILABILITY: WINTER

With its deep ruby brown color and light wispy head, the aroma showcases a faint roasted malt quality that gives way to rich caramel malt, a touch of cream and butter, followed by a slight earthy quality. The medium-bodied beer continues with a lightly sweet toasted malt character, a roasted malt hint, followed by a residual creaminess that works well against slight yeast bitterness. The mellow malt flavors remain quite drinkable and smooth throughout.

Anchor Bock

ANCHOR BREWING COMPANY
SAN FRANCISCO, CALIFORNIA
WWW.ANCHORBREWING.COM
ALCOHOL CONTENT: 5.5% ABV
GLASSWARE: PINT OR MUG
AVAILABILITY: SPRING

With its deep burgundy shimmer and wheat toast tan head, Anchor Bock is a charming number and its nose brims with lush toasted caramel malt sweetness with brushes of brown sugar and a dash of fruitiness. The velvety feel of the medium body rises to meet the aroma, again displaying a bready caramel quality that boasts a complex brush of flavors, from molasses to nuts and brown sugar again. Smooth and clean throughout, Anchor Bock is an excellent spring release.

Uff-Da Bock

NEW GLARUS BREWING COMPANY
NEW GLARUS, WISCONSIN
WWW.NEWGLARUSBREWING.COM
ALCOHOL CONTENT: 6.75% ABV
GLASSWARE: PINT OR MUG
AVAILABILITY: LIMITED RELEASE

Named after a Scandinavian phrase exclaiming surprise, befitting of its Midwestern roots, this Bock from New Glarus pours deep chestnut-amber with ruby hues and a sizable off-tan head. The beautifully malty aroma pools together sweet molasses, brown sugar, and a touch of chalky dryness, followed by a distinct fruitiness and a light Christmas spice. The flavor matches with a velvety, luscious, and medium- to full bodied mouthfeel that rolls over the tongue with light alcohol notes, hints of black currant and raisins, and a slight tang that balances out the robust malt flavor.

Goat's Breath Bock Ale

O'FALLON BREWERY
SAINT LOUIS, MISSOURI
WWW.OFALLONBREWERY.COM
ALCOHOL CONTENT: 6.2% ABV
GLASSWARE: PINT OR MUG
AVAILABILITY: FALL

Best served at a slightly warmer temperature, this Bock displays a rich, deep brown color with hints of auburn and orange at the edges, and balances a well-formed off-tan head. Fresh baked bread and toasted malts fill the nose, followed by a hearty basket of dried fruits, including figs and a touch of nuttiness, as well as powdered chocolate. The flavor strikes you as directly as the complex aroma, with big molasses and bready sweetness balanced by a dry fruity quality, all wrapped around light chocolate and caramel swaths. Goat's Breath Bock Ale is a highly nuanced and drinkable autumnal companion.

Schokolade Bock

MILLSTREAM BREWING COMPANY
AMANA, IOWA
WWW.MILLSTREAMBREWING.COM
ALCOHOL CONTENT: 5.7% ABV
GLASSWARE: PINT
AVAILABILITY: YEAR-ROUND

With its deep ruby amber color and solid fingers of tan foam, Schokolade certainly looks the part. Millstream's Bock is traditional in all accounts, starting with its mixture of bready and caramel malts in the nose aided by a touch of powdered cocoa. The medium body opens up with a moderately sweet blend of molasses and bready malts, flanked by flits of dark roasted malt and chocolate, all drizzled over dried fruit notes. A slight woody and earthy quality arrives late to the scene but provides additional structure.

DOPPELBOCK

Where bocks celebrate a judicious balance of malt strength, doppelbocks celebrate a bit of excess in the malt and alcohol departments. To be sure, these are not over-the-top, sugary sweet malt bombs. To the contrary, doppelbocks, or double bocks as they are sometimes referred to, are a descendent of the seasonal brewing activities of German monks. With elevated alcohol and malt levels, expect a stronger, fuller experience, but as with all German beers, restraint and balance remain key elements. Doppelbocks are generally dark brown or ruby in color, but paler versions exist, and offer an off-white, sustained head. The aromas are strongly of deep, robust Munich grains with occasional faint traces of roasted or chocolate malts. The mouthfeel is understandably full, with velvety malt waves cascading in the body over enhanced, warming alcohol notes.

Pioneer Bourbon Barrel Double Bock

PIONEER BREWING COMPANY
FISKDALE, MASSACHUSETTS
WWW.HYLANDBREW.COM
ALCOHOL CONTENT: 8.5% ABV
GLASSWARE: GOBLET OR TULIP
AVAILABILITY: SPRING

With its deep auburn brown color and sturdy tan head, Pioneer Double Bock breathes of sweet Munich and European malts, bready and alcohol soaked at times, mixed with a touch of vanilla draped over a mildly spicy and grassy hop character. A slight woody note underlies the pleasant composition of sweet and toasted malts, alcohol, and another light dose of vanilla, with an herbal bitterness rounding out the edges for a creamy and slightly slick and velvety finish.

Sudwerk Doppel Bock

SUDWERK RESTAURANT AND BREWERY
DAVIS, CALIFORNIA
WWW.SUDWERK.COM
ALCOHOL CONTENT: 8.0% ABV
GLASSWARE: GOBLET OR TULIP
AVAILABILITY: WINTER

Primarily a brewer of lagers and German-style beers, Sudwerk can be expected to make an excellent Doppelbock, and indeed it does. The light tannish brown hued body gives way to a dense several fingers of rigid foam and showcases rich aromas of sweet molasses, toasted toffee, dark chocolate hints, all mixed over a faint fruity quality, including figs, dark cherries, and prunes. The almost port-like aroma trends into a milder yet potent flavor combination of figgy sweet grains, a slight roasted dryness, and a caramel malt base, with a touch of alcohol for warmth.

Bayern Doppelbock

BAYERN BREWING, INC.
MISSOULA, MONTANA
WWW.BAYERNBREWING.COM
ALCOHOL CONTENT: 8.4% ABV
GLASSWARE: GOBLET OR TULIP
AVAILABILITY: WINTER

From Missoula, Montana, comes a traditional Doppelbock from a German-focused American craft brewery. Offering a dark copper brown tone, strikingly clear, and with a moderate wheat tan head, the beer is all caramel and sweet European malt, with hints of darker roasted malts. Translated into the glass, the beer continues the malty chords with additions of breadier elements and a light residual sweetness mixed over a creamy and velvety consistency. A light carbonation keeps the sweeter elements in line.

Liverator

THE LIVERY
BENTON HARBOR, MICHIGAN
WWW.LIVERYBREW.COM
ALCOHOL CONTENT: 9.0% ABV
GLASSWARE: GOBLET OR TULIP
AVAILABILITY: LIMITED RELEASE

An occasional and often hard to come by release from this small Michigan brewpub, this eponymously named Doppelbock pours dark burgundy with an impressive and tacky foam head, which offers up wave upon wave of dark caramel and chocolate mixed with brown sugar and a slight spice character. Equally alluring in the glass, the full-bodied flavor reveals bold layers of dark caramel, toffee, and chocolate, along with dark fruits, including grape and figs. Smooth in style and velvety on the tongue, the Liverator is a treat worth seeking out.

Samuel Adams Double Bock

BOSTON BEER COMPANY
BOSTON, MASSACHUSETTS
WWW.SAMUELADAMS.COM
ALCOHOL CONTENT: 9.5% ABV
GLASSWARE: GOBLET OR TULIP
AVAILABILITY: YEAR-ROUND

One of Boston Beer's most popular offerings, converted to a year-round product, the juicy and sweet Double Bock pours with a deep burgundy tone and a tannish ivory head that appears creamy and tacky. Soulful is a proper way to describe the liquid bread aroma, filled as it is with toasted grain, hints of chocolate and fig, and touches of roasted malt. Nearly full-bodied and a slow drinker in its own right, the sturdy flavor relies upon the substantial bready Munich malt base, along with roasted caramel and chocolate, dried fruit, a wisp of smoke, and a warming, ever-present alcohol. At times a tad chewy and robust, each sip beckons another.

Autumnal Fire

CAPITAL BREWERY
MIDDLETON, WISCONSIN
WWW.CAPITAL-BREWERY.COM
ALCOHOL CONTENT: 7.2% ABV
GLASSWARE: GOBLET OR TULIP
AVAILABILITY: FALL

It's hard to argue with a brewery that makes four seasonal doppelbocks throughout the year. The Capital Brewery manages this hefty feat, with each offering providing a satisfying malt experience. With its flared orange-amber color and lofty, moussy foam, Autumnal Fire gets the nod due to its crossing of an Oktoberfest and a Doppelbock. The resulting aroma booms with toasted malt notes, a favoring alcohol warmth, fruit touches including honey and dates, and a slight spiciness from German noble hops. Despite its alcoholic heft, the full-bodied beer remains quite smooth, with substantial toasted and bready malt characters running with a complex array of citrus and honey, toffee, and even hints of powdered dark chocolate. Autumnal Fire is a powerfully seductive fall seasonal.

DUBBEL

Taking the celebration of malt in a different direction, the Dubbel is a feisty blend of intricate malt flavors and layered spicy hints. Complex in both aroma and flavor, dubbels are closely associated with monastic brewing in Belgium but are brewed across the United States. Medium brown with reddish hints in hue, the medium- to full-bodied dubbels, sometimes called Abbey, exhibit a vigorous carbonation level, with bountiful and persistent off-white heads, and a slight bite from the bubbles. The aromas possess strong dark fruit and phenolic notes, with hints of plums and raisins, slight peppery tinges from Belgian yeast strains, and a well-balanced but present warm alcohol touch. Actual spices are not usually used. The flavor largely follows the aroma, with the addition of complex, rich bready malt flavors and light residual sweetness.

Dubbel

FLYING FISH BREWING COMPANY
CHERRY HILL, NEW JERSEY
WWW.FLYINGFISH.COM
ALCOHOL CONTENT: 7.0% ABV
GLASSWARE: GOBLET OR TUMBLER
AVAILABILITY: YEAR-ROUND

This New Jersey offering pours with a bright copper color and a light tan head, with an intriguing and mildly and phenolic spicy aroma that moves between allspice and pepper mixed with a sizable caramel and toasted malt base, with a touch of booze. Dubbel's flavor starts with a light yet drawn out dose of sweet malt but transitions gradually to a light tang and then quickly into a phenolic spiciness. Light alcohol and vanilla flavors in the base mix with the sweeter malt notes in this lighter bodied version of the style.

Brother Thelonious

NORTH COAST BREWING COMPANY
FORT BRAGG, CALIFORNIA
WWW.NORTHCOASTBREWING.COM
ALCOHOL CONTENT: 9.3% ABV
GLASSWARE: GOBLET OR TULIP
AVAILABILITY: YEAR-ROUND

Brewed in honor of jazz impresario Thelonious Monk, this hazy burgundy-toned Dubbel possesses a loose breed of cloudy foam and sets free oodles of dark fruit, including ripe cherries and figs, roasted caramel, a spicy and fresh mixture of cloves and a touch of anise. In a deep glass, the flavors swirl together to create a complex profile including mashed dark fruits, dry and leafy tobacco, hints of citrus, and then another round of spice from, among other things, yeast. The body stays firm but medium and balance and order are kept from start to finish in this highly drinkable strong Belgian-style ale.

Ommegang

BREWERY OMMEGANG
COOPERSTOWN, NEW YORK
WWW.OMMEGANG.COM
ALCOHOL CONTENT: 8.5% ABV
GLASSWARE: GOBLET OR TULIP
AVAILABILITY: YEAR-ROUND

A deep, hazy rouge-amber hue with a pillowy white head of foam, the namesake brand from one of America's foremost brewers of Belgian-style ales flowers with a complex fusion of black cherries, bananas, anise, caramel malt, and a hop spice and peppery yeast quality. With its tight carbonation level, the first sip imparts a slight bite, followed by a wash of residual, toffee sweetness, honey, black licorice, and a mild but ever-present and rounding spiciness. Slight dark chocolate and powdered cocoa elements show up from time to time in this stellar and well-priced offering.

Abbey Belgian Style Ale

NEW BELGIUM BREWING COMPANY
FORT COLLINS, COLORADO
WWW.NEWBELGIUM.COM
ALCOHOL CONTENT: 7.0% ABV
GLASSWARE: GOBLET OR TULIP
AVAILABILITY: YEAR-ROUND

Best known for its ubiquitous Fat Tire Amber Ale, New Belgium also brews a varied portfolio of other flavorful ales, including its signature Abbey offering. With its deep mahogany color and its robust tan head, this Dubbel possesses a decidedly spicy nose, filled with dried fruits and a touch of anise and black licorice; alcohol warms the edges alongside some earthy noble hops. The flavor is decidedly malty, defined best by a fig flavor mixed with a touch of candi sugar dryness and punctuated by a substantial hop and yeast bite and character. Growing in strength as it warms, the fruit and spice flavors balance well with dark malt into a dry finish.

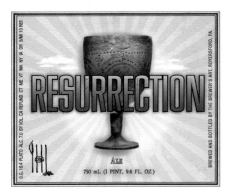

Resurrection

THE BREWER'S ART
BALTIMORE, MARYLAND
WWW.THEBREWERSART.COM
ALCOHOL CONTENT: 7.0% ABV
GLASSWARE: GOBLET OR TULIP
AVAILABILITY: YEAR-ROUND

Available in cork-finished bottles or on tap at the downtown Baltimore brewpub, Resurrection pours with a mildly hazy countenance, with dark amber to brown tones, and with a healthy dollop of tan foam. The aroma tingles with slight dried fruit, Belgian candi sugar, a mild peppery spice and perhaps a hint of anise. The flavor carries on a spirited discussion between the sweeter, dark fruit malt elements and the spicy, complex yeast flavors, finished off with phenolic notes of clove over candi sugar. A soft carbonation level accentuates the flavors.

Siamese Twin Ale

UNCOMMON BREWERS
SANTA CRUZ, CALIFORNIA
WWW.UNCOMMONBREWERS.COM
ALCOHOL CONTENT: 8.5% ABV
GLASSWARE: GOBLET OR TULIP
AVAILABILITY: YEAR-ROUND

A bit of a curveball amongst these more traditional selections, Siamese Twin Ale starts ordinary enough with a strong boost of carbonation behind its cloudy mahogany brown base coat and tall, spacious tan head. The first sign that this is an American take on the classic Dubbel style starts when the usual sweet caramel base malts and residual spiciness are joined by hints of citrus lime. The brewers blend in Thai spices, including lemongrass and kaffir lime, which results in sweet caramel malt covering a slowly building geyser of spicy citrus and coriander. Siamese Twin Ale is perhaps a little out in left field for the conventional, but it's certainly worth a taste.

MAIBOCK

One of the noblest and most under-represented lager styles, Maibock is a spring seasonal that epitomizes sweet, soulful malt goodness. The light-colored maibocks perhaps have more in common with lighter lager styles, such as Helles, than they do with their Bock brethren. Popular at spring festivals in Germany, the style is assertive both in terms of malt flavor and hop underpinning, with continental malt notes giving way to a judicious noble hop balance. Sometimes known as a heller or pale bock, the style is mild straw to glorious golden in color with a sweet, bready malt aroma. Maibocks are usually medium- to full-bodied, with prominent malt flavors and a noticeable noble hop presence, and a robust but not overpowering alcohol level. Maibock's beauty is in the balance of these challenging elements, a feat it manages with grace, resulting in a highly drinkable final product.

Mai Bock

SPRECHER BREWING COMPANY
GLENDALE, WISCONSIN
WWW.SPRECHERBREWERY.COM
ALCOHOL CONTENT: 6.0% ABV
GLASSWARE: MUG OR PINT
AVAILABILITY: SPRING

First brewed by the heavily German-influenced brewery in 1986, this Maibock starts with a bright cloudy copper color and a modest pale cream head, mixing in sweet touches of caramel and toasted malts, alongside hints of fresh bread and fruit. Medium bodied, Sprecher's version of the style imparts a rich, sweet caramel malt flavor with occasional spritzes of noble hops from the use of Tettnanger. A touch fruity and light at times, this remains clean and smooth until the last sip.

Maibock

CAPITAL BREWERY
MIDDLETON, WISCONSIN
WWW.CAPITAL-BREWERY.COM
ALCOHOL CONTENT: 6.2% ABV
GLASSWARE: MUG OR PINT
AVAILABILITY: YEAR-ROUND

This bready beauty of a classic lager starts orange amber in tone with a substantial frothy off-white head and an aroma that that boasts massive doses of Munich malt, with toasted notes, and a chalky wheat character. Very clean in aroma and flavor, the rounded bready malt sweetness rolls into a toasted touch followed by a slight tang from the alcohol and a little reserved pepper spice. Finishing firm bodied and never cloying, Capital's Maibock is a classic in its own right.

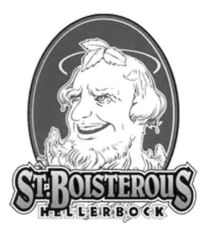

Spring Bock

SAINT ARNOLD BREWING COMPANY
HOUSTON, TEXAS
WWW.SAINTARNOLD.COM
ALCOHOL CONTENT: 6.4% ABV
GLASSWARE: MUG OR PINT
AVAILABILITY: SPRING

Pouring with a dull amber orange color and a pale white whip of foam, the aroma is of lightly toasted malts mixed with a bit of caramel and light, floral alcohol notes. The flavor corresponds with a mix of cotton candy sweetness, bready malts, light earthy hoppiness, and residual malt sugars that pervade the medium body from start to finish. A touch grainy at times, the Bock remains drinkable to the end.

St. Boisterous

VICTORY BREWING COMPANY
DOWNINGTOWN, PENNSYLVANIA
WWW.VICTORYBEER.COM
ALCOHOL CONTENT: 7.3% ABV
GLASSWARE: MUG, GOBLET, OR PINT
AVAILABILITY: SPRING

With its light pale yellow color and robust off-white head, you'd be forgiven for mistaking this strong lager from Victory for a delicate Pilsener beer. Instead, the aroma propounds the beauty of malt, with prodigious Munich sweetness, clean toasted expressions, and a surprisingly exuberant alcohol note. After the strong malt flavor, the body is surprisingly even keeled, with lighter flavor representations of each of the aromatics, along with a zesty, noble hop balance that makes St. Boisterous among the most dangerously drinkable big beers you'll ever come across.

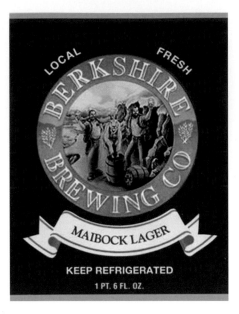

Andygator

ABITA BREWING COMPANY
ABITA SPRINGS, LOUISIANA
WWW.ABITA.COM
ALCOHOL CONTENT: 8.0% ABV
GLASSWARE: MUG, GOBLET, OR PINT
AVAILABILITY: YEAR-ROUND

With a big, brilliant, and bright golden yellow color with a beautifully frothy white head, Andygator's aroma is loaded with Munich malt, bready but not toasted in nature, with a slight sulfur vegetal hint alongside mildly grassy notes. The flavor combines a doughy and yeasty character with clean Munich malt expressions, and a mild yet complex layer of booziness, resulting in a clean natured, strong Maibock.

Maibock Lager

BERKSHIRE BREWING COMPANY
SOUTH DEERFIELD, MASSACHUSETTS
WWW.BERKSHIREBREWINGCOMPANY.COM
ALCOHOL CONTENT: 6.5% ABV
GLASSWARE: MUG OR PINT
AVAILABILITY: SPRING

This central Massachusetts brewery produces some of the most traditional lagers in New England and its Maibock is no exception. With a deep orange color and substantial white head, Maibock starts with the familiar breath of bready Munich malts but add to that a light alcohol note, slight citrus hints, and light yeast bite. The medium-body translates the aroma into liquid form, with the additions of a slight malt tang that helps round out the edges, leaving a clean, consistent, and highly drinkable mug of beer.

WEE HEAVY SCOTCH-STYLE ALE

In the Mellow and Malty section you learned about the standard Scottish-style Ale offerings. Now it's time to introduce their beefy big brother. At the 70 schilling level and higher, Scottish-style Heavy Ales, known as Wee Heavys, turn the flavor dial to eleven. The color deepens to a darker amber or ruby brown and the aroma packs a powerful wallop of near-cloying malt syrupyness, often balanced by smoky hints from specialty malts. The Wee Heavy's flavor and aroma develops through a particularly long kettle boil, resulting in a strong caramelization of the wort. The additional malt bill results in elevated alcohol levels and a much fuller body, with sweet malt arriving in cascading layers. So hold onto your kilts, as American versions routinely run up to 8 or 9 percent alcohol.

Fat Scotch Ale

SILVER CITY RESTAURANT AND BREWERY
SILVERDALE, WASHINGTON
WWW.SILVERCITYBREWERY.COM
ALCOHOL CONTENT: 9.2% ABV
GLASSWARE: GOBLET OR TULIP
AVAILABILITY: YEAR-ROUND

A dominating garnet color with a powerful flourish of foam, this Scotch Ale bubbles with potent aromatics ranging from dark caramel malts to roasted biscuits, plum and fig fruits, and a touch of earthy hops. Full-bodied and robustly constructed, the flavors start with a wave of sweet toffee malt followed by washes of dark fruits, a hint of smoke, and hearty alcohol flourishes. At 9 percent alcohol, you can often feel the burn, but no single element ever overwhelms the palate, instead bringing a new level of complexity to the mix.

Warped Speed Scotch Ale

LAKE LOUIE BREWING COMPANY
ARENA, WISCONSIN
WWW.LAKELOUIE.COM
ALCOHOL CONTENT: 7.0% ABV
GLASSWARE: MUG, PINT, OR GOBLET
AVAILABILITY: YEAR-ROUND

This amber hued beauty with ruby ridges casts off a profound tan head and displays a wonderfully sweet caramel malt presence, full and expressive, with unusual and interesting tropical citrus fruits alongside a soothing smoky character. The medium- to full-bodied Scotch Ale starts near-syrupy sweet, filled with caramel malts, and a complex mélange of light smoke, dry wheat, earthy hop bitterness, and a surprisingly long and dry finish.

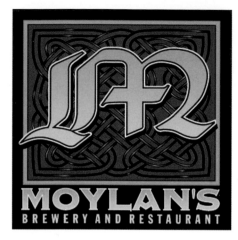

Kilt Lifter Scotch Ale

MOYLAN'S BREWERY & RESTAURANT
NOVATO, CALIFORNIA
WWW.MOYLANS.COM
ALCOHOL CONTENT: 8.0% ABV
GLASSWARE: PINT, MUG, OR GOBLET
AVAILABILITY: YEAR-ROUND

Weighing in at a hefty 8 percent alcohol, this Wee Heavy shines with a mildly hazy amber color and a soft beige head, with big notes of sweet caramel mixed with a touch of cotton candy and hints of spicy hops. The flavor offers strong tones of sweet, chewy caramel malts, with loads of residual sweetness boxed in by a slight resiny hop bite, a wispy note of smoked malt, and a healthy alcohol base. Soft and smooth in body, this fine Moylan's offering tantalizes your tongue without overwhelming your palate.

Tasgall Ale

HIGHLAND BREWING COMPANY
ASHEVILLE, NORTH CAROLINA
WWW.HIGHLANDBREWING.COM
ALCOHOL CONTENT: 8.0% ABV
GLASSWARE: MUG, PINT, OR GOBLET
AVAILABILITY: YEAR-ROUND

With a burgundy-brown body and an ivory foam crown, this Highland offering starts with a highly nuanced bouquet of rich, sweet malts, from molasses and treacle to brown sugar, along with some residual dark fruit and raisin notes. A bready malt flavor pervades the body, with quick flits of doughy sweet caramel malts and then a barrage of molasses, dark chocolate, fusel alcohol, and fruit waves. Full bodied with some thick, sticky moments, Tasgall Ale is a robust American take on a traditional style.

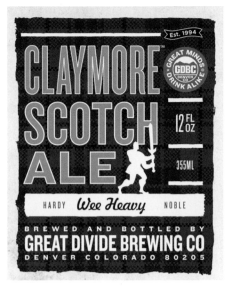

Wee Heavy Scotch Style Ale

THE DUCK-RABBIT CRAFT BREWERY
FARMVILLE, NORTH CAROLINA
WWW.DUCKRABBITBREWERY.COM
ALCOHOL CONTENT: 8.0% ABV
GLASSWARE: GOBLET
AVAILABILITY: FALL

Deceptively dark red, bright and luminous in spots and a touch hazy in others, Duck-Rabbit's version of the style is a model of restrained potency, a firecracker in a box waiting to be set off. Pouring with a sizable off-tan head, the Scotch Ale smells strongly of sweet toasted and bready malts, with noticeable alcohol esters, hints of dark fruits, and a touch of reserved bitterness that stops the onslaught from tipping into cloying. Medium to full bodied, the flavor is where this beer really shines. While the aroma suggests some reserve, the body booms with a cacophony of flavors, ranging from a toffee, treacle, and raisiny sweetness to a dry and slightly earthy bitter finish that rounds out the edges. Never flabby, Duck-Rabbit's Scotch Style Ale remains surprisingly balanced compared to many cloying versions of the style.

Claymore Scotch Ale

GREAT DIVIDE BREWING COMPANY
DENVER, COLORADO
WWW.GREATDIVIDE.COM
ALCOHOL CONTENT: 7.7% ABV
GLASSWARE: MUG, PINT, OR GOBLET
AVAILABILITY: YEAR-ROUND

A less heralded offering from this popular Colorado craft brewery, Claymore Scotch Ale pours with a vibrant and beautifully bright dark ruby color, a decent-sized pillow of off-tan foam, and a captivating aroma of mocha mixed with peat smoke notes and a near-syrupy sweet caramel malt wash that is curtailed by an earthy bitterness. Claymore is substantial in form, with a full body that simply coats the tongue in malt. An excellent Scotch-style Ale, it represents with a full but not cloying frame and a dizzying array of elements traditionally found in the best versions of this style.

GLUTEN-FREE BEER

Millions of people suffer from a physical inability to process a protein in wheat and other grains, including barley and rye, called gluten, known as Celiac Disease. Understandably, Celiac sufferers have long avoided commercially produced beers. In fraternity with these thirsty yet beer poor souls, craft brewers have started producing palatable beers made with 100 percent gluten-free ingredients such as sorghum, buckwheat, maize, corn, rice, or sunflower.

American gluten-free beers are passing a new standard for drinkability. Gluten-free beers tend to be a little unusual in flavor, yet possess a light sweetness so they can be enjoyed by individuals looking to experiment a bit. Brewed with sorghum, hops, water, rice, and gluten-free yeast grown on molasses, the New Grist, a gluten-free beer produced by the Lakefront Brewery in Milwaukee, Wisconsin, is a leading product. Possessing a pale gold color, the beer's flavor is slightly sweet and faintly of cotton candy, and the aroma is mildly fruity, lightly reminiscent of cherries, melon, and passion fruit.

The Sprecher Brewing Company, also in Milwaukee, brews the Shakparo Ale, an unfiltered beer made with sorghum and millet. Brewed in a traditional sub-Saharan African style, where barley and wheat are in short supply, the beer possesses decided cider, fruit, and phenolic spice notes that help balance the harsher grain notes. Slight banana and fruit flavors mix with a spiciness to complement the light, crisp malt undertones for a very drinkable beer.

The Bard's Tale Beer Company produces Dragon's Gold, an American lager with a mild golden amber color and creamy aromas of caramel and a touch of earthiness. The body is correspondingly creamy with touches of sweet toffee and a slight balancing bitterness.

HEAVENLY HOPPY

A 180-degree shift from the maltier beers reviewed earlier, the ales and lagers in this collection herald and pay homage to the God of Hops, the ultimate flavoring agent in beer. A role player on a team with a deep bench, hops influence the aroma and flavor of beers in myriad ways. Far from a one-dimensional experience, hoppiness comes in three main forms: aroma, flavor, and perceived bitterness. Depending upon the brewer's hand and recipe design, hops can add grapefruit juiciness or earthy nobility to the aroma, cotton candy sweetness or spicy bitterness to the body, and similar to lines in a children's coloring book, can provide some structure and order to malt sweetness. Once used primarily for their preservative qualities, hops have developed in the modern era into a popular focal point of their own. Some hopheads, as devoted fans are known, encourage their favorite brewers to push the limits of hop solubility to tongue-blistering levels with their extreme offerings. While bitter may have developed a bad name among some beer drinkers, hops are about much more than sharp contrasts. Far from some futile exercise in creating the least balanced beer possible, the beauty of hops rests in the complexity that judicious use can add to a well-crafted beer. A fantastic pairing with spicy foods, hoppy beers cut through heavy flavors in ways that other beverages fear to approach.

AMERICAN PALE ALE

The style that made American brewing famous is also one of the first ales that many drinkers experience. Ranging from golden to light copper in color, the charming style is more reserved than its boastful brother IPA. The best examples manage equilibrium between citrusy American hop aromas, fruity flavors, moderate bitterness and mild yet expressive pale malt sweetness. It's getting harder to tell which beers qualify as American Pale Ale versus India Pale Ale. Several of the selections could have qualified as IPAs, and are often marketed that way. The modern American Pale Ale has come a long way from Sierra Nevada's classic example. The ubiquitous American Pale Ale, produced by nearly every American brewpub and craft brewery, remains a very approachable style for novice drinkers.

Alesmith X

ALESMITH BREWING COMPANY
SAN DIEGO, CALIFORNIA
WWW.ALESMITH.COM
ALCOHOL CONTENT: 5.5% ABV
GLASSWARE: PINT
AVAILABILITY: YEAR-ROUND

Known as makers of big, bruising, and beautiful beers, Alesmith also knows how to brew some keenly subtle offerings. Its confounding X pours with a bright golden orange color and tiny hints of yeast with a rocky and big bubbled cap. The aroma is of mild but potent citrus hops with occasional earthier hints balanced by a nice pale malt sidecar. A surprisingly toasted and even biscuit like malt sweetness dominates the first sip, followed by some zesty citrus hops that provide a moderate but earthy and sustained bitterness. On the easier side of IPA, this one qualifies as an easy-drinking hoppy alternative to its palate-bruising cousins.

Two Hearted Ale

BELL'S BREWERY, INC.
KALAMAZOO, MICHIGAN
WWW.BELLSBEER.COM
ALCOHOL CONTENT: 7.0% ABV
GLASSWARE: PINT
AVAILABILITY: YEAR-ROUND

I know the good folks at Bell's consider this masterpiece to be an IPA, but I've also thought it was better suited as a grand representative of the APA category. If you could bottle the nose as a house air freshener or a perfume, hopheads would buy that by the crate as well. A dullish yellow tone with shades of orange making an appearance and a touch cloudy, Two Hearted boasts nothing but Centennial hop goodness, brimming with sticky and sweet cotton candy notes covering citrus beats. The resulting flavor has been described by some as oddly intoxicating, in a mystical sort of way, with more sweet cotton candy hops mixed with grapefruit and a teasing touch of sweet pale malt that creates a stunner of a beer.

IPA

SWEETWATER BREWING COMPANY
ATLANTA, GEORGIA
WWW.SWEETWATERBREW.COM
ALCOHOL CONTENT: 6.7% ABV
GLASSWARE: PINT
AVAILABILITY: YEAR-ROUND

Although advertised as an India Pale Ale, this beer packs a powerful aroma but mellows out considerably in the flavor, resulting in a perfect American Pale Ale. Pouring a luminous and slightly hazy amber-orange hue with a choppy white crown, the aroma explodes with sweet malt and sugar covered grapefruit notes. A work of art, the nose is so filled to the brim with floral and fruity notes that you half expect a hop bomb in the body. Thankfully, the brewers exercised artful control, resulting in a swirling mixture of sweet pale malts, floral hop flavors, and a mild mannered but omni-present earthy and minty bitterness. It is a real pleasure to find such a classic example of a style so often lost in the hop shuffle.

Alpha King Pale Ale

THREE FLOYDS BREWING COMPANY
MUNSTER, INDIANA
WWW.THREEFLOYDS.COM
ALCOHOL CONTENT: 6.0% ABV
GLASSWARE: PINT
AVAILABILITY: YEAR-ROUND

If not for Sierra Nevada's classic version, this might be the standard by which all American Pale Ales are set. With a hazy orange and golden tint and a straightforward off-white and lacey head, the aroma cruises with citrus hops, ranging from orange to mild grapefruit, and a touch of pale sweet malt. The flavor is accordingly quite citrusy, with limited pine notes, and deliberately smooth and clean. A healthy dose of malt helps keep the substantial but not overpowering hop bitterness in check from start to finish.

Torpedo Extra IPA

SIERRA NEVADA BREWING COMPANY
CHICO, CALIFORNIA
WWW.SIERRANEVADA.COM
ALCOHOL CONTENT: 7.2% ABV
GLASSWARE: PINT
AVAILABILITY: YEAR-ROUND

From the makers of the style-setting Sierra Nevada Pale Ale comes a new entry that helps stretch the boundaries of the American Pale Ale designation. The deep orange-amber presentation asserts a wheat-tinted head and starts with a slightly resiny and assertive hop assault on the nose, with a lush base of caramel malt. From the first sip, you know this is no weak-kneed Pale Ale but one that comes dangerously close to IPA territory. Its sharp hoppiness, however, is so well balanced by the underlying malt flavors as to render it famously drinkable and deserving of a place within the pantheon of great pale ales.

Angler's Pale Ale

UINTA BREWING COMPANY
SALT LAKE CITY, UTAH
WWW.UINTABREWING.COM
ALCOHOL CONTENT: 5.8% ABV
GLASSWARE: PINT
AVAILABILITY: YEAR-ROUND

With its bold mixture of orange and even mahogany colors, Angler's Pale Ale's pale wheat foam maintains its structure and stability throughout the experience of enjoying it. With a reserved nose that tends towards a toasted malt horizon, bits of orange hinted hops shine through as well. The medium-bodied combination of flavors jut back and forth between the caramel malt yin and the orange citrus and pine hop yang, resulting in balance, harmony, and a highly drinkable Pale Ale.

ENGLISH-STYLE BITTER

When the average drinker hears the word bitter, negative thoughts start to well up. Now, imagine seeing a beer with bitter in the name. Thus is the problem faced by brewers who want to brew this classic British beer style. Distinguishing Bitters from Pale Ales can also be trying, both personally and historically, and many American and British breweries use the terms interchangeably. American versions of the style range in color from pale golden to rich amber, with light carbonation and light to medium body, and possess a light fruity hop nose. Unlike IPAs, bitters are less mouth-puckeringly hoppy, with a complex mixture of floral hops, a touch of bitterness, rounded out by a light malt sweetness, and all with a low enough alcohol level, around 4 percent, to be sessionable. The Extra Special Bitter style is a touch hoppier and slightly fuller in body and alcohol.

Bridgeport ESB

BRIDGEPORT BREWING COMPANY
PORTLAND, OREGON
WWW.BRIDGEPORTBREW.COM
ALCOHOL CONTENT: 6.1% ABV
GLASSWARE: PINT
AVAILABILITY: YEAR-ROUND

One of America's longest running breweries, located in the heart of Oregon's West Coast brewing scene, the Bridgeport Brewing Company produces a few classic English beers, including its ESB. With a striking copper orange color topped off by a thin layer of tan foam, the aroma showcases mildly toasted and caramel tasting malt sweetness with a façade of earthy, woody, and grassy hops. The correspondingly malty flavor base, with its toasted hints, gives way to a mildly resiny and often fruity stream of hop character, counterbalanced by surprisingly robust hop bitterness.

Andrew's English Pale Ale

ANDREWS BREWING COMPANY
LINCOLNVILLE, MAINE
WWW.MAINEBREWERSGUILD.ORG/ANDREWS.PHP
ALCOHOL CONTENT: 5.5% ABV
GLASSWARE: PINT
AVAILABILITY: YEAR-ROUND

Located along a picturesque country road not far from the Atlantic Ocean in coastal Maine, the Andrew's Brewing Company is a throwback to the days when brewers lived to serve their local communities. From the bottle flows deep amber colored ale, with a soft but ample tan head, and possessing an aromatic mingling of English caramel malt flavors, with touches of earth and woodiness, and pine and citrusy hop additions. A touch of bready malt slips by the piney and earthy hops, with their restrained but notable bitterness. From the first sip, Andrew's has made a delightfully drinkable ale.

Best Bitter

GRITTY MCDUFF'S BREWING COMPANY
PORTLAND, MAINE
WWW.GRITTYS.COM
ALCOHOL CONTENT: 5.0% ABV
GLASSWARE: PINT OR MUG
AVAILABILITY: YEAR-ROUND

A small chain of Maine-based brewpubs, each with their own character, Best Bitter is the epitome of the classic English session ale. Designed to be full of flavor but easy drinking, the flagship Best Bitter pours with an amber-brown color with light beads of carbonation. It possesses a slightly grassy nose imparted by East Kent Goldings hops alongside a pale English malt character. Often served on cask for a stiller experience, the Best Bitter is quite understated in flavor, achieving a delicate balance between its use of English pale malts, a subtle and earthy hop bitterness, a sight yeast bite, and the occasional light and fruity flavors of cider or apples.

Phoenixx Double Extra Special Bitter

REAL ALE BREWING COMPANY
BLANCO, TEXAS
WWW.REALALEBREWING.COM
ALCOHOL CONTENT: 7.0% ABV
GLASSWARE: PINT OR MUG
AVAILABILITY: WINTER

Opening with a deep, inviting amber shade and a light white-tan head, the aroma booms with beautiful fruity, floral, and light citrus hop notes with earthy hints, balanced by the slightest touch of toffee sweet malt. With a medium body, this amped up ESB boasts a wallop of expressive hop and malt flavors, starting with a zesty and herbal bitterness akin to English tea, transitioning into a dry toffee sweetness and finishing a long, slow dance between the two driving flavors. A masterful blending of complex flavors.

Double Barrel Ale

FIRESTONE WALKER BREWING COMPANY
PASO ROBLES, CALIFORNIA
WWW.FIRESTONEWALKER.COM
ALCOHOL CONTENT: 5.0% ABV
GLASSWARE: PINT
AVAILABILITY: YEAR-ROUND

Finding a classically flavored English Bitter or Pale Ale from a West Coast brewery is a little like locating Titanic remnants in a local pond. As the award-winning Firestone Walker brewery's flagship beer, Double Barrel Ale sets itself apart from many hop heavy California beers by focusing on the beauty of English malt. Pouring a deep, rich amber copper color with a slight and quickly fading head, the beer boasts a complex array of toffee, caramel, and toasted malts, including the signature Maris Otter. The flavor is striking in its subtlety, with an unusually even-handed mixture of bready and nutty malts, light fruit esters, and an ever-so-slight earthy bitterness that is deep within this well-structured beer. The resulting masterwork offers something for novices and self-professed experts alike.

Sierra Nevada ESB

SIERRA NEVADA BREWING COMPANY
CHICO, CALIFORNIA
WWW.SIERRANEVADA.COM
ALCOHOL CONTENT: 5.9% ABV
GLASSWARE: PINT OR MUG
AVAILABILITY: LIMITED RELEASE

Internationally known for its signature Pale Ale and amongst beer geeks for its Celebration ale, Sierra Nevada's ESB is a sleeper amongst the cool kid brands. A deep tangerine orange color with a light tannish colored head, the aroma is an impressively well-structured array of light citrus notes, bits of toasted malt, and even a touch of gingerbread. Spot on for style in a way that would make British brewers blush, the malt hop interplay is subtle yet expressive, full of light earthy hop flavors that kick into a finishing fusion of bready malt and even modest chocolate expressions. ESB is a quiet star among Sierra Nevada's excellent regular lineup. Sadly, Sierra Nevada has announced that it is discontinuing this product as a seasonal product, although it will still occasionally be available at the brewery's tap room.

ENGLISH-STYLE INDIA PALE ALE

Perhaps no beer style's heritage is more debated amongst beer geeks and amateur historians than the India Pale Ale. Legend suggests that IPAs were first brewed as high-gravity, highly hopped beers in England to withstand the rough travel to India during the 1700s. Some claim the beer accidentally aged on the trip or that it was later watered down, while others suggest these stories are only myths. Moribund in its home country, the style has been resurrected and redefined in the United States, but examples of the subtler English style exist. In contrast to the American version, English IPA employs its native hop varieties, which generally place less emphasis on citrus and fruit and boast gentle earthy and even woody notes. A moderate bitterness mingles with a style-setting toasted Pale Ale malt foundation and earthy and flowery hop tinges to create a crisp, dry finish.

Dragonmead Crown Jewels India Pale Ale

DRAGONMEAD MICROBREWERY
WARREN, MICHIGAN
WWW.DRAGONMEAD.COM
ALCOHOL CONTENT: 7.0% ABV
GLASSWARE: PINT OR MUG
AVAILABILITY: YEAR-ROUND

The vibrant yet hazy orange colored beer from this multi-tap brewpub outside of Detroit captures yeast and your eyes in suspension, crowned by a flakey crag of almond colored foam. A vaguely musky and earthy English hop character pervades the nose, mixed with an appreciable level of mildly toasted and bready malts, and a touch of light fruitiness as a capper. The underlying English malt takes center stage on the first cue, with its toffee character and toasted bows, followed by a piquant, woody, and leafy hop finish that ends partially bitter on the tongue.

Impaled Ale

MIDDLE AGES BREWING COMPANY
SYRACUSE, NEW YORK
WWW.MIDDLEAGESBREWING.COM
ALCOHOL CONTENT: 6.5% ABV
GLASSWARE: PINT
AVAILABILITY: YEAR-ROUND

Hazy amber orange in appearance and with an ivory white tower of foam, Impaled Ale strings together tender citrus and floral hop tinges and the brewery's house diacetyl or butter character from its use of the signature Ringwood yeast strain. The flavor follows through with an English toffee character, mixed with buttery notes, and warming to a solid but balanced measure of citrus and earthy hop flavor and bitterness. Medium bodied and full of reserved English character, the Impaled Ale is a dry and hoppy treat.

Squatters India Pale Ale

SQUATTERS PUB AND BREWERY
SALT LAKE CITY, UTAH
WWW.SQUATTERS.COM
ALCOHOL CONTENT: 6.0% ABV
GLASSWARE: PINT
AVAILABILITY: YEAR-ROUND

This fantastic beer from Utah just straddles the edge between English- and American-style India Pale Ales. Bright copper with a light cream colored head, the nose is filled with juicy, earthy hop and intensely citrus fruit aromas, slightly armpit stinky at times (but in a good way), as is common with some American hops. But there is a British reserved quality amongst all this fruit bravado. Made with English barley, the Squatters IPA does not taste like an American IPA, preferring to linger much more on the British side. It still brims with citrus fruit esters, but they take on a dry quality that gives way into a European malt base and finishes clean and slightly earthy.

Ipswich Original Ale

MERCURY BREWING COMPANY
IPSWICH, MASSACHUSETTS
WWW.MERCURYBREWING.COM
ALCOHOL CONTENT: 5.4% ABV
GLASSWARE: PINT OR MUG
AVAILABILITY: YEAR-ROUND

One of the first craft beers I tried upon moving to New England, Ipswich's Original Ale is still one of the best craft beers in the region. Whether enjoyed directly from the bottle on a warm summer day or in a glass from a fresh growler, the dull and hazy apricot colored beer is a raw and thoroughly enjoyable English-style Pale Ale. Full of unfiltered charm, the aroma brims with a melody of toasted malt whispers aside a hop aroma possessed of earthy and woody yet reserved character. The medium-bodied flavor of toasted, biscuity malt notes, often a little grainy to the taste, balances against the very light but keenly hopped earthiness. Original Ale is indeed a New England classic.

India Pale Ale

ARCADIA BREWING COMPANY
BATTLE CREEK, MICHIGAN
WWW.ARCADIAALES.COM
ALCOHOL CONTENT: 5.9% ABV
GLASSWARE: PINT
AVAILABILITY: YEAR-ROUND

Boasting the Union Jack and an allusion to old British ships, this IPA's label lets you know right upfront that it is English in style. Coolly amber-orange in hue with a lightly sustained off-white head, the IPA's nose is filled with English reserve. Light fruity English yeast notes trickle over a touch of orange citrus notes and a toffee malt base tease. The flavor starts mildly creamy before building into an earthy yeast note, followed by a toasted malt kick, and finally heading into a long, drawn-out, minty bitterness. A biscuity malt character appears as the beer warms and it ends with a dry, nutty finish.

Cold Hop British-Style Ale

BOULDER BEER COMPANY
BOULDER, COLORADO
WWW.BOULDERBEER.COM
ALCOHOL CONTENT: 6.8% ABV
GLASSWARE: PINT
AVAILABILITY: SPRING

Pouring a bright golden color and with a soft ivory head and thick carbonation bubbles, this IPA is replete with English character, despite additions of German and Czech noble hops. The floral aroma is thick with pine, earth, wood, and an herbal quality that plays on the Marris Otter pale malt and English yeast base. The toasted and slightly nutty British malt character is quickly subsumed by a citrusy and then earthy hop flavor and then another round of tight, slashing hop bitterness, including a funky flavor added by dry-hopping with an unusual New Zealand variety. Cold Hop is a standout product in the Western lands of the United States, which are so dominated by American IPA varietals.

AMERICAN INDIA PALE ALE

Perhaps the most widely recognized beer style for American consumers, this version bears little resemblance to the original English IPA style. Filled with aromatic and bitter American hops, these orange to light amber colored beers boast prodigious grapefruit, orange, and floral aromas or sizable herbal and earthy notes. Medium bodied, the best American IPAs avoid fighting a one-sided hop battle against your palate by judiciously balancing a substantial pale malt backbone. The final results range from powerful and intensely juicy to milder yet deeply bitter hop finishes. The India Pale Ale style is best described as being a strong, expressive, and full-bodied hop experience that doesn't drift into the higher alcohol and bitterness levels associated with Double India Pale Ale. Many hop skeptics become dedicated hopheads when the right beer shows them that bitter isn't necessarily bad.

Smuttynose IPA

SMUTTYNOSE BREWING COMPANY
PORTSMOUTH, NEW HAMPSHIRE
WWW.SMUTTYNOSE.COM
ALCOHOL CONTENT: 6.9% ABV
GLASSWARE: PINT
AVAILABILITY: YEAR-ROUND

While many New England born IPAs tend towards the English style, Smuttynose's version is loaded with Simcoe and Santiam hops and balanced by the distinctive Amarillo hop. One of the brewery's most popular offerings, the beer opens with a hazy amber-orange color and a light off-white crown. The aroma is a strong mix of assertive earthy and grainy notes, with occasional clear grassy hints, and a touch of malt tang. This is not your usual American citrus bomb, instead the flavor tends towards the earthier, funkier hop flavor, with a slight malt undercurrent, and a long, drawn out bitterness.

Masala Mama India Pale Ale

MINNEAPOLIS TOWN HALL BREWERY
MINNEAPOLIS, MINNESOTA
WWW.TOWNHALLBREWERY.COM
ALCOHOL CONTENT: 6.0% ABV
GLASSWARE: PINT
AVAILABILITY: YEAR-ROUND

A hit among hop-crazed beer geeks, the Masala Mama from the Town Hall brewpub in the Seven Corners section of Minneapolis starts with a deep amber-orange tone and a crater-like tan crown of intricate foam. Packed with tons of grapefruit and citrusy chords and piney teems, this IPA celebrates the soulful potential of hops. The first sip bathes the taste buds in a rinse of bitter and sweet hop flavors, from grapefruit to mildly earthy resins, sticky throughout, and is counter-balanced by an unexpectedly substantial caramel malt base. The Masala Mama is a highly drinkable and even measured hop explosion in a glass.

IPA

ODELL BREWING COMPANY
FORT COLLINS, COLORADO
WWW.ODELLS.COM
ALCOHOL CONTENT: 7.0% ABV
GLASSWARE: PINT
AVAILABILITY: YEAR-ROUND

One of the most underestimated IPAs available, Odell's version focuses on intense hop flavor and aroma without going over the top. With a light copper shine and a well-sustained head, the first sniff is show-stopping in its potency, revealing a dizzying array of juicy and citrus notes, a light sweet crystal malt base, and a considerably stinky Amarillo hop presence. At times reminiscent of a liquid armpit, but in a very good way, the flavor gives off huge, sweet grapefruit and citrus bites, followed by a sweet malt middle, and finishing with an herbal, pungent hop cleanse. This IPA delivers substantial hop flavor without overpowering you with hop bitterness.

Address Unknown IPA

WILLIMANTIC BREWING COMPANY
WILLIMANTIC, CONNECTICUT
WWW.WILLIBREW.COM
ALCOHOL CONTENT: 6.7% ABV
GLASSWARE: PINT
AVAILABILITY: YEAR-ROUND

While New England is not particularly known for expressive American-style IPAs, the tiny Willimantic brewpub is the exception to that finicky rule. Located in an attractive converted post office, Willimantic brews several dozen different IPAs every year. The aroma is filled with essences of sweet, dense malts, rounds of citrus, and piney extracts. This tantalizing, perfectly balanced, and unfiltered IPA teases the palate with caramel and toasted malts, all while sucking every last essence out of the powerfully hoppy Columbus and Cascade varieties. A slight alcohol bite adds another layer of complexity to the pine and grapefruit fruit tones in the body.

Racer 5

BEAR REPUBLIC BREWING COMPANY
SANTA ROSA, CALIFORNIA
WWW.BEARREPUBLIC.COM
ALCOHOL CONTENT: 7.0% ABV
GLASSWARE: PINT
AVAILABILITY: YEAR-ROUND

This stalwart American IPA issues a slightly soft, hazy golden amber color with a moderate white head before unleashing a surprising fusion of sweet cotton candy hop and malt notes and citrus and pine touches. The fragrant nose translates to a complex wash of bubble gum malt sweetness that is immediately tempered by a persistent citrusy hop bite. The mouthfeel is a touch fuller than your average IPA but Racer 5 never overwhelms, with a lingering bitterness present to guide you to the last savored sip.

Furious

SURLY BREWING COMPANY
MINNEAPOLIS, MINNESOTA
WWW.SURLYBREWING.COM
ALCOHOL CONTENT: 6.2% ABV
GLASSWARE: PINT
AVAILABILITY: YEAR-ROUND

With the crush of excellent IPAs produced on the West Coast, hardcore hop heads might initially bristle at the idea of including two hop rockets from the Midwest, let alone from the same city. Let's see if they complain after trying this hop monster, which announces its arrival with a brilliantly hazy orange-rouge tint and a dollop of tacky foam. A fantastic mixture of sweet caramel malt is immediately smacked by a complex torrent of citrusy hops. Instantaneously discarding any notions of Midwestern reserve, the flavor unleashes a palate bruising flood of toffee like malt sugars that fight a losing battle for dominance with the funky citrus fruit onslaught and its reigning terror of bitterness. Both surly and furious, this IPA is not for the faint of heart, and represents the American style without entering extreme country.

BELGIAN-STYLE PALE ALE

Belgian pale ales are curious inventions, often difficult to define, but which preferably balance dry and biscuity malt notes with lightly spicy hop touches. A more widely available style in its home country, American brewers are slowly beginning to embrace Belgian pale ales, which are light golden to bright amber in hue and possess a sizable and sustained white to off-tan head. The style's aroma suggests its origins, with classic noble European hops mixing with an unusually phenolic but not fruity sweet yeast note. American brewers sometimes tend to branch out on their own with the addition of citrusy hops from the United States. Hoppier versions come closer to the India Pale Ale style and the most popular Belgian versions are heavily influenced by the American craft brewing renaissance.

Matilda

GOOSE ISLAND BREWING COMPANY
CHICAGO, ILLINOIS
WWW.GOOSEISLAND.COM
ALCOHOL CONTENT: 7.0% ABV
GLASSWARE: GOBLET, MUG, OR PINT
AVAILABILITY: YEAR-ROUND

Brewed as an homage to the classic Belgian Trappist Ale called Orval, this delightfully simple yet complicated ale starts with a dullish orange-amber color and finishes with a tacky foam crown that provides substantial lacing. As with its idol, the aroma is decidedly Belgian in character, with a blend of spicy and even fruity phenolics, a touch of funk, a hint of sweet candi sugar, all resulting in an impression of a tightly constructed and likely dry beer. Mimicking the aroma, Matilda glides over the tongue with cool pale malt and a touch of sweetness that isn't quite willing to be dry, and occasional earthy and spicy hop elements. Matilda remains an excellent and daring twist on a style-defining classic.

Luciernega

JOLLY PUMPKIN ARTISAN ALES
DEXTER, MICHIGAN
WWW.JOLLYPUMPKIN.COM
ALCOHOL CONTENT: 6.5% ABV
GLASSWARE: GOBLET, MUG, OR PINT
AVAILABILITY: SUMMER

Swirling in a dusty haze of orange luminescence, with a marble hued and tacky fop of foam, the beer known as "the Firefly" beams with a garden full of spices, from coriander, lemon, a touch of black pepper, and some barnyard funk. Bearing a peach and dull apple fruit essence, the grainy spice character demonstrates an unusual level of complexity, mixed with touches of alcohol, leading to a velvety character and a dry finish. There is a reserved hint of earthy hoppiness that underlies the beer without becoming more than a contributing player, allowing the Belgian-influenced flavor profile to shine.

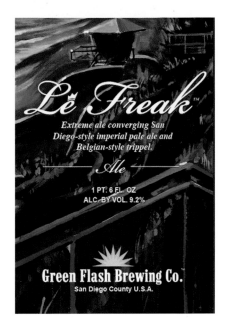

Fatty Boombalatty

FURTHERMORE BEER
SPRING GREEN, WISCONSIN
WWW.FURTHERMOREBEER.COM
ALCOHOL CONTENT: 7.2% ABV
GLASSWARE: GOBLET, MUG, OR PINT
AVAILABILITY: SPRING AND SUMMER

Another curious offering with an unusual name from the Wisconsin-based contract craft brewer. Initially conceived as a creative take on the traditional Belgian-style Witbier, things quickly went in a different direction, resulting in what can only be called a Belgian-style Pale Ale. Dashing off a golden to copper orange color with an exhibition of tacky alabaster foam, the estery nose divulges an organized jumble of citrus, coriander, wheat, and earthy hops, to Belgian effect. Like the marriage of two styles, the flavor momentarily confuses you with the clean, fruity essence of a Witbier, then smacks you with citrusy hops, and a touch of earthiness.

Le Freak

GREEN FLASH BREWING COMPANY
VISTA, CALIFORNIA
WWW.GREENFLASHBREW.COM
ALCOHOL CONTENT: 9.2% ABV
GLASSWARE: GOBLET
AVAILABILITY: YEAR-ROUND

Le Freak's dull but luminous burnished golden orange color and loose white pedestal of foam and nice lacing give way to a mildly candy sweet pale malt aroma, mixed with a spicy pepper and grain quality, and fruity American hops. On the boozier end of the Belgian spectrum, Le Freak blends two genres, with substantial Belgian influences sprinkled over a strong IPA base. The resulting flavor tends towards Belgian-style Tripel sweetness, balanced by orange and grapefruit esters, and zippy, grassy hop flavor and spicy pepper bitterness. Le Freak is an intriguing culture clash that results in a potent yet drinkable offering.

Lectio Divina

SAINT SOMEWHERE BREWING COMPANY
TARPON SPRINGS, FLORIDA
WWW.SAINTSOMEWHEREBREWING.COM
ALCOHOL CONTENT: 8.0% ABV
GLASSWARE: GOBLET
AVAILABILITY: YEAR-ROUND

It's a testament to the expansive growth of the craft beer movement that a small brewery in the macro-laden Gulf Coast of Florida could open and specialize in high quality, Belgian-influenced beers. Lectio Divina pours with a hazy reddish-orange color and a sizable crater of an alabaster head. The aroma catches your attention immediately, with mildly tart and sour darts jabbing out from dry, toasted malt sweetness, with an underlying funk and horse blanket character. The resulting experience combines the woodier elements with a Belgian-style flavor profile, with considerable spiciness from the yeast and hops, leading to a dry and moderately bitter finish. Lectio Divina is definitely on the funkier side of the Belgian Pale Ale ledger but is certainly worth a try if you're game.

Local 1

BROOKLYN BREWERY
BROOKLYN, NEW YORK
WWW.BROOKLYNBREWERY.COM
ALCOHOL CONTENT: 9.0% ABV
GLASSWARE: TULIP, SNIFTER, OR GOBLET
AVAILABILITY: YEAR-ROUND

So just how confusing and expansive a style is the Belgian Pale Ale category? Well, the Brooklyn Brewery produces a top-notch Belgian-style ale that defies categorization, looks and tastes nothing like the other beers discussed here, but that certainly meets many of the criteria describing this elusive style. Brewed with German malts, cane sugar, and subjected to a complete bottle refermentation, it pours a bright golden color with some haziness and an immense, stocky white head. The aroma pools together passion fruit, herbal and grassy hops, and a touch of Belgian funk in the yeasty nose, all mixed with a healthy alcohol jolt. The flavor tends more towards a smooth pale malt sweetness backed down by a peppery spiciness from yeast and hops, and a long, dry, and earthy bitter finish.

DOUBLE INDIA PALE ALE

Sometimes referred to as Imperial IPA, a borrowed reference from the strong stout style, these seriously amped up IPAs explode with a tongue melting cacophony of hops, alcohol, and malt. These atomic hop bombs started on the West Coast and quickly spread across the country. Deep orange or amber in color, the aromas pop with juicy, citrusy floral American hops, boom with boozy alcohol hints, and give off strong, sweet malt notes. Double IPAs offer intense hop bitterness and flavor, with alcohol levels ranging from around 8 to 11 percent ABV, and a substantial malt presence for balance and support. The best examples avoid a one-sided hop onslaught or the tendency to become pale malt booze bombs while managing to remain drinkable, a difficult task when juggling massive ingredient amounts.

Double Simcoe IPA

WEYERBACHER BREWING COMPANY
EASTON, PENNSYLVANIA
WWW.WEYERBACHER.COM
ALCOHOL CONTENT: 9.0% ABV
GLASSWARE: TULIP OR GOBLET
AVAILABILITY: YEAR-ROUND

A glowing fire orange color warns of the beast that lies within this pint, with its well-stacked tan head and its tempest of zesty, earthy, and at times citrusy aromas from the use of its stinky signature hop. Single hop beers allow drinkers an unparalleled opportunity to understand how individual ingredients influence the final product, and Double Simcoe gives imbibers a double dose of this potent hop. The resulting flavor keeps dense pale malt sweetness at bay as it attempts to advance on the flurry of complex Simcoe hop flavors, ranging from grapefruit to cotton candy and resiny earth and pine. A warming base of alcohol brews beneath the surface but never overwhelms the, at times, sticky-bodied ale.

Pliny the Elder

RUSSIAN RIVER BREWING COMPANY
SANTA ROSA, CALIFORNIA
WWW.RUSSIANRIVERBREWING.COM
ALCOHOL CONTENT: 8.0% ABV
GLASSWARE: PINT OR TULIP
AVAILABILITY: YEAR-ROUND

Perhaps the most revered Double IPA among hardcore beer geeks, who refer to its brewer as the "Hopfather," Pliny defines the Double IPA style for many fans. With its hazy orange hue and solid two-finger crown of foam, Pliny opens its arms wide and unleashes a torrent of hop goodness, with blasts of evergreen and pine, grapefruit and assorted citrus, and a tinge of resiny bitterness. Throw in a healthy dose of biscuity pale malt for balance and to boost the alcohol levels, and the well-rounded flavor smoothly flows with sweet and floral citrus before bursting into an extended jam session of dry, resiny hop bitterness that doesn't so much linger as build a timeshare on the edges of your tongue.

Heady Topper

THE ALCHEMIST PUB AND BREWERY
WATERBURY, VERMONT
WWW.ALCHEMISTBEER.COM
ALCOHOL CONTENT: 8.0% ABV
GLASSWARE: TULIP OR GOBLET
AVAILABILITY: LIMITED RELEASE

At the inventive Alchemist Pub in northern Vermont, visitors can sample a wide range of impressively flavored American ales. The bruising Heady Topper appears with a dull and mildly hazy apricot tone and a marble crest of foam. Engorged in hop aromas, from grapefruit to freshly cut citrus rind, and with some darker, resiny hints, the nose also hints at light pale malts and a touch of alcohol warmth. Wanting to please, the flavor continues with a tropical essence of hop flavors, with slick grapefruit tones and a moderate, lingering bitterness that hangs around the edge of your senses.

Racer X

BEAR REPUBLIC BREWING COMPANY
HEALDSBURG, CALIFORNIA
WWW.BEARREPUBLIC.COM
ALCOHOL CONTENT: 7.8% ABV
GLASSWARE: TULIP OR PINT
AVAILABILITY: YEAR-ROUND

This mild-mannered offering tugs you near with a mild copper color and a moderate white head, but the first sniff widens your eyes, opens your nasal passages, and fills you with an intense burst of fresh cut American citrus fruit. A waft of sweet pale malt, thankfully far from cloying, unlike many Double IPAs, balances the robust hop aroma. The aroma translates beautifully to the body, where a dizzying array of fruit and hop flavors vie for your attention, all while the pale malt acts as schoolmarm over the glorious liquid spectacle. Fresh, zesty hops contribute a lingering bitterness to the middle and finish, all nuzzled by a warming alcohol presence.

Pure Hoppiness

ALPINE BREWING COMPANY
ALPINE, CALIFORNIA
WWW.ALPINEBEERCO.COM
ALCOHOL CONTENT: 8.0% ABV
GLASSWARE: PINT OR TULIP
AVAILABILITY: LIMITED RELEASE

With loads of hops added to the boil, the hopback, and then later dry-hopped, this resilient base beer gets battered by hops from all sides. Pouring with a slightly hazy tangerine orange color and a sticky and craterous crown of foam, the aroma tingles with a fruit bowl full of citrus hints, with orange, lemon, and pineapple represented, and a touch of warming, sweet alcohol. Alongside its continual storm of floral fruit hops, a warming malt sweetness arrives to keep order in the hop world, resulting in a glorious candy-covered pineapple sensation. Smooth and surprisingly drinkable, Pure Hoppiness hits its mark in terms of flavor and naming.

Tricerahops

NINKASI BREWING COMPANY
EUGENE, OREGON
WWW.NINKASIBREWING.COM
ALCOHOL CONTENT: 8.8% ABV
GLASSWARE: PINT OR TULIP
AVAILABILITY: YEAR-ROUND

Cast in a heavenly bronze haze of hop particles and with a tacky and sustained tan head, this often overlooked specialty booms with the Double IPA fruit basket of orange, peach, lemon, and grapefruit, all with little trace of the elevated alcohol level. Far from a palate-abusing Double IPA of the kind that leaves you wrecked and wondering what happened, Tricerahops uses a careful hand with the sweet malt additions and leaves it to juicy citrus hops to cast their modest but abundant touch on the proceedings. With its final bow, the beer recedes from sight, leaving only a swath of drawn-out, dry bitterness in its wake.

ALTBIER

Closely associated with its home of Düsseldorf, the alt style is an enigmatic creature, promoting bitterness in a country where clean malty beers dominate. Sometimes brewed as a lager outside of the city, traditional alt beers are ales that are cold-conditioned at temperatures that suppress big, fruity aromas and flavors in favor of milder, more concentrated malt and hop notes. The resulting beer is usually light amber to light ruby-brown in color. An alt's aroma is defined by a potent but reserved discharge of earthy, spicy noble hops mixed with subtle touches of a light caramel sweetness. A seemingly difficult style to execute in the New World, American versions vary in their levels of interplay between bitterness and malt sweetness, but great examples let the noble hop bitterness shine through in nose and palate, with a nod towards a dry and smooth malt underpinning.

Altbier

BLUEGRASS BREWING COMPANY
LOUISVILLE, KENTUCKY
WWW.BBCBREW.COM
ALCOHOL CONTENT: 4.1% ABV
GLASSWARE: PINT
AVAILABILITY: YEAR-ROUND

Only the lighter orange side of crimson, Bluegrass's Altbier leads off with a thick, whipped froth of clean wheat colored foam and a nose that carefully blends caramel, raw and resiny noble hops, and a light spice character. A toasted malt flavor dominates the body, with touches of fruit and spice from the hops, and leads to some nutty grain hints, finishing with a smooth, creamy quality.

Altbier

BLUCREEK BREWING COMPANY
MADISON, WISCONSIN
WWW.BLUCREEK.COM
ALCOHOL CONTENT: 4.0% ABV
GLASSWARE: PINT
AVAILABILITY: YEAR-ROUND

A brownish-garnet colored beer with touches of citrus orange at the edges with a light wheat colored crown, BluCreek's version of the style looks spot on for tradition. The aroma abounds with caramel, flights of honey, and repeated nutty forays with the slightest hints of an earthy hoppiness. While the aroma suggests a mildly sweet flavor, Altbier actually takes a turn for the traditional and returns to its drier, hoppier roots. Embellished with shavings of dried fruit and a pleasant earthy hop flavor, BluCreek has brewed a little reminder of Düsseldorf.

Double Bag

LONG TRAIL BREWING COMPANY
BRIDGEWATER CORNERS, VERMONT
WWW.LONGTRAIL.COM
ALCOHOL CONTENT: 7.2% ABV
GLASSWARE: PINT, MUG, GOBLET
AVAILABILITY: YEAR-ROUND

The stronger, fuller big brother to the brewery's flagship Long Trail Ale, this Altbier pours a light amber-orange hue with a favorable dollop of creamy head. The aroma doesn't overwhelm, but instead contains some restrained nutty hints, a touch of European malt notes, and a quick glimpse of earthy hops. Well-balanced from start to finish, Double Bag tends more towards the Sticke Alt style, which is a limited edition and stronger version of the traditional Düsseldorf Alt beer. Filled with caramel and toasted malt notes that lay the groundwork for a pleasant patchwork of earthy and grassy hop notes, mixed with occasional touches of vanilla, chocolate, and even graham cracker.

Altbier

SOUTHAMPTON BREWING COMPANY
SOUTHAMPTON, NEW YORK
WWW.SOUTHAMPTONPUBLICKHOUSE.COM
ALCOHOL CONTENT: 5.3% ABV
GLASSWARE: PINT
AVAILABILITY: YEAR-ROUND

This fan favorite from the popular Long Island-based brewery may be the most widely available Altbier in America. Presenting with a deep chestnut hue with an off-whitish and well-laced and retained top, the aroma mixes dried fruit with a slight toffee malt character for an inviting result. The toffee elements translate into light caramel notes in the flavor mixed with a dry and herbal hop bitterness and additional apricot and dried fruit flavors.

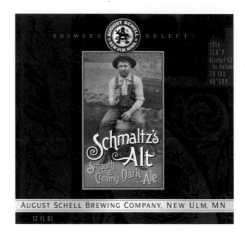

AUGUST SCHELL BREWING COMPANY, NEW ULM, MN

Headwall Alt

TUCKERMAN BREWING COMPANY
CONWAY, NEW HAMPSHIRE
WWW.TUCKERMANBREWING.COM
ALCOHOL CONTENT: 4.7% ABV
GLASSWARE: PINT
AVAILABILITY: YEAR-ROUND

A sometimes hard-to-find offering from Tuckerman, which is best known for its excellent Pale Ale, the Headwall Alt boasts a radiant chestnut color and a light earthy hop bite in the aroma. The brewers use dark Belgian specialty malts and domestic whole leaf hops to create their own take on the traditional brown ales of Düsseldorf. The smooth flavored ale is slightly peppery at times, with a balance of tempered malt sweetness and sustained and solid hop bitterness through to the lingering finish.

Schmaltz's Alt

AUGUST SCHELL BREWING COMPANY
NEW ULM, MINNESOTA
WWW.SCHELLSBREWERY.COM
ALCOHOL CONTENT: 5.1% ABV
GLASSWARE: PINT OR MUG
AVAILABILITY: YEAR-ROUND

A striking toasted brown color with faint orange highlights at the edges and rim, this classic Altbier from America's second oldest brewery casts quite a first look. The aroma shines through with hints of caramel and toasted almond mixed with a residual earthy bitterness and even a touch of chocolate. Caramel and cocoa powder go hand in hand for the malt side of things, with the addition of some dried fruit, all mixed together with an herbal and earthy hop flavor and drawn out bitterness that occasionally tosses an unexpected fruity hint at you.

GERMAN-STYLE PILSENER

Hardly content to let their Bohemian neighbors to the east enjoy all the hoppy credit, Germans created their own version of the Pilsener style. In addition to the herbal Saaz hop, the Germans relied upon their own varieties, including Hallertauer and Tettnanger. Zesty and herbal in their distinct ways, they are called noble, a concept as difficult to explain as *terroir* in wine. The noble hop label is generally given to a handful of specific hop varieties, including Hallertau, Spalt, Saaz, and Tettnanger, whose shared characteristics include low bitterness levels and substantial aromatics. The resulting beers are bright in color, from pale to deep golden, with deep, dense, thick heads. The clean and inviting aromas are spicy, grassy, and herbal and fuse with a modest pilsener malt balance to create a crisp, quenching beer.

Barmen Pilsner

BLUE MOON BREWING COMPANY
@ COORS FIELD
DENVER, COLORADO
WWW.BLUEMOONBREWINGCOMPANY.COM
ALCOHOL CONTENT: 5.5% ABV
GLASSWARE: PINT OR PILSENER
AVAILABILITY: YEAR-ROUND

Often credited to the Coors Brewing Company's Blue Moon brewing unit, this stunningly golden lager boasts a massive, rocky, and well-sustained white foam crown. The sweeping aroma cascades with clean, crisp, and fresh Saaz and German noble hops, with a distinctive and addicting spicy quality. The fresh and zesty hops start right in on the first sip, with a pleasant balance of slightly bready malt, followed by a long-lasting hop flavor and residual bitterness. Perhaps the only macro-brewed craft beer to be featured in this book, this fantastic example of the noble German-style Pilsener ranks as, perhaps, the best beer made by America's biggest breweries.

Elm City Lager

NEW ENGLAND BREWING COMPANY
WOODBRIDGE, CONNECTICUT
WWW.NEWENGLANDBREWING.COM
ALCOHOL CONTENT: 5.0% ABV
GLASSWARE: PINT OR PILSENER
AVAILABILITY: YEAR-ROUND

Another great canned beer option from New England Brewing Company, this spot-on German-style Pilsener shows that good, canned craft beer is far from an oxymoron. A dullish golden hue with a prodigious and frothy foam cap, the aroma cracks with a crisp, clean, and powerfully earthy and zesty noble hop presence with a mildly sweet malt base. This lager, brewed in the heart of New England ale country, is softer on the palate than some of the other more aggressive or Americanized versions of the classic style, effectively showcasing noble hops and bright European malts for a highly drinkable and clean experience.

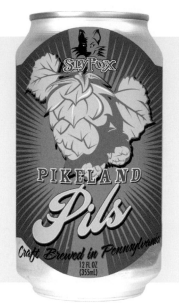

Pikeland Pils

SLY FOX BREWING COMPANY
PHOENIXVILLE, PENNSYLVANIA
WWW.SLYFOXBEER.COM
ALCOHOL CONTENT: 4.9% ABV
GLASSWARE: PINT OR PILSENER
AVAILABILITY: YEAR-ROUND

Hardly willing to be outdone by other great Pilsener beers made in Pennsylvania, Pikeland Pils is another outstanding German-style Pilsener. Sly Fox is known in part as a major supporter of canning craft beer and when you taste this offering, it'll change your opinion of canned beer forever. Pouring stark golden with a tight and tacky white foam head, the aroma swaggers with a rarely found combination of spicy noble hops and character-rich German malt to achieve greatness. The resulting flavor is both soft and rough at times, with a clean expression of both the hops and malt, but with an aggressive earthy bitterness resting on top of a substantial malt base. A joy to both smell and drink, Pikeland Pils will always have a home in my fridge.

Pilsner

AUGUST SCHELL BREWING COMPANY
NEW ULM, MINNESOTA
WWW.SCHELLSBREWERY.COM
ALCOHOL CONTENT: 5.6% ABV
GLASSWARE: PINT OR PILSENER
AVAILABILITY: YEAR-ROUND

Another laudable offering from an old German-American brewery, August Schell's Pilsner pours with a golden-amber color and a moderate off-white head. The aroma is earthy and grainy at times, with hints at both hops and malt in these instances. The malt plays the biggest role here, with a nicely toasted character to play foil to the mildly spicy and earthy hops. Clean, even with its grainier moments, and very drinkable throughout.

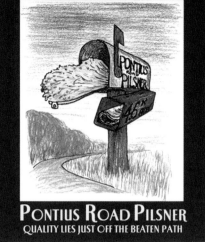

Prima Pils

VICTORY BREWING COMPANY
DOWNINGTOWN, PENNSYLVANIA
WWW.VICTORYBEER.COM
ALCOHOL CONTENT: 5.3% ABV
GLASSWARE: PINT OR PILSENER
AVAILABILITY: YEAR-ROUND

Lovers of sharp, piquant, and hoppy German-style pilseners should consider moving to Pennsylvania to get closer to America's greatest source of these beers. If a move won't work, try the excellent Prima Pils from Victory. Pouring a shade fainter than golden and with a persistent and mousse-like white head, the aroma defines clean, with tidy layers of spicy and earthy noble hops and slightly sweet and bready malts. Where some craft beers smell great but disappoint a bit in the flavor, the Prima Pils delivers in every possible way, with huge, spicy bitter hop flavors and residual bitterness, all balanced by a healthy dose of malt.

Pontius Road Pilsner

SHORT'S BREWING COMPANY
BELLAIRE, MICHIGAN
WWW.SHORTSBREWING.COM
ALCOHOL CONTENT: 4.8% ABV
GLASSWARE: PINT OR PILSENER
AVAILABILITY: YEAR-ROUND

Pouring with a decidedly pale yellow color and a slight wispy white head, this Pilsener may not look like much at first glance, but that only masks the flavor that lies underneath. The aroma mixes bready malt notes with waves of grassy, herbal noble hops, followed by a quick vegetal hint that adds a layer of complexity. The flavor punches through with sharp, piquant, and spicy hops from the very first sip, peppery at times, with a lingering, tangy bitterness that thankfully won't quit. Pontius Road Pilsner is a deceptively strong offering sinisterly masquerading as something much simpler.

CZECH-STYLE PILSENER

When people think of hoppy beers, their minds generally drift towards assertive India Pale Ales. Too often overlooked are the classic Pilsener styles, which offer some of the most sharp and zesty hop zings available. The granddaddy of all hoppy beers, the Czech or Bohemian-style Pilsener, laid the bright, brilliant groundwork for all Pilsener beers to come. Defined by the decidedly and lightly fruity Saaz hop, Czech Pilseners vary from pale straw to deep golden in color with impressive rocky white heads. Aromas of light hay and spicy noble hops are met with the soft, grassy aromas of Moravian malt. The flavor is simultaneously a touch malty sweet and vastly bitter, but in an intriguingly unusual way. Bracingly fresh and eminently drinkable, the Czech style is an excellent beer for hop neophytes and devotees alike to savor.

HUB Lager

HOPWORKS URBAN BREWERY
PORTLAND, OREGON
WWW.HOPWORKSBEER.COM
ALCOHOL CONTENT: 5.1% ABV
GLASSWARE: PINT OR PILSENER
AVAILABILITY: YEAR-ROUND

A relative newcomer to the vibrant Portland brewing scene, Hopworks specializes in brewing beers with organic ingredients. Even before Hopworks opened to the public, it won a World Beer Cup silver medal with this pale golden colored beer. In exploring its moderate creamy white head, you'll notice a resiny grain quality that gives way to a decidedly spicy and herbal noble hop character and even touches of bready malt and honey fruitiness. Brewed with whole leaf Saaz hops, the crisp body tingles with zesty hop bites that dance with a sizable malt sweetness. Zippy yet balanced, the HUB Lager is a highly drinkable offering from a talented young brewery.

Czech Pilsner

BOHEMIAN BREWERY
MIDVALE, UTAH
WWW.BOHEMIANBREWERY.COM
ALCOHOL CONTENT: 5.0% ABV
GLASSWARE: PINT OR PILSENER
AVAILABILITY: YEAR-ROUND

The story here, one of a German Reinheitsgebot-dedicated brewery located in the dry environment of Utah and named after a region in the Czech Republic, has the makings of a good joke. But you won't be laughing when you crack a can of this bright golden colored beer with its fluffy white head, which leads to a mild honey grain malt aroma followed by the low but solid hum of zesty noble hops and a mild fruitiness. Following its light aroma, Bohemian's flagship beer cracks with a crisp but aggressively zesty Saaz hop flavor and bitterness, one that dries the tongue even as soft malt seeps into the fold. Clean, crisp, and highly drinkable, the Czech Pilsner is a part of Europe right in Utah.

Pilz

LIVE OAK BREWING COMPANY
AUSTIN, TEXAS
WWW.LIVEOAKBREWING.COM
ALCOHOL CONTENT: 4.9% ABV
GLASSWARE: PINT OR PILSENER
AVAILABILITY: YEAR-ROUND

With its dull and lightly hazy yellowish-orange color and well-sustained and mildly carbonated white head, Live Oak's Pilz fills your nose with clean aromas of lightly toasted malt that give in quickly to earthy, spicy, zesty noble hops. Medium in body, the beer is tremendously complex in flavor, starting with a nice bready European malt flavor before kicking into an earthy, spicy, and zesty hop flavor, followed by a long sustained period of noble bitterness. Light fruit hints underlie the beer but give way to clean, crisp, and expressive hop flavors.

Reality Czech

MOONLIGHT BREWING COMPANY
SANTA ROSA, CALIFORNIA
WWW.MOONLIGHTBREWING.COM
ALCOHOL CONTENT: 4.8% ABV
GLASSWARE: PINT OR PILSENER
AVAILABILITY: YEAR-ROUND

A luminous golden-colored beer with softer hues at the edges and with sheets of downy alabaster lace, the aroma zings with fresh and earthy Saaz notes. While perhaps a touch mild in the aroma, the proof is in the glass, where zesty and musky hops flitter across the tongue, followed closely by a balancing sweet pale malt backbone. Always balanced and ever drinkable, this award-winning beer captures the soft yet sharp essence of the Czech-style Pilsener.

Torch Pilsner

FOOTHILLS BREWING COMPANY
WINSTON-SALEM, NORTH CAROLINA
WWW.FOOTHILLSBREWING.COM
ALCOHOL CONTENT: 5.3% ABV
GLASSWARE: PINT OR PILSENER
AVAILABILITY: YEAR-ROUND

A bright, brilliant golden tint leads your eye up to the strongly carbonated head, thick with fat, cascading bubbles of foam. The aroma balances pale malt, with some raw European grain hints, with an earthy and herbal hop quality that tends towards grassy at times. A touch light in body, this bone dry Czech Pilsener showcases a zesty hop quality that both teases and tangles with your tongue before getting wrapped up in a mild blanket of moderate malt sweetness. Torch Pilsner is a lively and standout stab at the classic style.

Summerfest

SIERRA NEVADA BREWING COMPANY
CHICO, CALIFORNIA
WWW.SIERRANEVADA.COM
ALCOHOL CONTENT: 5.0% ABV
GLASSWARE: PINT OR PILSENER
AVAILABILITY: SUMMER

Another of Sierra Nevada's less appreciated offerings, the hard-to-classify Summerfest skirts around the edges of the famed Czech-style Pilsener. A hazy marigold color with a polished ivory head, toasted grain at first pervades the aroma before a barrage of zesty, spicy noble hops reveal their presence. The flavor is a touch light for the style, which increases the overall drinkability of this seasonal offering, and gives the European malt base room to shine before handing the reins over to the earthy and piquant noble hop bitterness. A mild fruitiness lurks deep beneath the surface in an effort to add yet another layer of complexity.

HOP MONSTERS

Of all the crazy things American brewers have undertaken in their efforts to push the definition of beer to its outer limits, perhaps nothing tops the battle to brew the hoppiest beer. Ever since the debut of the first American Pale Ales, brewers here have been trying to ratchet up their offerings in terms of hop aroma, flavor, and bitterness. Their measuring stick is the International Bitterness Unit, known as the IBU, a method used to determine the level of hop bitterness in a beer. Technically defined as one part per million of an acid derived from hop, IBUs is the term brewers and beer geeks toss around to flex their respective muscles. In the great world of brewing, a standard American lager such as Budweiser might contain less than ten IBUs, while Sierra Nevada's Pale Ale hits the mid-thirties, once considered to be hop heaven. The breweries of today routinely brag of beers whose bitterness levels exceed 100 or even 200 IBUs.

In truth, the level of bitterness in a beer is little understood by many who use it, and the true impact of massive loads of hops on the flavor of beer and a consumer's ability to appreciate it remains a hotly debated topic among brewers and academics. Some brewing scientists contend that hops have a solubility level substantially lower than 100 IBUs, and suggest that breweries trying to break through the ceiling are simply wasting their hops. Other food science academics argue that consumers cannot discern bitterness levels in excess of sixty or seventy IBUs. Dedicated bitter beer fans call these points fighting words or at least dismiss them as attempts to rain on their hop parade. Despite the counterclaims, it's important to note that adding hops just for their own sake, like adding salt to a dish, is a bit silly if the ultimate drinkability of the final product is ignored.

Every year hopheads gather during the annual Great American Beer Festival in Denver, Colorado, to take part in the Alpha King Challenge. Sponsored by a hop distributor, this contest pits dozens of brewers against one another in a battle for hop supremacy. Some of the beers listed here have won medals in that competition.

There may be no more hop-crazy place in the world than San Diego, California. One of the local hop-obsessed breweries, the Port Brewing Company, brews a beer called Hop 15, made with fifteen different hop additions added every fifteen minutes to the boil. A big Double IPA weighing in at nearly 10 percent, the aroma is dominated by a blast of juicy citrus notes, including orange, grapefruit, and even lemon, mixed with a light piney quality and a restrained booziness. The malt addition is well-balanced and does not detract from the strongly flavored yet smoothly drinkable hop presence that tings with tropical fruit notes and a solid but not overpowering bitterness.

Located down the road from Port Brewing, the Ballast Point Brewing Company's Dorado Double IPA is another hop fan favorite. This deep orange colored beer packs a powerfully hoppy and oily aroma, with citrus fruit and floral touches. The flavor provides a pleasant caramel malt counterbalance to strong and lingering bitterness.

One of the beers most closely associated with the current hop craze is Ruination IPA, brewed by the Stone Brewing Company of, you guessed it, Southern California. Boasting more than 100 IBUs and packed with juicy Columbus and Centennial hops, Ruination, so named because of its palate assaulting properties, is packed with earthy, piney, and floral hops. While the flavor is defined by hops, running the citrus fruit gamut, it remains quite drinkable, even with its sizable bitterness levels.

In the surprising beer capital of Grand Rapids, Michigan, Founders Brewing Company produces a beer some claim has an IBU level exceeding 200 units. Putting that tomfoolery aside, Devil Dancer is touted as a "Triple IPA" and is brewed and dry-hopped with ten different hop varieties. It opens with a clean and zesty orange aroma with mild pine and hop oil aromas and a quick shot of alcohol and caramel malt. The alcohol and hops fight for control of your tongue from the first sip with a strong hop bite and smack of booze that continues in an estery tailspin to the final sip.

DARK AND ROASTY

With flavors akin to well-roasted coffee and silky milk and dark chocolates, beers in this formidable group provide a welcomed counterbalance to both malty and hop-centric offerings. Generously borrowing from both sides of the beer ingredient spectrum, dark and roasty beers can be at once sweet and deeply, soulfully malty while balancing a substantially bitter finish. Others in the category prefer to dive into the deep end of burnt coffee and dark chocolate flavors. Ranging in color from deep brown to opaque, brooding black, these are the "dark beers" people talk about disliking. But for all of the societal negativity and hand-wringing over dark beers, these offerings are perhaps the closest alcoholic equivalents to popular everyday beverages and desserts: coffee and chocolate. Dark and Roasty are adjectives easily applied to cappuccinos and espressos, let alone standard black coffee. Prefer cream and sugar in your daily cup? Why not try a sweet or Cream Stout? Prefer a big, unapologetically potent brew? Reach for a Porter or Imperial Stout and connect with these powerfully familiar flavors. And if you're not quite ready to throw yourself into the full-flavored roasted darkness, smooth glasses of Schwarzbier and lightly boozy Baltic Porter and Export Stout await an introduction. Great when paired with chocolate or fruit-based desserts or with a range of cheeses, these roasted beauties are food-friendly in ways that might surprise you. Through common, everyday flavor associations anyone can understand, you can begin to break down the barriers to some occasionally daunting styles.

PORTER

A product of eighteenth century London, the origins of the Porter style has led to many pub debates. When people say they don't like dark beer, Porter gets tossed under the bus along with Stout. That's a shame, as these same individuals likely rely upon coffee and its roasted fortitude to get through long days. By the mid twentieth century, Porter had all but died out in its home country. Enterprising American and British craft brewers later helped resurrect the moribund style, which celebrates dark, roasted, and rich flavors. Dark brown to black in color, occasionally with ruby hues along the edges, the aromas range from light roasted coffee notes to intensely bitter charred notes. A style subject to diverse interpretation, the resulting beers can possess sharply bitter roasted malt notes to milder chocolate and sweeter malt notes.

St. George Porter

ST. GEORGE BREWING COMPANY
HAMPTON, VIRGINIA
WWW.STGEORGEBREWINGCO.COM
ALCOHOL CONTENT: 5.0% ABV
GLASSWARE: PINT, MUG, OR GOBLET
AVAILABILITY: YEAR-ROUND

Ostensibly brewed in the London style, St. George's twist on the classic Porter is robustly brown to black with tiny chestnut hints along the extremes and pours with a creamy tan head. The aroma is richly malty, with touches of caramelized sugar, chocolate malt, and a faint whisper of smoke. Brawny in body and well-carbonated, smoothness characterizes the St. George drinking experience in this perfectly balanced Porter. A rich charred malt character matches with intricate layers of dark chocolate, espresso, and coffee notes, with the faintest hint of dark fruit intriguing you for another sip.

Robust Porter

SMUTTYNOSE BREWING COMPANY
PORTSMOUTH, NEW HAMPSHIRE
WWW.SMUTTYNOSE.COM
ALCOHOL CONTENT: 5.1% ABV
GLASSWARE: PINT OR SNIFTER
AVAILABILITY: YEAR-ROUND

Smuttynose Brewing Company of New Hampshire brews one of the most audaciously and richly flavored porters available. Nearly jet black in color, allowing little to no color at the edges, the aptly named Robust Porter informs you from the pour that it means business. Far from a weak-kneed version of the style, the aroma is strongly of cold coffee, deeply roasted malt, and expensive dark chocolate with light earthy notes. With its medium body, the Porter starts with a touch of sweetness that tempts you near but then smacks your palate by an onslaught of deep, dark roasted malts and a long, drawn out earthy and roasted bitter finish. Light powdered chocolate and black coffee notes soften the bitterness. Smuttynose's version is the quintessential Porter; unreserved and aggressive but not overbearing.

Mayflower Porter

MAYFLOWER BREWING COMPANY
PLYMOUTH, MASSACHUSETTS
WWW.MAYFLOWERBREWING.COM
ALCOHOL CONTENT: 5.5% ABV
GLASSWARE: PINT OR MUG
AVAILABILITY: YEAR-ROUND

An incredibly popular offering from this upstart brewery that is sure to please both novice drinkers and beer geeks alike. Pouring dark brown to ruby amber in color, Mayflower Porter possesses an aroma that is slightly British in origin, with light coffee notes and deep European malts. Medium bodied and very drinkable, almost like a cross between a Dunkel and a Porter, with an airy quality, a touch of sweeter malt, all resulting in a light mocha coffee finish. Very dry throughout, Mayflower Porter is made with a touch of peat malt for a hint of smokiness that aids drinkability.

Great Northern Porter

SUMMIT BREWING COMPANY
SAINT PAUL, MINNESOTA
WWW.SUMMITBREWING.COM
ALCOHOL CONTENT: 4.9% ABV
GLASSWARE: PINT OR MUG
AVAILABILITY: YEAR-ROUND

A little heralded offering from Summit, Great Northern Porter possesses a deep brown façade with reddish hues at the edges and a nice sized off-tan brown head. The aroma is faintly of roasted malt but remains very balanced, with a touch of creaminess. But do not let the mild-mannered aroma fool you; this hearty beer holds true to nature as a Porter. The whispers of earthy and even slightly spicy hops in the aroma come through in this sharply bitter and quite hoppy beer, with earthy flavors and a strong roasted bitterness shining. A lighter bodied Porter, a touch of molasses-like sweetness aids the balance, but its defining quality remains its earthy bitterness.

Black Butte Porter

DESCHUTES BREWERY
BEND, OREGON
WWW.DESCHUTESBREWERY.COM
ALCOHOL CONTENT: 5.2% ABV
GLASSWARE: PINT OR MUG
AVAILABILITY: YEAR-ROUND

A perennial favorite of craft beer fans in the Pacific Northwest, Black Butte Porter is perhaps a touch more dark brown than black with cranberry traces at the corners. Topped with a tightly carbonated and cascading brown head, the nose showcases a fusion of dark roasted and chocolate malts, a base creaminess, and a contributing level of hops, unsurprising for this region. The medium-bodied, smooth as silk flavor manages to balance all of the elements to become one of the most drinkable porters available.

London Style Porter

D.L. GEARY BREWING COMPANY
PORTLAND, MAINE
WWW.GEARYBREWING.COM
ALCOHOL CONTENT: 4.2% ABV
GLASSWARE: PINT OR MUG
AVAILABILITY: YEAR-ROUND

One of the oldest American craft breweries, Geary's Brewing has been producing quality English-style ales since 1986, when it was the thirteenth craft to open. The brewery has faithfully recreated a classic English Porter with this big brown colored beer with soft carbonation and a brownish head. The aroma exhibits a great deal of character from the Ringwood house yeast, with a slight acidic tang and creaminess. The medium bodied Porter starts with a light malt entrée but slowly, casually fades into a drawn out game in which multiple levels of dark roasted bitterness appear one at a time. Light malt sweetness from English two-row pale and crystal malts helps balance out the pleasant, dry bitterness from the black and chocolate malts.

BALTIC PORTER

It was in the Baltics near the North Sea that the Porter style took a turn. Enterprising Eastern European brewers boosted the beer's alcohol levels and occasionally inoculated them with a souring agent to create a slight acidic tang. Robust in aroma and flavor, Baltic porters have enjoyed a resurgence in interest, especially among adventurous American craft brewers. Often brewed in Eastern Europe with lager yeast and cold-fermented to achieve a distinctive smoothness, despite its rougher edges, many American versions are ales and exhibit fruitier notes. The complex aromas often include notes of figs, currants, plums, and licorice with a warming alcohol presence and moderate roasted notes. The Baltic Porter's flavor follows suit, with very little bitterness from hops or malt, ample molasses sweet, and fruit notes interacting with rich chocolate and complex roasted hints.

Dark Knight
BARLEY JOHN'S BREW PUB
NEW BRIGHTON, MINNESOTA
WWW.BARLEYJOHNS.COM
ALCOHOL CONTENT: 12.0% ABV
GLASSWARE: SNIFTER
AVAILABILITY: LIMITED RELEASE

Built in a renovated A&W fast food restaurant, the humble Barley John's is no stranger to high octane beers. The brewery's Rosie's Old Ale had beer geeks whispering that they'd heard it was 28 percent alcohol, a point that turned out to be a substantial exaggeration. Dark Knight is a much more modest 12 percent and pours jet black with a deep brown head. The aroma gives you fair warning, with big wine, oak, and bourbon barrel notes, with hints of vanilla and coffee mixed in for good measure. The flavor follows suit, with port-like qualities mixing with the bourbon notes, a touch of wood, and a slightly sweet mixture of European malts and a slight hop bitterness to balance the powerful alcohol and the malts. A bit big for the style, Dark Knight is a worthy adversary for those willing to face the challenge.

El Robusto Porter
PAPAGO BREWING COMPANY
SCOTTSDALE, ARIZONA
WWW.PAPAGOBREWING.COM
ALCOHOL CONTENT: 8.0% ABV
GLASSWARE: PINT OR GOBLET
AVAILABILITY: YEAR-ROUND

Opening with a foreboding black color and a creamy and tightly carbonated head, the aroma presents a powerful burst of sweeter malts, from deep caramel to lighter chocolate and hints of coffee. Despite its imposing name, El Robusto starts relatively mild and light on the palate, with a rotund sweetness that quickly gives way to more forceful deep roasted and burnt malt notes, touches of coffee, very faint earthy hops, and a dry, roasted, and slightly warm alcohol finish. A complex beer that manages to keep all of the elements playing well with one another.

Good people drink good beer. —Hunter S. Thompson

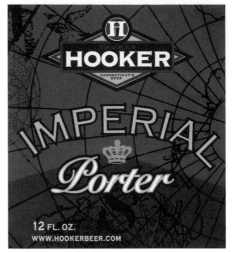

Gonzo Imperial Porter

FLYING DOG BREWING COMPANY
FREDERICK, MARYLAND
WWW.FLYINGDOGALES.COM
ALCOHOL CONTENT: 7.8% ABV
GLASSWARE: GOBLET OR SNIFTER
AVAILABILITY: YEAR-ROUND

Presenting with a deep, dark black color with very little color around the edges and an off-tan head, Gonzo's aroma is lightly boozy with a European malt hook that lies pretty flat alongside a light chalky dryness like hints of coconut. Near full bodied, the flavor of the beer does not match its relatively passive aroma, breaking free into big, sweet malt notes and a touch of roasted bitterness to make sure the experience does not suddenly go all Hunter Thompson (the adventurer after whom the beer is named) on the consumer. The flavor itself boasts a quick hit of dark fruits, followed by a large splash of sweet European malts, then by wave upon wave of roasted dryness, then alcohol, then roasted bitterness. Surprisingly complex, the rougher edges will likely lessen with age.

Imperial Porter

THOMAS HOOKER BREWING COMPANY
BLOOMFIELD, CONNECTICUT
WWW.HOOKERBEER.COM
ALCOHOL CONTENT: 7.8% ABV
GLASSWARE: SNIFTER OR GOBLET
AVAILABILITY: WINTER

Deep garnet brown in color and capped with a wheat brown fluffy head, Thomas Hooker's version of the style is an impressive sight. Made with eight different malts and a mixture of German and American hops, the aroma plays between dark fruits, mocha coffee, dark and milk chocolate, and a dry roasted nut quality. Brewed with lager yeast, the flavor is smooth yet nuanced, with a complex array of powdered chocolate, roasted malts with a smoky touch, along with a solid earthy bitterness from the hops. Imperial Porter finishes dry from the black patent malt inclusion, yet remains quite drinkable throughout.

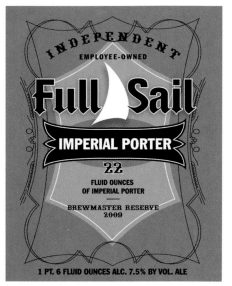

Killer Kapowski

**FLOSSMOOR STATION RESTAURANT
AND BREWERY
FLOSSMOOR, ILLINOIS
WWW.FLOSSMOORSTATION.COM
ALCOHOL CONTENT: 8.3% ABV
GLASSWARE: SNIFTER OR GOBLET
AVAILABILITY: LIMITED RELEASE**

In a southern suburb of Chicago quietly sits a brewpub of great renown, tucked away in an old railroad depot. Despite its inconspicuous appearance, Flossmoor Station is one of America's most highly decorated pub brewers. The brewpub's Baltic Porter, called Killer Kapowski, appears jet black with a substantial crown of mocha colored foam. Its aroma peaks with roasted and burnt malts, chocolates, dried dark raisins and cherries, and a touch of alcohol warmth. The flavor follows the advertised aroma menu with blasts of roasted grain, toffee and molasses, chocolate covered cherries, a bit of vanilla and sometimes honey, and a boozy alcohol addition. Killer Kapowski is a brilliant beer that would be a great accompaniment to many desserts.

Imperial Porter

**FULL SAIL BREWING COMPANY
HOOD RIVER, OREGON
WWW.FULLSAILBREWING.COM
ALCOHOL CONTENT: 7.5% ABV
GLASSWARE: SNIFTER OR GOBLET
AVAILABILITY: LIMITED RELEASE**

The employee-owned Full Sail Brewing Company is best known for making approachable, drinkable beers that boast strong character and wide appeal, namely the sort of thing hardened beer geeks ignore. For these jaded souls, the brewery also produces its Brewmaster Reserve series. Available early in the year, Imperial Porter pours with a deep, dark, luminous black color and a sizable off tan head that stays put. This barrel-aged offering demonstrates the expected wood notes but also a burnt coffee bitterness mixed with a light lactic acidity and even coconut hints. Medium to full bodied, it's full of fruity alcohol esters, green apples, vanilla mixing with cold coffee, and a light underlying bitterness to wrap it all together.

IRISH-STYLE DRY STOUT

The Stout designation once meant a stronger than average beer and even applied to pale beers. As the style developed in Britain and Ireland, including an early version by Guinness, Stout came to be known as a stronger version of brown Porter. Despite their foreboding appearance, opaque and dark with a sizable, sustained creamy head, modern incarnations are the polar opposite of heavy beers. With a light to medium body, these stouts have a mild carbonation when served from the bottle, or take on an airy, creamy consistency if served from a nitrogen tap system. The dry moniker of this low alcohol beer is apt as a distinct yet reserved bitterness imparted by roasted barley dominates the malt bill and gives off coffee and dark chocolate notes. Americanized versions can be a touch hoppier and sometimes bear closer resemblance to the Porter style.

Riley's Stout

PAPER CITY BREWING COMPANY
HOLYOKE, MASSACHUSETTS
WWW.PAPERCITY.COM
ALCOHOL CONTENT: 5.5% ABV
GLASSWARE: PINT
AVAILABILITY: YEAR-ROUND

The dark brown to black color with the slightest edges of red and a soft creamy tan head get things off to a great start for Riley's Stout. The aroma is lightly of European malt with a touch of sweetness and a dash of cream that quickly gives way to a light roasted malted milk ball flavor. The resulting flavor is quite creamy and smartly balances the darker and lighter malt flavors, resulting in a delight that alternates between milky creaminess and lightly burnt maltiness. The lightest touch of alcohol and fruity esters underlies this pleasant, drinkable beer.

Susquehanna Stout

APPALACHIAN BREWING COMPANY
HARRISBURG, PENNSYLVANIA
WWW.ABCBREW.COM
ALCOHOL CONTENT: 4.6% ABV
GLASSWARE: PINT OR GOBLET
AVAILABILITY: YEAR-ROUND

Available at Appalachian's several pubs throughout the state, its Susquehanna Stout is a classic representation of the Irish-style Dry Stout. Named after the local Susquehannock Indians, the beer pours deep brown to sable in color with a creamy mocha head. The aroma brims with dark roasted malt notes, nutty hints, and dark chocolate and coffee notes. This Stout's flavor follows with considerable charred malt notes that give off both light smoky and bitter flavors that mix with a toasted nuttiness and even a dash of sweet chocolate notes. Smooth from start to finish, this Stout is drinkable and roasty throughout.

Kozlov Stout

THIRSTY BEAR BREWING COMPANY
SAN FRANCISCO, CALIFORNIA
WWW.THIRSTYBEAR.COM
ALCOHOL CONTENT: 5.0% ABV
GLASSWARE: PINT
AVAILABILITY: YEAR-ROUND

Rich ebony in color with a plentiful tan head, Kozlov is a looker with the added layering cascade from the nitrogen tap push. The nose is filled with roasted malts, light oat notes, tinges of chocolate, and a smidge of alcohol. A medium-bodied beer, the roasted malts make themselves known before a kiss of earthy hops melds with a drawn out bitterness from the dark malts and finishes the job. The nitrogen infusion adds a base layer of creaminess to this roasty joy.

Old No. 38 Stout

NORTH COAST BREWING COMPANY
FORT BRAGG, CALIFORNIA
WWW.NORTHCOASTBREWING.COM
ALCOHOL CONTENT: 5.6% ABV
GLASSWARE: PINT
AVAILABILITY: YEAR-ROUND

With its dark brown color and light reddish hues at the extremes, the pale cream head with slight retention gives off notes that are lightly creamy with mild pale malts and a slight lactic tang. The flavor is slightly bitter from dry roasted malts. It fades into a hint of creaminess and into a dark roasted finish, all very light and airy on the palate. At no point overwhelming, Old No. 38 Stout is approachable yet full-flavored.

Brewed in honor of the life & times of Michael Faricy.

Faricy Fest
Irish Stout

12 fl. Oz—MI 10¢ Deposit

Faricy Fest Irish Stout

ARBOR BREWING COMPANY
ANN ARBOR, MICHIGAN
WWW.ARBORBREWING.COM
ALCOHOL CONTENT: 4.5% ABV
GLASSWARE: PINT
AVAILABILITY: YEAR-ROUND

From the heart of Wolverine country, this Stout pours with a deep coffee brown color, with touches of burgundy around the fringes, and a creamy tan head. The aroma is filled with lightly smoked notes, occasionally peaty in nature, mixed with roasted grains, bitter chocolate, and a nutty conclusion. Similarly minded, the flavor starts with a mildly acrid base that gives way to chocolate, coffee, and espresso notes with a touch of black licorice. With its relatively low-alcohol level, Faricy Fest packs a lot of flavor into a tight, slippery little package.

Onward Irish Stout

YAZOO BREWING COMPANY
NASHVILLE, TENNESSEE
WWW.YAZOOBREW.COM
ALCOHOL CONTENT: 3.8% ABV
GLASSWARE: PINT
AVAILABILITY: YEAR-ROUND

Pouring pitch black to the eye and with a wavy thick cascade of a tan head, this Nashville pride boasts rich espresso coffee notes, dry and roasted malt kicks, and bits of smoke. The head rests in sheets on the glass as the flavors of sweeter molasses and oatmeal mix with the black patent malt's inherent bitterness to create a dry and roasted delight. A very sessionable beer at only 3.8 percent alcohol, Onward Irish Stout adds some coffee and espresso flavors to create a deeper, more complex take on the traditional Stout.

OATMEAL STOUT

A quirky style mixing chocolate and caramel roasted malt flavors, Oatmeal stouts derive a gentility and lightness of body from the use of oatmeal in the grist mill. Deep brown to pitch black in color and with sustained, tan heads, these stouts bridge the gap between the Dry Irish-style and the Sweet or Foreign Export Stout versions. Beyond the aromas and flavors of roasted malts, which tend more towards chocolate and even nutty hints, a moderate bitterness is used for balance. Depending upon the level of oatmeal employed, these stouts can possess creamy notes and the resulting flavors can be silky smooth in texture. Balance is key here and the best Oatmeal Stouts are highly drinkable and not heavy on the palate.

Wolaver's Oatmeal Stout

WOLAVER'S BREWING COMPANY
MIDDLEBURY, VERMONT
WWW.OTTERCREEKBREWING.COM
ALCOHOL CONTENT: 5.9% ABV
GLASSWARE: PINT
AVAILABILITY: YEAR-ROUND

One of America's leading organic breweries, Wolaver's has long been dedicated to making classic-styled beers with all-natural ingredients. Pouring a deep brownish-garnet hue with a toasted colored head, a tad light for the style, slight lacing is achieved. A pleasant lightness fills the aroma, with oat notes and plentiful well-roasted barley with touches of lightly roasted coffee beans and chocolate. The flavor matches the aroma with the additions of a tight bitterness from a combination of roasted grains and noble and American hops. Substantially dry to the taste, flairs of malt sweetness complete this offering.

Brass Knuckles Oatmeal Stout

BARLEY ISLAND BREWING COMPANY
NOBLESVILLE, INDIANA
WWW.BARLEYISLAND.TRIPOD.COM
ALCOHOL CONTENT: 4.9% ABV
GLASSWARE: PINT
AVAILABILITY: YEAR-ROUND

This burnt sable-hued beauty boasts a foreboding dark brown head with tight carbonation, very impressive to the eye. A bruiser indeed, Brass Knuckles smacks of charred malts and ground coffee beans mixed with dark chocolate, all melding well together. Not for the faint of heart, this Stout is light on the oatmeal and big on the scorched roasted malt character, coupled with the lightest tinges of cream and even vanilla, and finished off with some chocolate notes and a bit of earthy bitterness from the hops.

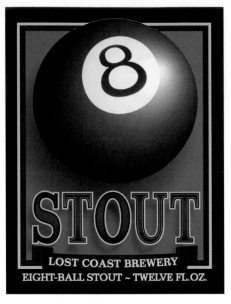

One Oatmeal Stout

DARK HORSE BREWING COMPANY
MARSHALL, MICHIGAN
WWW.DARKHORSEBREWERY.COM
ALCOHOL CONTENT: 8.0% ABV
GLASSWARE: PINT, MUG, OR GOBLET
AVAILABILITY: YEAR-ROUND

Brewed as one of five stouts the brewery produces around the winter holidays, this Oatmeal Stout starts with an opaque black color and is capped with a solid, spongy head of foam. One's nose is filled with big roasted malts mixed with charred baker's chocolate, burnt coffee beans, and a slight acidity and creaminess, all acting with restraint. A surprisingly rich and thick example, One Oatmeal Stout unleashes a mild torrent of bittersweet and roasted chocolate, black coffee, and a slightly smoky roasted malt character that also displays some lighter caramel malt qualities, all resulting in an unexpectedly soft and velvety mouthfeel. A bit of an enigma considering the style, Dark Horse lives up to its name with this beer.

8 Ball Stout

LOST COAST BREWERY & CAFÉ
EUREKA, CALIFORNIA
WWW.LOASTCOAST.COM
ALCOHOL CONTENT: 5.9% ABV
GLASSWARE: PINT OR MUG
AVAILABILITY: YEAR-ROUND

Lost Coast's 8 Ball pours with a blackish brown body and a moderate mocha cap. It smells of chocolate, coffee, a touch of molasses, and rich roasted malts. The flavor follows suit, with the addition of dry cocoa, a little treacle, a mild creaminess hidden amidst the dark malts, and the slightest hint of oats. A full-bodied Stout, the mouthfeel is creamy at times with a moderate carbonation balancing out the thick body. Befitting its West Coast heritage, the magical 8 Ball is a tinge hoppier than your average Stout.

Ipswich Oatmeal Stout

MERCURY BREWING COMPANY
IPSWICH, MASSACHUSETTS
WWW.MERCURYBREWING.COM
ALCOHOL CONTENT: 7.0% ABV
GLASSWARE: PINT OR MUG
AVAILABILITY: YEAR-ROUND

Menacingly black color for an Oatmeal Stout with a light tan head and very little color at the edges, Mercury's version, unlike many versions of the style, is hugely hoppy with big earthy and mineral notes from Pacific Northwest hops. The unexpected hop aromas add to the more standard dark roasted coffee notes and light espresso hints resulting in an earthy, clean experience. Surprisingly full bodied, Ipswich Oatmeal Stout booms with flavor, choosing to rely on the side of burnt roasted strength instead of lighter creamy touches. The roasted malt flavor starts slow, transitions into a touch of raisin malt sweetness, but then kicks into a long, pronounced, and never-ending burnt bitterness.

Barney Flats Oatmeal Stout

ANDERSON VALLEY BREWING COMPANY
BOONTVILLE, CALIFORNIA
WWW.AVBC.COM
ALCOHOL CONTENT: 5.7% ABV
GLASSWARE: PINT
AVAILABILITY: YEAR-ROUND

Anderson Valley's first gold medal winner at the Great American Beer Festival is also one of the brewery's most popular beers. With a two-finger deep light brown head that refuses to quit, Barney Flats is a classic Oatmeal Stout with a deceptively light brownish-rouge color. The brewery's yeast strain gives off a signature creamy aroma, a rare sign of true house character, which gives way to very light touches of roasted malt and hints of milk chocolate. The flavor remains quite reserved in terms of dark malts, instead yielding a complex array of coconut, yeast creaminess, roasted bitterness, and chocolate notes.

MILK STOUT

Sometimes a bit difficult to find, Milk Stouts fully give in to the lighter, creamier side of the roasted Stout world. But don't expect a cloying, unbalanced mess. Quite the contrary, these medium- to full-bodied stouts balance deeply roasted grains, with their cream coffee and milk to dark chocolate aromas, with a moderate level of sweetness to create a creatively and agreeably dissonant beverage. Deep and dark in color and with low carbonation, the high residual sweetness comes from unconverted sugars left in the beer and in the case of milk stouts, the addition of lactose, an unfermentable ingredient also known as milk sugar. Sometimes called Cream Stout, the flavor of these styles often focus on a downy, milky flavor reminiscent of sweetened coffee or espresso.

Veruca Stout

RED EYE BREWING COMPANY
WAUSAU, WISCONSIN
WWW.REDEYEBREWING.COM
ALCOHOL CONTENT: 5.3% ABV
GLASSWARE: PINT
AVAILABILITY: YEAR-ROUND

A nice offering from a small northern Wisconsin brewpub, the Veruca Stout pours dark brown to black color with garnet edges, and the aroma is lightly sweet mixed with oats and lactose creaminess. Medium bodied and with a jolt of lactose sweetness upfront, the flavor mixes additional pleasant touches of a balancing roasted bitterness. Hints of smoke and roasted coffee are hidden deep within this drinkable beer that finishes slightly sweet.

Special Double Cream Stout

BELL'S BREWERY
KALAMAZOO, MICHIGAN
WWW.BELLSBEER.COM
ALCOHOL CONTENT: 6.1% ABV
GLASSWARE: PINT OR MUG
AVAILABILITY: WINTER

Bell's Brewery of Michigan has a thing for stouts, having once produced ten different stouts in the month of November alone. Special Double Cream Stout is not some extreme version of the style but instead pours near black with tiny brown highlights and topped with a lightly carbonated deep brown head. This medium-bodied Stout smells of rich roasted malts with hints of coffee, vanilla, and creamy milk chocolate. The flavor tends more towards milk chocolate, with all its creamy and milky goodness, fused together with a dark roasted chocolate and burnt coffee base. A highly drinkable Milk Stout from a brewery that understands dark beers.

Milk Stout

LEFT HAND BREWING COMPANY
LONGMONT, COLORADO
WWW.LEFTHANDBREWING.COM
ALCOHOL CONTENT: 5.9% ABV
GLASSWARE: PINT
AVAILABILITY: YEAR-ROUND

This Milk Stout pours with a dark brown color with ruby hues at the edges and a light tan head. The aroma possesses a chalky, mocha like dryness with deep and dry roasted notes and a slight burnt malt character. The beer's flavor starts off slow, with a lightly toasted maltiness reminiscent of molasses, before diving into a moderate dark malt quality that plays well with a light lactose creaminess from the addition of milk sugars and flaked oats. Light-bodied and with an overall sweetness, the beer is a great entrant for dark beer wary novices, like a brown ale with lactic sweetness.

Steel Toe Stout

SKA BREWING COMPANY
DURANGO, COLORADO
WWW.SKABREWING.COM
ALCOHOL CONTENT: 5.4% ABV
GLASSWARE: PINT
AVAILABILITY: YEAR-ROUND

Steel Toe pours deep brown with light brownish-red hues around the trim. A bit unusual for the style, the beer leans more heavily on the roasted side of the ledger, with an aroma that also features a smattering of light cream traces. This Milk Stout, brewed with lactose, starts with a light roasted malt bite that lasts throughout the flavor but is joined near the end by a distinct, pleasant creaminess that finishes almost like chai tea with milk. A very enjoyable and drinkable flavor combination.

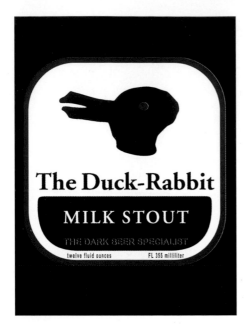

Milk Stout

DUCK-RABBIT BREWING COMPANY
FARMVILLE, NORTH CAROLINA
WWW.DUCKRABBITBREWERY.COM
ALCOHOL CONTENT: 5.4% ABV
GLASSWARE: PINT
AVAILABILITY: YEAR-ROUND

Run by a former college philosophy professor, Duck-Rabbit is a quirky brewery that focuses on brewing dark beers. The brewery's Milk Stout is dark brown in color with copper edges and a light wispy head. The aroma brims with dark roasted malt notes and a touch of sweetness and cream imparted by lactose sugars. The Stout is medium bodied and possesses a substantially roasted character filled with chocolate malt, which kicks into another gear of roasted bitterness mixed with a touch of lactic sweetness and creaminess. The intriguing and playful beer almost resembles a creamy, highly roasted brown ale.

Milk Stout

LANCASTER BREWING COMPANY
LANCASTER, PENNSYLVANIA
WWW.LANCASTERBREWING.COM
ALCOHOL CONTENT: 5.3% ABV
GLASSWARE: PINT
AVAILABILITY: YEAR-ROUND

Deep mahogany hues flash out in patches from this thick brownish black colored Stout with a booming toasted wheat foamy head. The aroma fills with light cream from lactose, roasted grains, dark and bittersweet chocolate, tiny coffee touches, and even a hint of vanilla on occasion. Packed with flavor from start to finish, Milk Stout begins with bittersweet chocolate that gives way to fresh roasted coffee beans, lactic sugars, powdered cocoa, vanilla, and an unusual bitterness, both from grain and from hops, that serves to keep everything in balance. Milk Stout is the pride of Lancaster.

EXPORT STOUT

This style offers amateur historians a rare glimpse at what traditional British stouts tasted like a century ago. Sometimes referred to as Foreign-style Stout, the style remains popular in many countries throughout Africa and southeastern Asia. Despite their pleasant, approachable flavors and aromas, Export Stouts are not commonly found in American markets. Deep brown to jet black in color, the style balances moderate roasted grain aromas, even slightly burnt coffee at times, with a novel fruitiness and a complex array of molasses, plums, and lightly boozy alcohol notes. While not cloying, residual sugars mix with higher alcohol levels and the roasted notes and fruity hints to create a very intriguing and drinkable beer, even on warm days. Some versions bear a slight acidity that balances the sweeter notes.

Steelhead Extra Stout

MAD RIVER BREWING COMPANY
BLUE LAKE, CALIFORNIA
WWW.MADRIVERBREWING.COM
ALCOHOL CONTENT: 6.0% ABV
GLASSWARE: PINT OR MUG
AVAILABILITY: YEAR-ROUND

The Extra Stout pours with a jet black color and a light tan head and smells of deep, rich, and sweet malt, with the lightest touches of roasted edge, but not bitterness. It possesses light mocha notes, even coconut at times, and the medium body also contains big roasted flavors competing with sweeter malt notes for dominance, with neither winning out in a balanced stalemate. The booze is very well-restrained compared to some alcohol-heavy examples of the style, and light mocha and coffee notes run alongside a hint of smoke.

Damn Good Stout

BRÜ RM @ BAR
NEW HAVEN, CONNECTICUT
WWW.BARNIGHTCLUB.COM
ALCOHOL CONTENT: 7.0% ABV
GLASSWARE: SNIFTER OR MUG
AVAILABILITY: YEAR-ROUND

Created from a mixture of seven different malts, this Stout actually manages to live up to its bold name. Appearing near opaque black with a thick tan head, the beer lets you know you are in for a treat with its rich, malty, and roasted swirls of coffee and chocolate. There is an initial burst of light alcohol flavors upfront, followed by a wash of mild roasted notes, and the beer finishes with a slight sweetness. Damn Good Stout possesses slight cocoa and coffee flavors but ends up best expressing some notable maltiness, which is typical for this sweeter style.

Tsunami Stout

PELICAN PUB AND BREWERY
PACIFIC CITY, OREGON
WWW.PELICANBREWERY.COM
ALCOHOL CONTENT: 7.0% ABV
GLASSWARE: PINT
AVAILABILITY: YEAR-ROUND

This rollercoaster of a beer starts chugging along with a deep jet black color and a dark brown, lightly carbonated head. The first spin tosses out rich milk chocolate and mocha notes, turning dry at times, fused with mild dark fruit hints, covered in chocolate. The flavor is impressively layered, starting with mocha-like dryness from flaked, unmalted barley, and then kicking into a deep, rich, and roasted bitterness akin to cold coffee, with a fair amount of alcohol warmth near the finish.

Obsidian Stout

DESCHUTES BREWERY
BEND, OREGON
WWW.DESCHUTESBREWERYCOM
ALCOHOL CONTENT: 6.4% ABV
GLASSWARE: PINT
AVAILABILITY: YEAR-ROUND

While not a sweet Stout in the general sense, Obsidian is a style bender. Big, deep, and thick, with a well-sustained brown head, the aroma is a mixture of dark roasted malts, substantial creaminess, and a touch of lactose sweetness with definite doses of American earthy hops. The flavor starts out decidedly sweet and has a lactose like creaminess that lines up with the style. With a medium body and silky smooth, the sweetness eventually gives way, but not totally, for a sizable roasted bitterness, a deeper roasted flavor, and an earthy hop flavor that makes this a very accessible yet complex offering. It remains very drinkable due to the lactose-like quality.

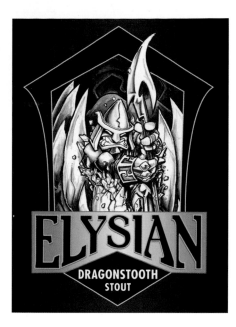

Dragonstooth Stout

ELYSIAN BREWING COMPANY
SEATTLE, WASHINGTON
WWW.ELYSIANBREWING.COM
ALCOHOL CONTENT: 7.2% ABV
GLASSWARE: SNIFTER, TULIP, OR PINT
AVAILABILITY: YEAR-ROUND

With a name referencing Greek warriors who sprang from the ground when the teeth of a slain dragon were sown, you know this Export Stout is going to be tough. Made with rolled oats, Dragonstooth pours with an ominous black tint and dark ruby edging, capped by a tan crown. The Stout's aroma glimmers with rich malt aromas, bouncing from caramel, toffee, and brown sugar to dark chocolate and a touch of coffee, and finishing out with hints of vanilla. The flavor adds the unusual touch of American citrus hops, which is a departure from the style but helps bring together the old and new worlds of brewing. A creaminess to the malt mixes with its substantial sweetness and the citrus hops to create a highly drinkable concoction.

Captain Swain's Extra Stout

CISCO BREWERS
NANTUCKET, MASSACHUSETTS
WWW.CISCOBREWERY.COM
ALCOHOL CONTENT: 8.0% ABV
GLASSWARE: PINT OR GOBLET.
AVAILABILITY: YEAR-ROUND

Named for one of the earliest settlers on Nantucket, a family from which the brewery's owner descends, this Extra Stout is a testament to the sea-faring world that holds this style so dear. A rich sable color with hints of garnet hues at the extremes underlies the moderately creamy tan crown. The nose fills with a slightly acrid dark roasted malt burst followed by waves of sweeter chocolate and burnt coffee and a touch of earthy hops. The roasted malt occasionally strays into a pleasant and somewhat unexpected acidity, not quite sour, before giving way to creamy swirls of caramel, milk chocolate, and charred grains. A hint of pine from Chinook dry-hopping balances out this full-flavored beer.

SCHWARZBIER

One of the world's least understood beer styles, Schwarzbier ("shvahrts-beer"), means "black beer" in German. Despite its deep menacingly dark brown to black color with ruby hues, Schwarzbier is incredibly light in mouthfeel and flavor, resulting in a drinkable and easily approachable style. As a lager, Schwarzbiers benefit from cold-conditioning, which smoothes out the rougher patches associated with other roasted styles, and the dark flavors and aromas are mild compared to most Porters. The clean aroma is lightly malty, with slight burnished hints and sweet and cream touches from Munich malt. The flavor balances lightly roasted malts with a mild bitterness and finishes long, dry, and smooth. A relatively low alcohol style, in the 5 percent range, Schwarzbiers are easily accessible for roasted beer novices.

Saranac Black Forest

THE MATT BREWING COMPANY
UTICA, NEW YORK
WWW.SARANAC.COM
ALCOHOL CONTENT: 5.3% ABV
GLASSWARE: PINT OR MUG
AVAILABILITY: YEAR-ROUND

One of the oldest regional breweries in the United States, the Matt Brewing Company has a long history of producing flavorful beers. Founded in 1888 by F.X. Matt, the brewery now focuses on producing a wide line of accessible craft brands. Its Black Forest is a stand-out, with its deep brownish-black color and substantial off-brown head. The aroma lightly fills with a quick burst of roasted malt followed by hints of caramel sweetness. True to style, the imposing color translates into a surprisingly mild body, with waves of slightly sweet caramel malt mixing with occasional roasted notes. A very slight noble hop bitterness and earthy character balances out the whole package.

Kidd Lager

FORT COLLINS BREWERY
FORT COLLINS, COLORADO
WWW.FORTCOLLINSBREWERY.COM
ALCOHOL CONTENT: 4.5% ABV
GLASSWARE: PINT OR MUG
AVAILABILITY: YEAR-ROUND

At its core, a true Schwarzbier should be dark enough to instill a little fear into your heart but light enough on the palate to confound your tongue and make you wonder about an eye appointment. With its Kidd Lager, Fort Collins achieves these lofty goals. A deep brown color with crimson highlights and a wheat brown head, the beer possesses a rich roasted malt nose that surpasses many other beers of the style. There is also a touch of light fruity hops mixed with powdered cocoa. The flavor matches but adds a faint fruity quality from the hops that gives way to a mild sweet yet dry roasted malt and cream quality, all in a smooth and clean package. A touch of smoked malt adds some additional character to this drinkable beer.

Black Noddy Lager

BUCKBEAN BREWING COMPANY
RENO, NEVADA
WWW.BUCKBEANBEER.COM
ALCOHOL CONTENT: 5.2% ABV
GLASSWARE: PINT OR MUG
AVAILABILITY: YEAR-ROUND

Poured from a pint-sized can, this offering from America's biggest little city starts with a deep brown color and substantial mahogany hues at the outskirts. The black lager's aroma is lightly roasted but is also brimming with creamy malt and caramel notes, a touch of smoke, and some additional light fruity hints. The resulting flavor is perhaps a bit fruity for the general style, but the rich malted barley flavors, which include a reserved smoky side, balance well together and include a chocolate side.

Samuel Adams Black Lager

BOSTON BEER COMPANY
BOSTON, MASSACHUSETTS
WWW.SAMADAMS.COM
ALCOHOL CONTENT: 4.9% ABV
GLASSWARE: PINT OR MUG
AVAILABILITY: YEAR-ROUND

One of the lesser heralded beers in Boston Beer's substantial portfolio of flavorful offerings, this to-style Schwarzbier is a credit to a big craft brewery that has never lost touch with its beer-loving roots. Black Lager presents with a disquieting blackish brown color with only the slightest edges of color at the margins and with a huge, tightly carbonated tan head. The beer's aroma boasts a panoply of lightly roasted dark malts blended with a big flash of cream and the slightest hint of dark fruits. The flavor continues to mix moderately roasted dark malts, a few dashes of cream, and a quick whiff of smoke, all finishing very dry and pleasant.

Death and Taxes

MOONLIGHT BREWING COMPANY
FULTON, CALIFORNIA
WWW.MOONLIGHTBREWING.COM
ALCOHOL CONTENT: 5.0% ABV
GLASSWARE: PINT OR MUG
AVAILABILITY: YEAR-ROUND

Easily the darkest Schwarzbier in this list, Moonlight's popular version checks in with an opaque black color and a dark cocoa foam top. The beer's aroma fills the nose with roasted malt akin to Stout, baker's chocolate, light smoky hints, and fresh ground coffee. Booming with character, Death and Taxes is smooth as silk with gentle cream notes and in contrast to its potent aroma, only touches of roasted malt that leaves the final product very easy to drink. A classic version of this misunderstood style.

Black Bavarian

SPRECHER BREWING COMPANY
GLENDALE, WISCONSIN
WWW.SPRECHER.COM
ALCOHOL CONTENT: 5.8% ABV
GLASSWARE: PINT OR MUG
AVAILABILITY: YEAR-ROUND

Brewed by owner Randy Sprecher for more than 35 years, since his return from a trip to Germany, the Black Bavarian is one of the most popular Schwarzbiers in America. The beer unleashes a massive onyx tint with only flecks of mahogany and a beige colored foam accent. Black Bavarian's aroma is a curious mixture of chocolate, caramel, and cream with a light molasses edge at times and only the slightest touch of darker malts. The flavor similarly confounds, with an array of notes from cream to burnt chocolate, to the faintest ground coffee hints, all mixed with a touch of sourness that plays well against the sweetness.

COFFEE BEER

Hundreds of millions of Americans reach for a cup of coffee every morning to help kick start their days. While some just take it black, billion dollar enterprises have sprouted up to meet the finicky needs of many coffee drinkers. From simple espressos to double grande soy milk half-caf mouthfuls, coffee is as much a national beverage as soda and beer. So it is with irony still dripping from the Starbucks-stirring straw that many Americans also decry dark beers, brushed aside in their entirety without a moment's thought as to how similar many might be to their favorite morning pick-me-up.

Beers made with coffee are the perfect foot soldiers in the battle to get people to drink with an open mind and mouth. Unlike the millions of Americans described above, I'm not a coffee drinker and, in fact, don't always enjoy bitter, dark roasted flavors. Despite this acknowledged prejudice, I'm a big coffee beer fan and they have helped me develop a passion for porters, a style I once avoided.

It is important to note that any beer style can include coffee as an ingredient, and beers made with coffee are not designated as their own separate style. With that said, brewers often prefer to use coffee-related products in beers that already possess darker hues, flavors, and aromas as a means of complementing the existing character or to add additional complexity. Depending upon the type of coffee and method of use in the brewing process, the resulting beer may possess light roasted aromas and flavors or strongly bitter hints. Some brewers tend to dump coffee beans or grounds into already flavor heavy imperial stouts. The beers profiled here tend to focus on maximizing coffee flavors and not using them as yet another palate assault weapon.

In Western Massachusetts, Berkshire Brewing Company works with a local fair trade coffee provider to transform its regular Drayman's Porter into the delectable Coffeehouse Porter. Using a robust coffee extract, this dark mahogany beer possesses a playful bouquet of caramel malt mixed with ground

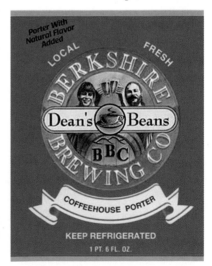

coffee, all with an off-tan head. With a light carbonation, the beer starts with a jolt of cold coffee roasted character mixed with a touch of coffee bitterness, all balanced by a lightly sweet caramel flavor. A complex yet drinkable beer that does not allow the coffee influence to overshadow the underlying style's flair.

In Minneapolis, Minnesota, the beer geek friendly Surly Brewing Company transforms its style twisting Bender, an oatmeal Brown Ale, into Coffee Bender with the use of coarsely ground, cold steeped Guatemalan beans. Dark ruby in hue, the beer bears some similarity to an iced coffee in aroma and flavor, with cascades of caramel, vanilla, chocolate, all mixed with the underlying brown ale.

Wisconsin-based contract brewer Furthermore Beer produces a surprisingly light amber colored beer called Oscura that contains an astoundingly potent and concentrated cold coffee character obtained from roasted Nicaraguan beans. With a toasted graham cracker-like malt lager base, the brewers use flaked maize and whole beans cold soaked and slow fermented to create an impressive and accessible new take on the coffee beer.

At nearly 9 percent alcohol, Terrapin Beer Company's Coffee Oatmeal Imperial Stout, playfully nicknamed Wake-n-Bake, bestows a powerful and potent coffee beer experience. Made with a blend of coffee from Costa Rica, Guatemala, and Zimbabwe, this coffee Stout pours slightly thick and smells of an intricate mixture of iced coffee, roasted malt, light smokiness, and a warming alcohol base. A touch of sweetness holds its own against the strong, lush roasted and creamy coffee flavors.

LUSH AND FRUITY

With their pleasing aromatics, eye-catching colors, and luscious flavors, fruit beers are popular both for their approachability and their individuality. Brewers in Europe and beyond have long used fruits to add sweet, sour, or tart flavors and aromas to their beers. While there are some historic brewing styles, such as Framboise (raspberry) and Kriek (cherry), which are defined by their use of particular fruits, "fruit beer" is not solely its own style. Instead, creative brewers now use a variety of fruits, from classics to downright obscurities (gooseberry, plumcots, and prickly pear), as ingredients in the production of any style of beer.

Once considered gimmicks that smelled and tasted like sugary soda pop, today's best fruit beers can charm even the most ardent lover of hoppy, bitter beer. Often made with real fruit instead of extract or essence, the leading examples offer a swirling dance between sweet, sour, and acidic notes, and rival wine in terms of complexity and character. Offerings in the Lush and Fruity group also often serve as gateway beers for drinkers who profess to dislike beer and quietly nurse hard ciders and adult lemonade drinks. These beers offer familiar and accessible flavors, including sweet cherry hints, tart cranberry notes, and milder pear and apricot aromas. Drinkers of all experience levels can agree that Lush and Fruity beers make refreshing accompaniments to summertime activities and warmer weather.

As fruit can be added to any style of beer, the base beers that underlie these selected offerings are also sometimes highlighted to give you a little more information about what flavors and aromas to expect along with your fruit experience.

CHERRY BEER

One of best known of all fruit beer styles, cherry beers (sometimes referred to by the French word for cherry, 'kriek') strike an impressive figure when served in the proper fluted glassware. Often luminous and vividly red, the appearance of a cherry beer is enough to turn heads in restaurants. As with other fruit beers, brewers usually add whole cherries, puree, or juice to a base beer as it ferments. The resulting products range in terms of sweetness, with some standout beers offering a welcomed balance of tartness and even light acidity imparted by the fruit.

Phoenix Kriek

SELIN'S GROVE BREWING COMPANY
SELINSGROVE, PENNSYLVANIA
WWW.SELINSGROVEBREWING.COM
STYLE: BELGIAN-STYLE SOUR ALE
ALCOHOL CONTENT: 8.0% ABV
GLASSWARE: TULIP OR FLUTE
AVAILABILITY: LIMITED RELEASE

This limited release offering by the small central Pennsylvania brewpub is a stunner, and obtaining it earns beer geeks a merit badge. It pours a hazy rose color with very light beads of carbonation. The aroma is solidly of black cherries with earthy, yeasty hints. Edgier than some examples in this category, due to its homage to the classic lambic style, Phoenix Kriek is tart and fruity, and the flavor finishes with a slightly sour bent. The beer opens up to reveal some funkier notes as it warms.

Hanami Ale

SMUTTYNOSE BREWING COMPANY
PORTSMOUTH, NEW HAMPSHIRE
WWW.SMUTTYNOSE.COM
STYLE: CHERRY ALE
ALCOHOL CONTENT: 5.7% ABV
GLASSWARE: PINT OR TULIP
AVAILABILITY: SPRING

Hanami Ale is a quick dash in a new direction for Smuttynose, which is best known for its style-appropriate, traditional ales and lagers. Inspired by the Japanese tradition of gathering together in parks to contemplate the arrival of the cherry blossoms, often accompanied by food and a drink, Hanami is made with fresh cherries and four different malt varieties. The rose colored beer offers subtle, tart cherry aromas and hints of a very mild malt base. The flavor is surprisingly gentle, with only the mildest hints of fruit, and is light, earthy, and dry from the middle to the finish.

Wisconsin Belgian Red

NEW GLARUS BREWING COMPANY
NEW GLARUS, WISCONSIN
WWW.NEWGLARUSBREWING.COM
STYLE: CHERRY WHEAT ALE
ALCOHOL CONTENT: 5.1% ABV
GLASSWARE: FLUTE OR SNIFTER
AVAILABILITY: YEAR-ROUND

An ale the brewers call a "marriage of wine and beer," Wisconsin Belgian Red is one of the world's most award-winning beers. Brewed with more than a pound per bottle of whole Montmorency Cherries from nearby Door County, the beer pours with a luminous, hazy ruby red tint. The aroma is strongly of tart cherries with light acidic hints. Belgian Red is well-balanced, mixing vinous, woody flavors with sweeter fruit notes. The tight beads of carbonation cleanse the palate after each sip. This legendary ale is easily one of America's top fruit beers.

Cascade Kriek Ale

CASCADE BREWING COMPANY
PORTLAND, OREGON
WWW.RACLODGE.COM
STYLE: FLANDERS RED ALE
ALCOHOL CONTENT: 8.1% ABV
GLASSWARE: TULIP
AVAILABILITY: LIMITED RELEASE

A small brewery with a growing reputation for sour and barrel-aged beers, Cascade's Kriek Ale is based upon the storied red ales of the Flanders region of Belgium. Colorful beers, occasionally brewed with fruit and taking some sourness from barrels or inoculation with bacteria, the Cascade version of the style pours with murky, hazy brownish amber color and a great deal of carbonation in its auburn-pink head. The room immediately fills with the tart results of nine months lactic fermentation with fresh whole Northwest cherries in French oak. Pungent dried cherries and a woody funk mark the way for a crispness from the beer's acidity, staying dry on the palate but with a distinctly full flavor. The sour and tart qualities play well against the lightly sweet cherry fruit flavor to a fantastic end.

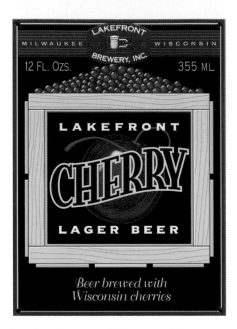

The Mad Elf Holiday Ale

TRÖEGS BREWING COMPANY
HARRISBURG, PENNSYLVANIA
WWW.TROEGS.COM
STYLE: STRONG ALE
ALCOHOL CONTENT: 11.0% ABV
GLASSWARE: GOBLET
AVAILABILITY: WINTER

Brewed with Pennsylvania honey, West Coast cherries, and a healthy dose of chocolate malts, Mad Elf Holiday Ale is a powerful holiday ale that would warm Santa's heart and home. The ruby red beer gently cascades into the wide-rimmed goblet, releasing scents of fruits and subtle spices. The warming alcohol level is noticeable in the aroma and in the flavor itself, along with a complex mélange of caramel and dark malts. Never cloying, the mix of several ingredients builds a substantial and hearty seasonal ale.

Lakefront Cherry Lager

LAKEFRONT BREWERY
MILWAUKEE, WISCONSIN
WWW.LAKEFRONTBREWERY.COM
STYLE: CHERRY LAGER
ALCOHOL CONTENT: 5.5% ABV
GLASSWARE: PINT
AVAILABILITY: SPRING

Another fine Wisconsin offering that uses cherries harvested from local Door County. Founded near downtown Milwaukee in 1987 by brothers Russ and Jim Klisch, Lakefront makes a wide range of ales and lagers. As its name suggests, this lager selection differs from most of the fruit beers discussed in this chapter. The beer has a bright, dark red appearance with a lighter pink head. This is not an over-the-top fruit beer, but one whose aroma is only mildly reminiscent of cherries. As with many other lager beers, Cherry Lager is a mellower flavored fruit beer, with a mild cherry flavor throughout that is balanced by a light tartness.

RASPBERRY BEER

Raspberry may have debuted a little later in the world brewing scene as a brewing ingredient than cherry, but it has become one the most popular of all fruit adjuncts. Brewers use an assortment of raspberry products, including extracts, purees, and whole raspberries, in an array of beer styles, from light wheat ales to foreboding imperial stouts. In the finest beers, the deep, luminous purple tones imparted by the use of actual raspberries are eye-catching, and the aromas are unmistakable. A beautiful match with desserts, especially chocolate-based treats, raspberry-infused ales offer a subtle and pleasing reward for fruit beer fans.

Raspberry Tart

NEW GLARUS BREWING COMPANY
NEW GLARUS, WISCONSIN
WWW.NEWGLARUSBREWING.COM
STYLE: WHEAT ALE
ALCOHOL CONTENT: 4.0% ABV
GLASSWARE: FLUTE OR TULIP
AVAILABILITY: YEAR-ROUND

Not to be outdone by its better-known sibling, Wisconsin Belgian Red, Raspberry Tart has garnered plenty of critical acclaim itself. A winner of several gold medals at the Great American Beer Festival, the Raspberry Tart is brewed with Oregon raspberries and is spontaneously fermented in oak vats. This indigo purple-colored beer's playfully aromatic bouquet throws waves of raspberry sorbet. As the name implies, this ale offers a balance of delightful raspberry flavor mixed with a balance of tartness and light acidity. Raspberry Tart packs an expert mixture of flavors into a neat, tight beverage, complete with an effervescent carbonation kick.

Rübæus

FOUNDERS BREWING COMPANY
GRAND RAPIDS, MICHIGAN
WWW.FOUNDERSBREWING.COM
STYLE: WHEAT ALE
ALCOHOL CONTENT: 7.0% ABV
GLASSWARE: GOBLET
AVAILABILITY: SUMMER

This unusually named beer packs in fresh raspberries at no less than five different stages of the brewing process. The result is an orange-red hued beer whose aroma is surprisingly balanced between wheat and mild raspberry notes. The flavor is more complex than the aroma suggests, with a slight tanginess upfront, followed quickly by a spritzy tartness, mild fruit sweetness, and a pleasant, tart finish. Rübæus has a medium to full body, and the relatively high alcohol content is at times noticeable. If you like the strength of this beer, try its imperial sibling, Blushing Monk, which is brewed with four times more raspberries than Rübæus.

Raspberry Strong Ale

BERKSHIRE BREWING COMPANY
SOUTH DEERFIELD, MASSACHUSETTS
WWW.BERKSHIREBREWINGCOMPANY.COM
STYLE: STRONG ALE
ALCOHOL CONTENT: 9.0% ABV
GLASSWARE: GOBLET OR TULIP
AVAILABILITY: WINTER

For those who equate fruit beers with Zima-drinking wimps, Berkshire's Raspberry Strong Ale will slap you back into line. The beer pours with a substantial, well-sustained, off-white head and smells strongly of raspberries and sharper acidic notes. Add to the mix its radiant, reddish-orange hue and you know this is no average fruit beer. The flavor is a mix of big malts, a sizable alcohol presence, and a slightly mouth-puckering balance of sweet and tart notes from a half-pound of fresh raspberries per gallon of beer.

New Belgium Frambozen

NEW BELGIUM BREWING COMPANY
FORT COLLINS, COLORADO
WWW.NEWBELGIUM.COM
STYLE: BROWN ALE
ALCOHOL CONTENT: 7.0% ABV
GLASSWARE: TULIP
AVAILABILITY: WINTER

Made with a brown ale base, New Belgium's late-year holiday seasonal ale is a complex take on the fruit beer. Frambozen, which is taken from the Flemish word for raspberry, is comprised of more than 10 percent raspberry juice by volume. The deep ruby-colored ale's aroma is of ripe raspberries, followed by the base beer's hints of cocoa and toasted malts. The beer's flavor closely resembles its aroma, just in reverse. The mildly carbonated, medium-bodied ale offers notes of powdered chocolate and toasted hints, followed by light flavors of raspberry.

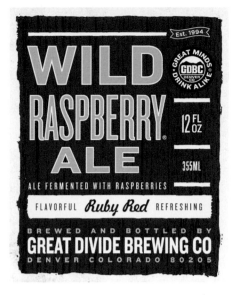

Wild Raspberry Ale

GREAT DIVIDE BREWING COMPANY
DENVER, COLORADO
WWW.GREATDIVIDE.COM
STYLE: BLONDE ALE
ALCOHOL CONTENT: 5.6% ABV
GLASSWARE: PINT
AVAILABILITY: YEAR-ROUND

Great Divide Brewing Company, located in a warehouse on the edge of downtown Denver, is known for making big, strong, and edgy beers. While the Wild Raspberry Ale is refreshingly none of those three, it does adhere closely to the brewery's mantra, "real fruit makes real beer." Fermented with several hundred pounds of red and black raspberries, the beer pours clear with a clean, reddish hue and a slight head. The aroma offers an intriguing mixture of sweet and tart raspberries, underpinned by a substantial biscuit maltiness. The beer is never cloying or sugary, but delivers a solid fruit experience.

Railway Razz

WILLOUGHBY BREWING COMPANY
WILLOUGHBY, OHIO
WWW.WILLOUGHBYBREWING.COM
STYLE: WHEAT ALE
ALCOHOL CONTENT: 4.2% ABV
GLASSWARE: PINT
AVAILABILITY: YEAR-ROUND

The brewpub's flagship wheat-based Raspberry Beer is a low alcohol beer whose reserved flavor allows it to qualify as the rare fruit session beer. A frequent medalist at the Great American Beer Festival, Railway Razz pours a dark amber red color and with a thin, wispy head. The aroma is dominated by raspberries with some other light fruit hints. While possessing sweet and tart raspberry notes, the flavor also showcases a substantial, balancing malt presence. The beer avoids cloyingness and finishes with a quick, dry fruit fade.

BLUEBERRY BEER

Blueberry beers tend to divide beer drinkers into three groups: people who love them, people who think they are wimpy beverages not worthy of their time, and self-loathing members of the second group who lie about not liking them. These offerings range from sickly sweet beers that taste like syrupy alcopops to drier, balanced offerings that gently highlight the powerful fragrance and taste of the tiny blueberry. Brewers frequently call upon a small area in craggy eastern Maine for the wild blueberries they use. Praised for their antioxidant qualities and ability to improve nearly every breakfast food, blueberries remain one of the most popular fruit adjuncts in American beer.

Blueberry Ale

DOWNTOWN BREWING COMPANY
SAN LOUIS OBISPO, CALIFORNIA
WWW.DOWNTOWNBREW.COM
STYLE: BLONDE ALE
ALCOHOL CONTENT: 4.2% ABV
GLASSWARE: PINT
AVAILABILITY: YEAR-ROUND

Downtown Brewing Company, of California's central coast, and its popular Blueberry Ale have seen quite a few changes in their short history, transitioning from a local operation to a national brand under the SLO Brewing Company name and run by a beverage marketing company in Connecticut and then back to a small brewing operation. Although most of its brands are only available in California, SLO claims that its Blueberry Ale is the "best-selling blueberry ale in America." Brewed with blueberry juice, the ale pours with a hazy orange color and a sizable head. The aroma is of freshly pressed blueberries and an unusual underlying spiciness. The flavor is more reserved, with a balance between fruit hints and pale malt notes.

Blueberry Ale

WACHUSETT BREWING COMPANY
WESTMINSTER, MASSACHUSETTS
WWW.WACHUSETTBREW.COM
STYLE: BLONDE ALE
ALCOHOL CONTENT: 4.4% ABV
GLASSWARE: PINT
AVAILABILITY: YEAR-ROUND

Founded and run by three friends, Wachusett Brewing is a mid-sized brewery with an intensely local focus and following. As the brewery has grown in size, so has the popularity of its blueberry offering, which now stands as the company's flagship. A pale blonde-colored ale with a simple, wispy head, the beer's aroma is of pale wheat and mild, muted blueberries. The flavor is light, with a consistent blueberry flavor through to the faintly bitter finish.

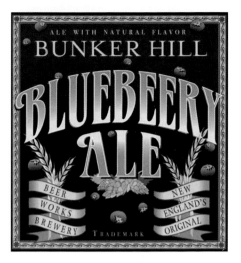

Blue

SWEETWATER BREWING COMPANY
ATLANTA, GEORGIA
WWW.SWEETWATERBREW.COM
STYLE: BLONDE ALE
ALCOHOL CONTENT: 4.9% ABV
GLASSWARE: PINT
AVAILABILITY: YEAR-ROUND

A shining star on the southern brewing scene, Sweetwater Brewing has been brewing since 1997. Pouring a golden amber color, this is a beer that lets you know upfront that it is all about the blueberry. The initial aroma is of blueberry pancakes, although it may not be the best breakfast of champions. The substantial fruit aroma remains present throughout the pint, but the flavor doesn't quite match the beer's bouquet. Consistent blueberry flavors permeate the beer, with a light, dry middle and finish.

Bunker Hill Bluebeery Ale

BOSTON BEER WORKS
BOSTON, MASSACHUSETTS
WWW.BEERWORKS.NET
STYLE: BLONDE ALE
ALCOHOL CONTENT: 4.0% ABV
GLASSWARE: PINT
AVAILABILITY: YEAR-ROUND

Located across the street from historic Fenway Park in Boston's Kenmore Square, this brewpub understandably attracts a great deal of visitors. Beer Works' most famous beer, Bluebeery Ale, offers both a pleasing fruit flavor and a fascinating visual element. The brewers age a golden-based ale on top of a foundation of Maine blueberries. To complete the process, the bartender pours two spoonfuls of fresh blueberries into each pint. The result is a cascade of dancing blueberries that bob up and down in the glass as they float against currents of carbonation. The beer itself is medium-bodied, with light wheat and caramel malt notes that finishes slightly bitter.

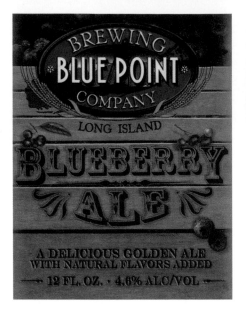

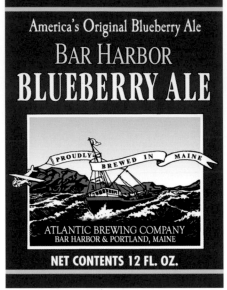

Blueberry Ale

BLUE POINT BREWING COMPANY
PATCHOGUE, NEW JERSEY
WWW.BLUEPOINTBREWING.COM
STYLE: BLONDE ALE
ALCOHOL CONTENT: 4.6% ABV
GLASSWARE: PINT
AVAILABILITY: YEAR-ROUND

Blue Point Brewing's popular Blueberry Ale has spread like wild fruit over tap handles across New York's Long Island. The vibrant and translucent Blueberry Ale offers a tiny white head and juicy, fragrant aromas of fresh blueberry. The flavor is predominantly a wheaty, biscuity maltiness with a light, zesty hop bitterness. Created with 130 pounds of blueberries, the beer's fruit character is mainly focused in the nose, while the flavor is dry and mildly fruity.

Bar Harbor Blueberry Ale

ATLANTIC BREWING COMPANY
BAR HARBOR, MAINE
WWW.ATLANTICBREWING.COM
STYLE: BLONDE ALE
ALCOHOL CONTENT: 5.2% ABV
GLASSWARE: PINT
AVAILABILITY: YEAR-ROUND

Operating out of an old farmhouse on the outskirts of Bar Harbor, Atlantic's estate brewery is a popular destination for tourists and beer lovers in the area. Made with Maine wild blueberries, Atlantic's Blueberry Ale is a classic case of breweries using their local ingredients to create cult favorites. Bar Harbor Blueberry Ale is a light fruit ale focused on blueberry aromatics, but shunning the sweet, cloying blueberry aftertaste found in many artificially sweetened beers.

PUMPKIN BEER

American brewers have a long history of brewing with pumpkins and squash. Early colonial recipes included pumpkin as an ingredient as a less expensive, local way to replace costly imported malt. Commonly released as a fall seasonal beer, the aroma and flavor of Pumpkin Beers vary widely depending upon the brewer's aims. Some brewers add hand-cut or pureed pumpkins into the mash, while others employ a variety of spices, including nutmeg, cinnamon, ginger, and allspice. The resulting beers range in flavor from mild autumn delights to over-spiced, pumpkin pie nightmares. The best Pumpkin Beers, which can be very time consuming to brew, require a brewer's steady hand in controlling the spice dial. When done right, the final products can be some of the most enjoyable and widely anticipated seasonal releases of the year.

Cottonwood Pumpkin

CAROLINA BEER COMPANY
MOORESVILLE, NORTH CAROLINA
WWW.CAROLINABEER.COM
ALCOHOL CONTENT: 6.0% ABV
GLASSWARE: PINT
AVAILABILITY: FALL

A rare southern pumpkin seasonal, Cottonwood Pumpkin is promoted by Carolina Beer Company as "grandma's pumpkin pie with a kick." The beer pours with a dark copper color and consistent white lacing. The aroma is decidedly of autumn spices, with notes of pumpkin, cinnamon, ginger, and allspice and a modicum of toasted malt. Cottonwood Pumpkin manages to walk the tightrope between spicing and malt balance without falling off into the protective netting below. Crisp at times, the substantial malt balance makes the beer very enjoyable.

Imperial Pumpkin Ale

WEYERBACHER BREWING COMPANY
EASTON, PENNSYLVANIA
WWW.WEYERBACHER.COM
ALCOHOL CONTENT: 8.0% ABV
GLASSWARE: GOBLET OR PINT
AVAILABILITY: FALL

Make no mistake: Weyerbacher's Imperial Pumpkin Ale is a thoroughbred of a beer. The brewery is known for taking otherwise delicate fruit beers and juicing them up to powerhouse strength. The beer smells strongly of cinnamon and nutmeg, along with the somewhat unusual addition of cardamom, which gives it a chai tea character. A steady, toasted malt flavor pervades the beer, mixing with occasional caramel notes and the potpourri of spices. A wonderful imperialization of the standard pumpkin beer for your Halloween drinking pleasure.

Pumking

SOUTHERN TIER BREWING COMPANY
LAKEWOOD, NEW YORK
WWW.SOUTHERNTIERBREWING.COM
ALCOHOL CONTENT: 9.0% ABV
GLASSWARE: GOBLET
AVAILABILITY: FALL

This big, bruising seasonal ale is brewed as an ode to Puca, a mythical creature of Celtic folklore who was said to take unsuspecting travelers for the ride of their lives. The beer pours a deep copper color with a sizable wheat colored head. The Imperial pumpkin ale's aroma is striking, mixing pie spices, brown sugar, mild citrus notes, and hints of graham crackers. Pumking's fantastic flavor mimics its outstanding aromas, with brown sugar and caramel malts interplaying with vanilla, spices, and delightful pumpkin notes. At 9 percent alcohol, the beer's strength is at times present in the flavor, though not overwhelming.

Night Owl Pumpkin Ale

ELYSIAN BREWING COMPANY
SEATTLE, WASHINGTON
WWW.ELYSIANBREWING.COM
ALCOHOL CONTENT: 6.1% ABV
GLASSWARE: PINT
AVAILABILITY: FALL

Brewed with more than 150 pounds of pumpkin in the mash, boil, and fermenter, including roasted pumpkin seeds, and spiced in conditioning with nutmeg, clove, cinnamon, ginger, and allspice, this beer worships in Charlie Brown's neighborhood pumpkin patch. The aroma is gently of sweet pale malt with a light spice. Night Owl's flavor matches its aroma, with mild spicing mixing with smooth malt flavors and a pleasant pumpkin element. If you can find it, Elysian produces an Imperial and impeccably strong version of the Night Owl, playfully called The Great Pumpkin.

Pumpkin Ale

THE SAINT LOUIS BREWERY
SAINT LOUIS, MISSOURI
WWW.SCHLAFLY.COM
ALCOHOL CONTENT: 8.0% ABV
GLASSWARE: GOBLET OR PINT
AVAILABILITY: FALL

Popular with locals, the Saint Louis Brewery is bringing the fight for better beer directly to the geographic heart of corporate brewing in America. While infinitesimally smaller than hometown rival Anheuser-Busch, the small craft brewery and its lines of Schlafly beers have proven a powerful counterpoint to mainstream, macro lagers. Pumpkin Ale is a full-bodied, deep amber beer made with a mixture of pumpkin, butternut squash, nutmeg, clove, and cinnamon spices. The aroma expectedly matches the list of ingredients without overpowering the senses with spice overload. While the spicing is notable in the beer's flavor, a pervasive toasted malt character makes Pumpkin Ale very drinkable, even at a hefty 8 percent alcohol.

Punkin Ale

DOGFISH HEAD CRAFT BREWERY
LEWES, DELAWARE
WWW.DOGFISH.COM
ALCOHOL CONTENT: 7.0% ABV
GLASSWARE: PINT
AVAILABILITY: FALL

You can build up a pretty good thirst creating a machine that hurls pumpkins more than four thousand feet. Or at least that's what the folks at Dogfish Head thought when they created their popular seasonal ale. Located near the site of the World Championship Punkin Chunkin Contest, the brewery produced a pumpkin beer that you can enjoy while watching air compressors, catapults, and trebuchets toss around this Halloween gourd. The Punkin Ale's aroma is strongly of pumpkin and brown sugar. The base brown ale provides an underlying support structure for this pleasantly malty beer with caramel notes.

HONEY BEER

The use of honey as a brewing ingredient, both in beer and mead, is an old and storied practice. A honey-based drink called Braggot is referred to in Chaucer's *The Canterbury Tales*, dating back to the late 1300s, with occasional earlier references dating even further back to Ireland in the 1100s. In modern brewing, honey is often used as a means for softening and sweetening beers, and contributes to several summer seasonal products. The best beers use a careful hand in employing honey, which when added in bulk can make a beer taste sickly sweet. Brewers often call upon local farmers and bee keepers to provide the honey for their lush and layered offerings.

Slippery Slope

THE PEOPLE'S PINT
GREENFIELD, MASSACHUSETTS
WWW.THEPEOPLESPINT.COM
ALCOHOL CONTENT: 9.0% ABV
GLASSWARE: SNIFTER OR FLUTE
AVAILABILITY: WINTER

Located in the heart of Greenfield's small downtown, this community brewpub opens its doors and shares beers with the whole town. In addition to its excellent range of English-style ales, the People's Pint also produces an unusually potent blend of cider, malted barley, honey, and ginger called the Slippery Slope. Brewed in the Braggot style, this winter offering presents a wispy off-white head, mild carbonation, and a pretty copper hue. It has a fruity aroma with tart cider and wine notes and hints of honey, earth, and mildly spicy ginger. The flavor tends more towards cider than beer, with kicks of honey over alcohol as it warms along with an intriguing herbal apple quality.

Leinenkugel's Honey Weiss

JACOB LEINENKUGEL BREWING COMPANY
CHIPPEWA FALLS, WISCONSIN
WWW.LEINIE.COM
STYLE: WHEAT ALE
ALCOHOL CONTENT: 4.9% ABV
GLASSWARE: PINT OR WEIZEN
AVAILABILITY: YEAR-ROUND

Although the brewery was sold to Miller Brewing Company in 1988, Leinenkugel's remains under the operational direction of the Leinenkugel family as it has been for five generations and more than 140 years. One of this historic brewery's most popular beers, Leinenkugel's Honey Weiss, is a big part of the company's success. Made with pale and wheat malts and Wisconsin honey, the beer pours a yellowish gold hue with a short head of bright white foam. The aroma is mildly sweet with a tinge of honey, and the resulting flavor is strong on wheat with a balance of sweet yet dry honey and fruit flavors. Daring drinkers can mix the Honey Weiss with its sibling, Berry Weiss, to create a Honey Bear.

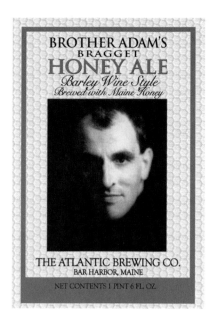

Brother Adam's Honey Bragget Ale

ATLANTIC BREWING COMPANY
BAR HARBOR, MAINE
WWW.ATLANTICBREWING.COM
STYLE: BARLEY WINE ALE
ALCOHOL CONTENT: 11.8% ABV
GLASSWARE: SNIFTER OR FLUTE
AVAILABILITY: LIMITED RELEASE

Produced only once a year, Atlantic's Bragget Ale is a beer with few peers. The brewers use a simple malt and hop schedule but add 2,000 pounds of wildflower honey in the boil to create this special ale. Atlantic then cellars the beer for a year before bottling it. The resulting product is a complex mix of flavors, ranging from coconut and oak to passion fruit. Similar to a barley wine in presentation, the beer is lightly carbonated, and at nearly 12 percent alcohol by volume, it remains best enjoyed as a sipping drink.

JW Dundee's Original Honey Brown

HIGH FALLS BREWING COMPANY
ROCHESTER, NEW YORK
WWW.JWDUNDEE.COM
STYLE: BROWN LAGER
ALCOHOL CONTENT: 4.5% ABV
GLASSWARE: PINT
AVAILABILITY: YEAR-ROUND

While High Falls appears content to fly under the radars of most beer enthusiasts, a billboard campaign for its popular JW Dundee's brand garnered some attention. From upon high, a stern, stone figure called the Beer God would stare down at the public and offer his direct advice, such as, "That not wife in car! You buy Honey Brown Lager or Beer God tell!" One of the pioneers in the honey beer segment, Original Honey Brown pours a golden amber color with solid lacing. The nose is lightly of honey sweetness and the resulting flavor, while sweet at times, mixes caramel malt flavors and a strong honey finish.

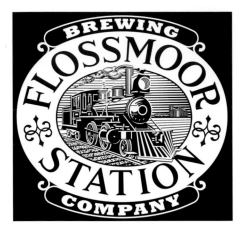

Gandy Dancer Honey Ale

**FLOSSMOOR STATION RESTAURANT AND
BREWERY
FLOSSMOOR, ILLINOIS
WWW.FLOSSMOORSTATION.COM
STYLE: HYBRID RYE AND HONEY ALE
ALCOHOL CONTENT: 7.0% ABV
GLASSWARE: PINT
AVAILABILITY: YEAR-ROUND**

Located in the town's former train stop for the Illinois Central Railroad, Flossmoor Station is one of America's most highly decorated brewpubs. Made with a blend of aromatic rye and a touch of Orange Blossom honey, Gandy Dancer is dark pale with a simple head. The aroma is strongly of malt with a slight hint of sweet honey and a welcomed note of hops. The flavor closely resembles the aroma, with a fortifying alcohol undercarriage supporting this moderately carbonated beer. A touch stronger and hoppier than your average honey beer, the Gandy Dancer remains complex and drinkable.

Midas Touch

**DOGFISH HEAD CRAFT BREWERY
LEWES, DELAWARE
WWW.DOGFISH.COM
STYLE: HYBRID HONEY ALE
ALCOHOL CONTENT: 9.0% ABV
GLASSWARE: GOBLET OR FLUTE
AVAILABILITY: YEAR-ROUND**

The product of this experimental brewery's deranged ways, Midas Touch is based upon a recipe for the oldest-known fermented beverage. After analyzing samples from a drinking vessel found in the tomb of King Midas, the brewers and a scientist attempted to replicate the contents using barley, white Muscat grapes, honey, and saffron. The beer pours with a luminous, hazy orange color and a bright white head. The aroma fuses citrus and white wine notes, with defined alcohol whispers. Midas Touch is a wonder to drink, very effervescent, with tight carbonation and a slight Belgian yeast aftertaste. Lightly fruity, smooth, and dry, it can serve as a special occasion replacement for Champagne.

··PEACH, APRICOT, AND TANGERINE BEER··

While brewers use dozens of different fruits in their beers, those that offer juicy, citrusy aromas and flavors blend well with a variety of beer styles, from dry India Pale Ales to subtle wheat ales. Beers brewed with fruits such as peach, apricot, and tangerine, often remain quietly anonymous, use uncanny abilities to camouflage their true identities and surprise unsuspecting beer drinkers with their pleasant, agreeable flavors.

Audacious Apricot

PYRAMID BREWERIES, INC.
SEATTLE, WASHINGTON
WWW.PYRAMIDBREW.COM
STYLE: WHEAT ALE
ALCOHOL CONTENT: 5.1% ABV
GLASSWARE: PINT
AVAILABILITY: YEAR-ROUND

Pyramid's style-defining Apricot Weizen has the power and charisma to bring together lovers of sickly sweet fruit beers and those who gruffly protest any fruit beer. The brewery boils California apricots into a syrupy reduction, which is then added to the American wheat ale base beer before bottling. The final product is left unfiltered and unpasteurized and the resulting nose is strongly of sweet apricot fruit. The cloudy beer and its dense white head give way to a positive blending of caramel malts, earthy Nugget hops, and a dry, unrelenting fruit flavor. Crisp and sharp at times, the beer is great as a warm day refreshment.

Tangerine Wit

KUHNHENN BREWERY & WINERY
WARREN, MICHIGAN
WWW.KBREWERY.COM
STYLE: WITBIER
ALCOHOL CONTENT: 4.2% ABV
GLASSWARE: TUMBLER
AVAILABILITY: SUMMER

The tiny Kuhnhenn Brewery's reputation is quickly growing among hard-core beer geeks. Brewing several dozen styles in small batches, the brewery's specialty releases are difficult to come by. One of the more accessible brands is the brewery's popular summer seasonal, Tangerine Wit. Based on the Belgian white ale style known as Witbier, the beer blends the flavors of tangerine, chamomile, and coriander. It pours a hazy yellow with the Witbier style's signature bright white head and solid retention. The aroma is strongly of citrus, tending more towards familiar orange hints and a mix of yeast. The tightly-carbonated Tangerine Wit's flavor is decidedly citrusy with a mild, style-appropriate wheatiness.

#9

MAGIC HAT BREWING COMPANY
BURLINGTON, VERMONT
WWW.MAGICHAT.NET
STYLE: PALE ALE
ALCOHOL CONTENT: 4.6% ABV
GLASSWARE: PINT
AVAILABILITY: YEAR-ROUND

Accounting for nearly 80 percent of Magic Hat's production, the flagship 'not quite pale ale' #9 has been the subject of debate among consumers. Some argue that it's named for the Beatles' song, Revolution No. 9, others claim it's for The Clovers' Love Potion No. 9. The apricot-infused beer pours a light orange hue with a faint and fleeting nose of meaty citrus fruit. The flavor playfully bounds between dry English-style Pale Ale and a more exotic American fruit beer, with little residual sweetness, but enjoyable apricot hints.

Stinson Beach Peach Ale

MARIN BREWING COMPANY
LARKSPUR, CALIFORNIA
WWW.MARINBREWING.COM
STYLE: AMERICAN WHEAT ALE
ALCOHOL CONTENT: 5.0% ABV
GLASSWARE: PINT
AVAILABILITY: YEAR-ROUND

A pleasant marriage of the peach flavoring and the brewery's base Wheat Ale, Marin's Stinson Beach Peach Ale pours with a light straw color and wispy white beads of carbonation. The aroma is soundly of fresh, meaty peaches and an underlying bready wheat base. The flavor follows suit, with peach notes rolling off the tongue from the beginning through to the finish. Daring to run up to the edge, the beer never drops off into cloying, and a light bitterness keeps order to the end.

Apricot Wheat

DUNEDIN BREWERY
DUNEDIN, FLORIDA
WWW.DUNEDINBREWERY.COM
STYLE: AMERICAN WHEAT ALE
ALCOHOL CONTENT: 4.6% ABV
GLASSWARE: PINT
AVAILABILITY: YEAR-ROUND

Located due west of Tampa on Florida's Gulf Coast, the tiny Dunedin Brewery celebrates the town's Scottish history, but is not a slave to tradition. Brewed with apricot puree harvested in the Willamette Valley of northwestern Oregon, Dunedin's Apricot Wheat is golden in color with occasional pinkish tints and a substantial white head. The aroma is a potent play of apricots and peaches, and it hardly subsides as the beer warms and opens up. While the flavor doesn't quite match the strong aroma, its smooth balance and solid fruit flavor make it a very popular refuge for visitors and locals.

Arizona Peach

FOUR PEAKS BREWING COMPANY
TEMPE, ARIZONA
WWW.FOURPEAKS.COM
STYLE: WHEAT ALE
ALCOHOL CONTENT: 4.0% ABV
GLASSWARE: PINT
AVAILABILITY: YEAR-ROUND

With its cloudy blonde frame and gentle, cascading white head, the aroma brims with pureed peaches, like a jammy marmalade, with soft floral and citrus notes over wheat. The flavor moderates a touch on the fruit side, with a steadier hand of toasted malt and slight additions of spice and hops to balance out the presence of the peaches. A lingering dryness finishes out this refreshing and interesting summer favorite.

STRONG, DARK, AND FRUITY BEERS

American brewers have especially enjoyed exploiting the interplays between the sweeter flavors and aromas of fruit and the richer, sharper notes of roasted porters. In Minnesota's great frozen north, near the banks of Lake Superior, Fitger's Brewhouse specializes in promoting independent musicians and producing nearly 100 different beers, including Blitzen's Blueberry Porter. At a sessionable 5.4 percent alcohol, the dark brown representation of the classic English-style bursts with a curious blend of blueberry and roasted malt aromas. The fruit is dry throughout as it works with the coffee elements of the Porter style. In downtown Columbus, Ohio, Barley's Brewing Company's year-round Cherry Porter is made with cherries and hops from the Pacific Northwest. The brewpub  heavily focuses on real ale, and the mahogany-colored Porter, with its potent aromas of roasted malts and hint of cherries, is often featured on cask when available.

On the opposite end of the taste spectrum, Weyerbacher Brewing Company's Raspberry Imperial Stout bursts with bold, roasted malt flavors and aromas, and finishes with a sweet, tart raspberry flourish. The beer is also worthy of aging, with each year stripping away another layer of raspberry to reveal more subtle, caramelized malt flavors. In the historic fishing town of Gloucester, Massachusetts, Cape Ann Brewing Company brews its quirky Fisherman's Pumpkin Stout. Exhibiting more of the traditional roasted qualities of the Stout style, the beer offers occasional hints of pumpkin seeds and allspice, mixed with roasted malts.

A handful of fanatical brewers have done some pretty masochistic things with fruit. Touting itself as the world's strongest fruit beer, Dogfish Head's 18 percent alcohol Fort (French for strong) is a robust fruit beer to be sure. Brewed with more than a ton of pureed Oregon and Delaware raspberries during a slow, two month primary fermentation, the beer produces a collage of fruit and malt flavors and aromas.

NIGHTCAPS AND NURSERS

It's time to break out the snifters and funky shaped specialty glassware for this lot. Big, brash, and boozy, Nightcaps and Nursers call out to be savored slowly. A proper substitute for an end of the evening glass of single malt Scotch, brandy, or port, these beers demand for leisurely, thoughtful contemplation. The headier alcohol qualities contribute another dimension of depth and complexity to these beers, with some offering warming cognac, woody bourbon, and rich vanilla aromas. The polar opposite in flavor and experience from session beers, there is no need to hurry here. Each sniff offers a rush of intricate, inviting aromatics. Each sip provides a velvety wash of character, some subtle and elusive, others robust and forceful. As with a glass of reserve spirits, the mind quietly works to decipher the experience. As with an aged Cabernet or Burgundy, these beers are also highly capable of improving and evolving with age. The higher hopped varieties lose their sharp potency, just as time reduces bitter tannins in Bordeaux wine. While some people prefer to drink the strong, assertive, young versions, added layers of flavor that develop with age compel some to counsel stashing a bottle or two away in a dark, cool hiding place for future enjoyment. The ultimate Slow Food beers, Nightcaps and Nursers allow the world to flash by while you think, "What's the hurry?"

BARLEY WINE

Barley Wines are strong ales possessing far above average alcohol levels. And while alcohol plays a prominent role in most beers of the style, sometimes reaching 12 percent, it is not the defining characteristic. A storied British-style and the ultimate nightcap sipper, the term "Barley Wine" covers a broad swath of strong ales. The style is characterized by a dizzyingly complex array of alcohol and fruit esters, with a mix of deep caramel malt and light hop aromas. While English versions tend to exhibit greater balance, American Barley Wines range from restrained to delightfully out of balance. Malt sweetness often takes a backseat to strongly bitter American hops. Versions of both styles generally age well for years or even decades, resulting in beers with less hop character and whose malt profiles develop rich sherry or port-like characters through slow oxidation.

Third Coast Old Ale

BELL'S BREWERY
KALAMAZOO, MICHIGAN
WWW.BELLSBEER.COM
ALCOHOL CONTENT: 10.2% ABV
GLASSWARE: SNIFTER OR TULIP
AVAILABILITY: WINTER, LIMITED SPRING

This mash-up of the American Barley Wine and English Old Ale styles projects a dullish orange-red hued base with a flourish of off-tan, sticky foam and oozes with cotton candy sweet caramel malt, with a light almond nutty quality, followed by a little boozy jolt and a touch of caramel. The flavor is where things really get started, as the Old Ale starts with a complex and aggressive mixture of sweeter pale malts, revealing juicy pineapple and coconut flavors, all topped by a strongly hopped and bitter layer of earthy hops. As the beer ages, the bitterness imparted by the hops fades, revealing a port and sherry like flavor and dryness.

Doggie Claws

HAIR OF THE DOG BREWING COMPANY
PORTLAND, OREGON
WWW.HAIROFTHEDOG.COM
ALCOHOL CONTENT: 11.5% ABV
GLASSWARE: SNIFTER OR TULIP
AVAILABILITY: FALL

With its peach-amber color and modest off-white head, this decidedly hazy number introduces an intense combination of potent aromas, starting with a dark, sweet honey tone, immediately followed by some cotton candy pale and caramel malt syrup, a light citrus tinge, and a pepper spice quality. In the glass, the assortment of flavors vying for your attention range from citrus, fruit, and honey to a light spicy quality from the hops and a thawing alcohol warmth. Developing a thick, syrupy character as it ages, additional elements of cotton candy are revealed in this age-worthy offering.

Triple Exultation

EEL RIVER BREWING COMPANY
FORTUNA, CALIFORNIA
WWW.EELRIVERBREWING.COM
ALCOHOL CONTENT: 9.7% ABV
GLASSWARE: SNIFTER OR TULIP
AVAILABILITY: WINTER

A bit of a difficult beer to characterize, Triple Exultation displays a mild mannered amber-brown base coat, with a light off-tan wisp of head, followed by surprisingly strong aromatics of molasses, vanilla, slight citrus, and warming alcohol. The aromas contribute all of these notes and more to the full-bodied finish, which showcases an intricate array catalog of sweet malt dashes, including molasses and vanilla, followed by a light mocha character and dryness and a mildly earthy bitterness that serves to shape the diverse chords into a fine sonata of flavor.

Bearded Pat's Barleywine

BLUEGRASS BREWING COMPANY
LOUISVILLE, KENTUCKY
WWW.BBCBREW.COM
ALCOHOL CONTENT: 11.0% ABV
GLASSWARE: SNIFTER OR TULIP
AVAILABILITY: WINTER

Rolling about in a snifter, this Kentucky classic greets you with an inviting amber nod and a tacky dollop of ivory foam before extending its hand with offers of deep caramel sweetness, followed by sugary citrus fruit and a quick whiff of earthy and bitter hops. Firm in body, the well-structured strong ale develops a caramel sweetness as it warms, while the more bitter elements play off to the sides before coming together in a citrusy jumble of sweetness. Soothing and precocious at times, bold and forthright at others, this Barley Wine displays its American heritage without forgetting its Old Ale style origins.

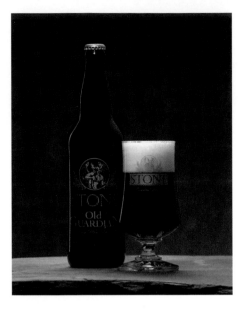

Old Guardian Barleywine

STONE BREWING COMPANY
ESCONDIDO, CALIFORNIA
WWW.STONEBREW.COM
ALCOHOL CONTENT: 11.3% ABV
GLASSWARE: SNIFTER OR TULIP
AVAILABILITY: WINTER

One of the kings of Stone's mile-wide portfolio of challenging beers, Old Guardian starts with a ruby-orange tint that cascades into a craggy beige head, giving off huge waves of sweet caramel and sugar covered grapefruit, doses of citrus and pine resin, and a calming alcohol fruit note. After a few swirls, the flavor corresponds with a resounding smack of bitter citrus hops, followed by softer layers of potent caramel malt sugar, a touch of roasted malt, and a bit of earth from the hops. Upon its initial release, this bruiser is not for the faint of heart, but after a few months of rest, it awakens with a friendlier countenance. As both personalities appeal, it all depends upon which fellow you want to spend the evening with.

Old Backus Barleywine

FREE STATE BREWING COMPANY
LAWRENCE, KANSAS
WWW.FREESTATEBREWING.COM
ALCOHOL CONTENT: 10.5% ABV
GLASSWARE: SNIFTER OR TULIP
AVAILABILITY: SEASONAL

Exhibiting a jolting crimson color with a snappy and well-retained crest of tan foam, this Kansas Barley Wine loads up on dark fruits, with freshly picked cherries sharing the ride with figs, prunes, and a touch of sweet grapefruit, along with toffee and brown sugar swirls and a Burgundy wine alcohol character. The flavor tends more towards the Old Ale side of the ledger, with big toffee and caramel malt sweetness beating back attempts by the dark fruits to take over the texture, all while earthy hop bitterness sneaks in to join the party. Full-bodied and a bit creamy in texture, the sizable alcohol content becomes more pronounced as the beer warms.

WINTER WARMER

The Winter Warmer label has been applied to styles as diverse as spiced beers, sometimes called Wassails, to Old Ales, and many in-between. While some beer geeks debate whether any distinctions truly exist between Old Ales and Barley Wines, beers of the Winter Warmer style include these malt-forward beers whose alcohol levels do not reach the boozy Barley Wine stratosphere. With colors ranging from dullish rouge to deep brown, these strong ales possess deep, sweet malty notes ranging from caramel, molasses, treacle, and toffee, and when aged take on some pleasant, nutty oxidized notes. Light herbal spicing may be present in Wassails, and these beers possess a dose of fruit esters in the aromas and bodies. Malty sweet with a mix of light alcohol heat throughout, Winter Warmers are well-attenuated and finish dry.

The First Snow Ale

RJ ROCKERS BREWING COMPANY
SPARTANBURG, SOUTH CAROLINA
WWW.RJROCKERS.COM
ALCOHOL CONTENT: 6.0% ABV
GLASSWARE: MUG OR GOBLET
AVAILABILITY: WINTER

While I'm not sure that South Carolina residents ever have to deal with much snow, if it does come along they'll be well fortified with the help of this hazy amber offering. The nose offers a host of spices, including cinnamon and allspice, ground into the caramel malt base along with tinges of toffee. The Christmas spicing continues for a little while into the flavor but then excuses itself for the introduction of layers of caramel and toasted malt sweetness, bready brown sugar notes, and a light grassy hop character. A touch spicy in the finish, the creamy medium-body also displays a wonderful nutty quality that makes it a slow sipper.

Old Monkeyshine

NIMBUS BREWING COMPANY
TUCSON, ARIZONA
WWW.NIMBUSBEER.COM
ALCOHOL CONTENT: 8.2% ABV
GLASSWARE: MUG OR GOBLET
AVAILABILITY: YEAR-ROUND

Essentially a supped-up English Brown Ale, this southwestern Winter Warmer starts with a deep mahogany tone, followed by a swirl of ivory-tan foam, and a wandering nose of sweet roasted malts, contributing baked brown sugar, toffee, and caramel malt, followed by a light, dry earthy English hop character. In the glass, the beer opens up with further bursts of sweet roasted malt, mainly caramel, followed by a quick dry boom of earthy hops, along with touches of the well-camouflaged alcohol heat.

Hampshire Special Ale

D.L. GEARY BREWING COMPANY
PORTLAND, MAINE
WWW.GEARYBREWING.COM
ALCOHOL CONTENT: 7.0% ABV
GLASSWARE: MUG OR GOBLET
AVAILABILITY: YEAR-ROUND

Once limited to being brewed "when the weather sucks," Geary's now offers the superb Hampshire Special Ale on a year-round basis. Brewed with classic English pale, crystal, and chocolate malts, and a touch of American Cascade and Mt. Hood hops, along with traditional East Kent Golding hops, the Hampshire draws ruby brown in color with a tight wad of dense foam, and is packed with toasted malt character along with a touch of butter. The beer's toasted malt flavors and warming alcohol notes help balance a light fruitiness along with mildly grainy malt notes. Beer lovers throughout New England remain quite happy to no longer have to wait for junky winter weather to enjoy this offering.

Our Special Ale

ANCHOR BREWING COMPANY
SAN FRANCISCO, CALIFORNIA
WWW.ANCHORBREWING.COM
ALCOHOL CONTENT: 5.5% ABV
GLASSWARE: MUG OR GOBLET
AVAILABILITY: WINTER

One of the first seasonal beers ever produced by an American craft brewery, Anchor's Our Special Ale was also one of the first American beers to be actively cellared by beer enthusiasts. Vintages go back to the 1970s, with most maintaining great complexity and character long after their release. The specific recipe for this dark brownish-amber ale changes a touch from year to year but usually involves a strong earthy nose, touches of pine and wood, along with deep, dark malt character. The flavor profile often touches upon darker flavors mixed with some mild and changing spice quality and evened out by a decidedly piney and evergreen taste component. Stash a bottle or two away for future enjoyment to see how the beer develops and evolves.

Old Jubilation

AVERY BREWING COMPANY
BOULDER, COLORADO
WWW.AVERYBREWING.COM
ALCOHOL CONTENT: 8.5% ABV
GLASSWARE: MUG OR GOBLET
AVAILABILITY: WINTER

One of the oldest offerings from this rapidly evolving and creative craft brewer, Old Jubilation strikes a mature note in a lineup often dominated by wonderfully quirky and strong offerings. With its deep ruby color and deep tan, moussy foam peak, this winter strong ale is imbued with abiding character, running the gamut from baked apples, raisins, and plums to chalky and mocha dry dark malts, along with hazelnut. With no spices added, the deeply complex ale mainly continues without the aid of the dark fruits, instead relying upon an attention grabbing mélange of dark and roasted malts, assisted by the occasional trace of toffee and caramel. Definitely a beer to take your time over, Old Jubilation brings great holiday cheer to its fans.

Jubelale

DESCHUTES BREWERY
BEND, OREGON
WWW.DESCHUTESBREWERY.COM
ALCOHOL CONTENT: 6.7% ABV
GLASSWARE: MUG OR GOBLET
AVAILABILITY: WINTER

Pouring with a dense, bright, and slightly burnished caramel color and a rich wallop of ivory foam, Jubelale is a strikingly attractive Winter Warmer. Nearly defining the style as applied in America, the strong winter offering starts with a delicate and well-choreographed dance of caramel and dark roasted malts that usher in a very light Christmas spice character, followed by another wash of clean toffee malt and the faintest hints of warming alcohol. Similar in construction, the medium body well balances its sweeter caramel tones with its mildly earthy and spicy hop ripples, all for a dry and slightly bitter finish.

TRIPEL

Hardly content to leave the strong ale game to the British and Americans, Belgian brewers produce a beautifully balanced and brilliantly hued contender in the Tripel. Often bottle-conditioned, with yeast re-fermenting the beer after packaging, Tripels boast striking golden colors and a sizable and sustained white head. Deceivingly complex, the aromas combine juicy passion fruit and even mild banana notes, phenolic yeast hints, sizable pale malt hints, and robust yet coy alcohol traces. The Tripel's body is equally mesmerizing, converting all of the aromas into an intricate web of playful flavors, with spicy yeast notes tempering warm malt, sugar, and fruity alcohol elements. The multiple fermentation stages result in a dry finish with only fleeting touches of sweetness, well-hiding the near 10 percent alcohol levels.

Xtra Gold Tripel

CAPTAIN LAWRENCE BREWING COMPANY
PLEASANTVILLE, NEW YORK
WWW.CAPTAINLAWRENCEBREWING.COM
ALCOHOL CONTENT: 10.0% ABV
GLASSWARE: TULIP
AVAILABILITY: YEAR-ROUND

Swirling in a deep tulip glass, this bright Captain Lawrence offering projects a bold, confident golden color and soft, downy white head and contains a complex mixture of fruits, with passion fruit, dried apricots, and a slight wheaty note. The alcohol is well hidden as the medium body starts with an initial sweetness that leads into a mild wheat character and citric bite, where the alcohol finally reveals itself just before the dry, slightly yeasty finish.

Final Absolution Trippel

DRAGONMEAD MICROBREWERY
WARREN, MICHIGAN
WWW.DRAGONMEAD.COM
ALCOHOL CONTENT: 8.5% ABV
GLASSWARE: TULIP
AVAILABILITY: YEAR-ROUND

This free-spirited offering from the little brewpub that could starts with a clear flash of golden and soft color and simple white head, determinedly followed by neatly trimmed rows of sweet flowers, honey, ripe fruit, and a clove spiciness. The glass fills with apricot and mild banana flavors, rolling over the clove's phenolic qualities, occasionally flitting off with some pepper spiciness, and a light candi sugar sweetness. Relatively light bodied and well concealing its alcohol warmth, the Final Absolution rates among the easiest drinking Tripels.

Black Tulip Trippel

NEW HOLLAND BREWING COMPANY
HOLLAND, MICHIGAN
WWW.NEWHOLLANDBREW.COM
ALCOHOL CONTENT: 8.8% ABV
GLASSWARE: TULIP
AVAILABILITY: YEAR-ROUND

With a light and playful golden color and wispy white head, Black Tulip projects a mild citrus first note, followed by rounds of banana, clove phenolics, and a fair amount of sweet malt and booze with a dry wheat finish. Hefty in body and character, this Tripel starts with a warming pale malt and Belgian sugar sweetness, followed by a slightly peppery tone, matched by another round of fruity alcohol and pale base malt. Soothing to the palate and humble in its approach, this New Holland offering breezily balances complex elements and remains remarkably drinkable.

Trade Winds Tripel

THE BRUERY
PLACENTIA, CALIFORNIA
WWW.THEBRUERY.COM
ALCOHOL CONTENT: 8.0% ABV
GLASSWARE: TULIP OR FLUTE
AVAILABILITY: SUMMER

With its hazy light golden color and full crest of white foam, Trade Winds looks the traditional part. The aroma and flavor that follow creatively depart a little from the traditional standards, imparting a range of strongly sweet European base malts along with a light citric tang and touches of warming alcohol. The flavor sets forth a wash of sweet and dry alcohol, within a tight body of mild pepper spice over a drawn out noble hop flavor. The blend of different elements finishes both sweet and dry, calling for another go at its intriguing character.

Solstice

PISGAH BREWING COMPANY
BLACK MOUNTAIN, NORTH CAROLINA
WWW.PISGAHBREWING.COM
ALCOHOL CONTENT: 9.5% ABV
GLASSWARE: TULIP
AVAILABILITY: YEAR-ROUND

With its bright golden hued countenance and sliver of white, lacy foam, the simply named Solstice entreats you to breathe in its layers of sweet fruit, with baskets of pears, apricots, and bananas served up with a dish of Belgian candi sugar dryness and a light dollop of peppery spice. A lighter bodied Tripel but with the benefit of strong carbonation, the strong ale develops more fruit character followed by a slightly bready and candy coated malt experience, all in a highly drinkable and dry finishing form.

Panty Peeler Tripel

MIDNIGHT SUN BREWING COMPANY
ANCHORAGE, ALASKA
WWW.MIDNIGHTSUNBREWING.COM
ALCOHOL CONTENT: 8.5% ABV
GLASSWARE: TULIP
AVAILABILITY: YEAR-ROUND

Perhaps a touch more charming when its name is considered in the original French, previously known as *E'pluche-culotte*, this rambunctious Tripel starts with a peachy-golden color, moderately hazy to the eye, and a lacy white head. The juicy aroma teems with ripe fruit, including a touch of banana, peach, apricot, and even coconut, before heading to an earthy pasture of scents, followed by coriander and black pepper spicing from the yeast. A touch candied at times, the full-bodied flavor imparts honey, and pale malt sweetness along with a litany of fresh fruit notes, including orange peel and coriander.

QUADRUPEL

A curious style inspired and influenced by Belgium's Trappist monk brewers, the Quadrupel is a potent, herbal, and bready style that boasts considerable alcoholic warmth and fruit complexity. Dark amber to deep brown in hue, boozy alcohol notes swarm the nose, mixed with rich, phenolic yeast notes and dark fruit hints, including plums, cherries, and figs. Often aided by the addition of sugar, which ferments quickly, Quadrupels reach soaring alcohol heights of 8 to 12 percent. Despite these numbers, the style is surprisingly dry, and a high carbonation level keeps everything in check. The texture is unusually light and medium bodied, especially compared to the more cloying Winter Warmer and Barley Wine styles, and the multiple fermentation cycles fight against flabbiness. Creamy and bready sweet at times, the nuanced phenolics and fruit flavors result in a particularly challenging slow sipper.

Abbot 12

SOUTHAMPTON PUBLICK HOUSE
SOUTHAMPTON, NEW YORK
WWW.SOUTHAMPTONPUBLICKHOUSE.COM
ALCOHOL CONTENT: 10.5% ABV
GLASSWARE: SNIFTER OR TULIP
AVAILABILITY: WINTER

With its cascading flow of light ruby brown hues and a mild meringue of soft white foam, this Southampton classic opts for a slightly clove flavor and mildly alcoholic introduction, tempered with plum fruit esters. Always balanced and even reserved at times, the medium-body balances a light banana and prune and plum dark fruit character with loads of slightly sweet Belgian yeast and candi sugar character. A light phenolic pepper spice dials through the body to rein in any elements that consider talking out of turn. Masking its alcohol level, Abbot 12 is a devilishly drinkable and refreshing beer.

Quadfather

IRON HILL BREWERY AND RESTAURANT
NEWARK, DELAWARE
WWW.IRONHILLBREWERY.COM
ALCOHOL CONTENT: 10.0% ABV
GLASSWARE: SNIFTER OR TULIP
AVAILABILITY: LIMITED RELEASE

Disgorged from a cork-finished bottle, the cleverly named quad pours with a surprisingly thick flow of deep brown liquid, tinged at the extremes by ruby hints, along with a modest carbonation level and beige foam core. The nose is filled with molasses coated dark fruits, with plums and prunes mixing with treacle and sweet malts over light black pepper spicing and a hit of peppercorn and coriander. The bready sweet body continues with raisin flavors, brown sugar, and a touch of anise, mixed over some dark cherries. Complex yet approachable, Quadfather is a very worthy take on the classic strong dark beers of Belgium.

Grand Cru

GREEN FLASH BREWING COMPANY
VISTA, CALIFORNIA
WWW.GREEFLASHBREW.COM
ALCOHOL CONTENT: 9.0% ABV
GLASSWARE: SNIFTER OR TULIP
AVAILABILITY: WINTER

With its ruddy, hazy dark brown color and finger of tan foam, Grand Cru, a wine term usually reserved for a producer's finest offering, starts with a sweet bouquet of raisins and plums mixed with herbal hops and touches of clove spice. The medium-bodied flavor corresponds with a maze of Belgian influenced flavors, straying from a phenolic and spicy yeast character to dark fruits, including plums, and a pronounced dark chocolate malt and light candi sugar component. The finish approaches with a tight level of carbonation and an earthy hop bite that leaves some welcomed, lingering bitterness.

Baby Tree

PRETTY THINGS BEER & ALE PROJECT
HOLYOKE, MASSACHUSETTS
WWW.PRETTYTHINGSBEERTODAY.COM
ALCOHOL CONTENT: 8.6% ABV
GLASSWARE: SNIFTER OR TULIP
AVAILABILITY: SPRING

A substantial offering from a brewer and his wife who produce a quirky line of beers by renting time on other people's brewing systems. Despite the absence of a brick-and-mortar brewery, Pretty Things manages to brew some great beers, including this deep brownish ruby colored beer with light tan foam, which is made with forty pounds of dried California plums in the kettle. The aroma booms with plums, prunes, and other dark fruit, as well as some phenolic spice character, a touch of powdered cocoa, and a lilt of alcohol warmth. Similarly situated, the flavor continues with loads of dark, sweet fruit flanked by a spicy, warming yeast and alcohol character, finishing slightly dry.

FOUR

ALLAGASH BREWING COMPANY
PORTLAND, MAINE
WWW.ALLAGASH.COM
ALCOHOL CONTENT: 10.0% ABV
GLASSWARE: SNIFTER OR TULIP
AVAILABILITY: YEAR-ROUND

With its soulful blend of garnet colored hues and dense whip of frothy beige foam, Allagash's quad is a looker bent on capturing your attention. Breathing deeply of dark fruits layered in cocoa powder and with a dark Belgian candi sugar quality that mixes with a touch of molasses, FOUR plays fits on your tongue. The wonderful aroma hardly does justice to the even more expressive body, which in its rich fullness expresses loads of fruit, including banana, blackberry, and plums, alongside a honey sweetness and a lightly spicy and herbal hop balance. FOUR is definitely worth taking some time to swirl.

The Sixth Glass

BOULEVARD BREWING COMPANY
KANSAS CITY, MISSOURI
WWW.BLVDBEER.COM
ALCOHOL CONTENT: 10.5% ABV
GLASSWARE: SNIFTER OR TULIP
AVAILABILITY: YEAR-ROUND

Cleverly named after a literary reference to a Hans Christian Anderson tale decrying the ills associated with getting to the half-dozen drink marker, this estimable quad pours with an impassable quality, mixing deep burgundy and ruby tones with a sharp, tall cream head. The aroma tingles with deep, dark, sweet fruits, including fat, juicy plums, and a lingering black pepper spiciness that adds character on top of the considerable Belgian yeast notes. Slightly phenolic to start, waves of dense, juicy fruit wash forward in a full-bodied mouthfeel that reveals hints of spice and deep, dark alcohol.

IMPERIAL STOUT

The Imperial Stout style is the kingfish of big, bold and dark beers, designed to simultaneously scare and intrigue the average drinker. In beer lore, British brewers long ago produced these strong beers for the Czarist courts in Russia. Their foreboding pitch-black color and unusually deep brown head serve as warning signs to the wary: enter at your own peril. Imperial Stouts burst with massive malt notes, from powerfully roasted malts to cloyingly sweet port notes, usually balanced by a healthy addition of strong, earthy hops. Alcohol heat, ranging from 8 to 12 percent or even higher, is also usually present as the beer's body remains dense and silky from the use of so much malt. The best versions avoid the cloying trap, instead offering nuanced jumbles of licorice, treacle, dark fruits, raisins, chocolate, coffee, and dozens of other flavors.

Happy Ending

SWEETWATER BREWING COMPANY
ATLANTA, GEORGIA
WWW.SWEETWATERBREW.COM
ALCOHOL CONTENT: 9.0% ABV
GLASSWARE: SNIFTER
AVAILABILITY: YEAR-ROUND

The big deep black color and a lightish tan head portays the earthy, minerally aroma booming right out of the bottle. It is very clean and has a light boozy alcohol note. Near full bodied, the beer starts incredibly complex, with a pop of deep roasted and sweet malt flavors, then kicks into an earthy, minerally hop flavor that is incredibly pleasant and very unusual for this style, including the presence of light green apples. This is not a booze or hop bomb, nor alcohol bomb, but instead a minerally sweet experience. Malt flavors are quite complex, mixing with dark fruit and alcohol, but the main event is the pleasant hop flavor and bitterness.

Speedway Stout

ALESMITH BREWING COMPANY
SAN DIEGO, CALIFORNIA
WWW.ALESMITH.COM
ALCOHOL CONTENT: 12.0% ABV
GLASSWARE: SNIFTER OR TULIP
AVAILABILITY: YEAR-ROUND

Not a beer to be underestimated, Alesmith's Speedway Stout handily captures the essence of the American Imperial Stout with this mystifyingly black beer with a dense pillow of brown foam. The aroma wallops your nose with loads of fresh dark roasted coffee, deeply burnt malts, dark chocolate, and light earthy hops. Serving up a double espresso shot, the coffee angles play heavily in the full-bodied Stout, with layers of dark roasted malt following slight molasses sweetness and the faintest hints of dark, chocolate covered fruits. Velvety and smooth despite its alcoholic girth, Speedway Stout eases to victory in the all-encompassing Imperial Stout experience.

Black Chocolate Stout

BROOKLYN BREWERY
BROOKLYN, NEW YORK
WWW.BROOKLYNBREWERY.COM
ALCOHOL CONTENT: 10.0% ABV
GLASSWARE: SNIFTER OR TULIP
AVAILABILITY: WINTER

With its opaque black body and striking cocoa brown colored frothy head, the Black Chocolate Stout exudes a cool charm. The active nose sings with a melody of chocolate and mocha coffee flavors of all ranges, with the additions of hazelnut and light alcohol warmth. The full-bodied flavor masks the alcohol content and pours forth with layers of velvety dark chocolate, with milk chocolate notes wrapping around mocha, and fueled by a slight earthy bitterness. A beer that ages incredibly well, try stashing a few bottles in a cool, dark space and opening them alongside newer vintages of this well-valued prize.

B.O.R.I.S. The Crusher Oatmeal-Imperial Stout

HOPPIN' FROG BREWERY
AKRON, OHIO
WWW.HOPPINFROG.COM
ALCOHOL CONTENT: 9.4% ABV
GLASSWARE: SNIFTER OR TULIP
AVAILABILITY: WINTER

With a jet black shade and a light wispy mocha head, B.O.R.I.S. makes a fairly timid first impression. The shyness lulls you into a state of calm, which is shattered by powerful shouts of chocolate, toasted malt, vanilla, and alcohol in the bouquet. The full-bodied beer responds with a slightly syrupy mouthfeel filled with deep, dark chocolate and coffee notes, a light toasted and dry oatmeal quality, mild alcohol heat, tannic hints, and touches of vanilla. Sturdy and strong, this hybrid Imperial Stout beautifully blends ingredients into an inviting and evenly nuanced performance.

Ten Fidy

OSKAR BLUES GRILL AND BREWERY
LYONS, COLORADO
WWW.OSKARBLUES.COM
ALCOHOL CONTENT: 10.0% ABV
GLASSWARE: SNIFTER OR TULIP
AVAILABILITY: WINTER

Promoting itself as the ultimate Rocky Mountain Winter Warmer, this Oskar Blues offering, as with all major offerings from the brewery, is available in aluminum cans. To see an opaque black colored and thick liquid issue forth into a glass, with a deep brown head, definitely catches your attention after a lifetime of being taught to expect fizzy, yellow lager. The aroma is filled with sweet molasses, light mocha coffee, and leather. The full-body explodes with flavor at a pace far exceeding the aroma, with hammering notes of sweet dark malt and molasses mixed against a crushing hop and roasted malt bitterness. Slight alcohol warmth serves to lighten the experience, allowing all of the elements to gel before finishing in a flourish.

Dark Lord Russian Imperial Stout

THREE FLOYDS BREWING COMPANY
MUNSTER, INDIANA
WWW.THREEFLOYDS.COM
ALCOHOL CONTENT: 13.0% ABV
GLASSWARE: SNIFTER OR TULIP
AVAILABILITY: LIMITED RELEASE

At the far horizon of the Imperial Stout spectrum lurks a beer whose flavor and motor oil consistency have made it perhaps the most geeked out craft beer on the planet. Three Floyds sells much coveted bottles of its near-mythical Imperial Stout on one day per year, appropriately deemed Dark Lord Day. Appearing completely jet black and rivaling week-old coffee sludge in appearance, Dark Lord's nose roars with dark chocolate, burnt toffee and molasses, roasted coffee, and sherry-soaked dark fruits. If you can get beyond marveling over its incredibly thick mouthfeel, the flavors invoke notes of dark and burnt chocolate, molasses, tobacco, chicory, and hints of earthy hops.

EISBOCK

Brewers in Germany, either through planning or more likely accident, learned a curious way of making stronger beers. By freezing their stronger beers, such as doppelbocks, and then removing the ice (as alcohol freezes at a lower temperature than water) the brewers were able to highly concentrate the flavor and alcohol levels of their products. As the resulting product, called Eisbock after the German word for ice, tends to boom with alcohol and sweet malt, brewers lagered the beers for extended periods of time to smooth out the flavors. A rare treat, either in America or Germany, eisbocks are characterized by a rich and sweet malt aroma mixed with warming, dark fruit alcohol notes. Despite its substantial size, generally ranging from 9 to 14 percent alcohol but sometimes much higher, balance remains central to the Eisbock experience. A mixture of toasted or caramel malts, with occasional roasted touches, dominates the sweet but not cloying malt backbone and full body, which mixes with substantial chocolate and fruit esters, ranging from plums to grapes.

Considering the work involved in the brewing, freezing, and lagering processes, it should not be surprising that eisbocks remain pretty rare. American brewers who embrace the extreme edge of brewing prefer the simpler route of employing hardy champagne and wine yeasts to masochistically ratchet up the alcohol levels in their big beers.

In Warren, Michigan, the tiny Kuhnhenn Brewery & Winery serves up a range of beers that make beer geeks salivate in anticipation. At nearly 12 percent alcohol, the brewery's Raspberry Eisbock is a highly charged beer with a powerful aroma of ripe raspberries, bittersweet chocolate, and fruit liqueur.

The High Point Brewing Company of New Jersey also specializes in classic German ales and lagers, and its rare Winter Wheat Eisbock, a take-off on its popular Doppelbock, is a boozy delight. A deep mahogany color, the beer showcases a flurry of dark fruits, including cherries, prunes, and plums, mixed with light treacle hints and a touch of smokiness, all with mild alcohol warmth. The flavor thankfully follows the aroma, with the addition of some molasses notes and a light, figgy dryness.

FUNKY FLAVORS

As with experimental theatre, modern art, and avant-garde jazz, beers of this flock may not be to everyone's immediate liking. As distant as they get from the standard American lager, these beers serve up an initial shock to the system and senses. Aromas of earthy farmhouse funk, acrid smoked ham and sausage, or spicy rye bread are not what television commercials have taught you to expect in a pint or bottle of beer. But given the right circumstances and selection, you might be surprised at just how quickly you can acquire a taste for tart, sour ales, or a lightly smoked lager. Funky Flavors are playful, quixotic beers, often deeply grounded in ancient brewing history and dating to methods used before modern techniques emerged. Like the polka dot elephant on the Island of Misfit Toys, the flavors celebrated in these beers are considered to be flaws by modern brewing authorities. Borrowing from regional preferences in small parts of Germany, Belgium, and other places, enterprising American brewers have resurrected these unusual beers and delivered them to an entirely new audience. To the modern palate, these beers are designed to be a little surprising. But with a measured hand, talented and forward-thinking brewers turn shock into awe and skepticism into joy in their courageous customers. A great conversation starter to break out at parties, these beers push the limits of what average consumers think about beer. Despite their quirky nature, the best funky beers are built on a strong foundation that serves not to overwhelm, but to please your palate with their unexpected drinkability. A fun pairing for food, this diverse group offers something for nearly every type of food and occasion.

AMERICAN WILD ALE

Taking a page from the Belgian brewing book, American brewers have embraced the use of particularly funky agents that most brewers strive hard to eradicate from their brewing vessels. These little organisms, including Brettanomyces, Lactobacillus, and Pediococcus, whether used as part of a spontaneous fermentation or through barrel inoculation, each contribute different, unusual characteristics to beers. Aromas range from mildly tart to acid sour, with some exhibiting light wheat or farmhouse notes, and others a pungent and shocking funkiness. Some brewers employ mild fruits, such as apricots, to balance the acidity and sourness. The flavors vary from soft tartness and light acidity to mouth-puckering sourness and deep, dank barnyard notes with dry, fruit hints.

Cuvee du Jongleur

CASCADE BREWING COMPANY
PORTLAND, OREGON
WWW.RACLODGE.COM
ALCOHOL CONTENT: 8.41% ABV
GLASSWARE: FLUTE, SNIFTER, OR TULIP
AVAILABILITY: LIMITED RELEASE

This small Portland, Oregon, brewpub is making a big name for itself with its line of sour and barrel-aged beers. Cuvee blends select barrels of Flanders Red ale and soured Tripel aged in oak, as well as a huge Quadrupel, and then bottle-conditioned with lactic acid. With its cloudy amber-brown color and light tan colored two fingers of foam, this ale extends a bouquet filled with tart, lactic acid qualities, mixed with a young, ripening fruit scent, followed by a light bready quality. In the glass, the tartness expands in all directions, with sour plums and woody oak dominating, followed by a light bready malt character covering flits of dark cherry fruit tones. More vinous and less funky than some other American Wild Ales, Cuvee is refreshing and quite approachable.

Cuvee de Castleton

CAPTAIN LAWRENCE BREWING COMPANY
PLEASANTVILLE, NEW YORK
WWW.CAPTAINLAWRENCEBREWING.COM
ALCOHOL CONTENT: 8.0% ABV
GLASSWARE: FLUTE, SNIFTER, OR TULIP
AVAILABILITY: LIMITED RELEASE

With its light pale yellow-orange color and neatly packaged layer of white foam, this Captain Lawrence offering starts with a neatly sour lactic nose, very toasty at times and sour, but not puckering, mixed with funky, earthy tea and grass characters and a slight nutty quality. A medium body and a tight level of carbonation stand up well to the layers of dry flavor, including a vinous and herbal funk with hints of leather and earth, followed by light dried apricot fruit hints over a woody oak base. Ever so slightly tart at times with far less sourness than many versions of the style, Castleton is an inviting Wild Ale.

Brute

ITHACA BREWING COMPANY
ITHACA, NEW YORK
WWW.ITHACABEER.COM
ALCOHOL CONTENT: 6.5% ABV
GLASSWARE: FLUTE, SNIFTER, OR TULIP
AVAILABILITY: LIMITED RELEASE

Pouring into a Champagne flute with a slightly hazy golden-yellow hue and a solid, effervescent white head, the aroma breathes deeply of soft fruits, with peaches and pears, as well as a slight orange peel character, all before a long, lingering cleanse of tart and puckering sourness. The springy flavor starts with a bolt of mouth-puckering tartness that catches you at the jaw line, tart and dry in character, followed by a orange rind fruit quality, a touch of oak, and a light pepper spice, all finishing decidedly sour, tart, and refreshing. Brute is an excellent and well stage-managed sour from this talented New York brewery.

Gueuze

UPSTREAM BREWING COMPANY
OMAHA, NEBRASKA
WWW.UPSTREAMBREWING.COM
ALCOHOL CONTENT: 6.5% ABV
GLASSWARE: FLUTE, SNIFTER, OR TULIP
AVAILABILITY: LIMITED RELEASE

One of the great unexpected finds of my research process, this under-the-radar Nebraska brewery produces some excellent sour beers. With its hazy dull orange-amber color and decently carbonated, moderate off-tan head, Gueuze's aroma is a mind-blowingly complex mixture of light, tart sour notes and an ever so slight touch of oaky wood, along with lactic acid sourness and light hints of vanilla. The farmhouse character of the aroma is enough to counsel buying this beer, but the flavor gets even better with an array of sour and acidic notes of different levels and densities, vanilla and lightly sweet malt notes, and a tang of light carbonation, all bridled by a slight toasted malt flavor. The beer's bright acidity shines throughout and casts a slight citrus and green apple fruitiness in a dry finish

Interlude

ALLAGASH BREWING COMPANY
PORTLAND, MAINE
WWW.ALLAGASH.COM
ALCOHOL CONTENT: 9.5% ABV
GLASSWARE: FLUTE, SNIFTER, OR TULIP
AVAILABILITY: LIMITED RELEASE

From the only American brewery to create its own koelschip (an open fermenter in which fresh wort is exposed to wild yeast and microfauna), Allagash invites the funk into its operation. The same can certainly be seen in its Interlude, with its hazy yet brilliant orange hue, streams of gentle bubbles rising up to a billowy off-white head. Fermented with farmhouse yeast, conditioned with Brettanomyces, and then aged in French Merlot and Sirah barrels, the aroma sings with strong and funky fruit character, woody and earthy at times, with some juicy apricot fruit notes tossed in for good measure. The flavor begins soft, with a slight pale and honey malt character, followed by dull fruit, then an intense tart and slightly sour element that injects wood, earth, and a vinous funk into the mix for a dry finish.

Supplication

RUSSIAN RIVER BREWING COMPANY
SANTA ROSA, CALIFORNIA
WWW.RUSSIANRIVERBREWING.COM
ALCOHOL CONTENT: 7.0% ABV
GLASSWARE: FLUTE, SNIFTER, OR TULIP
AVAILABILITY: LIMITED RELEASE

Another in a long line of stellar wood-aged offerings from Russian River, Supplication starts with a dull rose color and creamy off-tan head, before unleashing Tsunami sized waves of sparkling and tart Brettanomyces character followed by woody oak, sour and acidic pale wheat, with dull bready qualities, and with hints of green apple and apricot fruits. The first sip overpowers with mouth-puckering sourness before relenting and allowing a lightly fizzy texture to scrub the acidic notes away, leaving tart fruit, an earthy and musty dryness, followed by another dose of oak drawn out long in the finish. The occasional dry, cinnamon-like spiciness can provide a pleasant heat on the palate in this American classic.

BIÈRE DE GARDE

Slightly less in-your-face funky than the Wild Ale bunch, the French style Bière de Garde are a rare breed in this country. Light to deep golden in color, these beers possess a vast earthy and musty sensibility that pervades from the aroma down through the body. A light toasted malt nose hints at a slight sweetness with fruit edges, but gives way to the farmhouse elements. The medium-bodied beer tastes of pale toasted malt mixed with earthy notes and a mild noble hoppiness. Above average in alcohol, weighing in at 5 to 8 percent, the beers are often bottle-conditioned, which leads to a dry, quenching finish.

Biere de Mars

BREWERY OMMEGANG
COOPERSTOWN, NEW YORK
WWW.OMMEGANG.COM
ALCOHOL CONTENT: 6.5% ABV
GLASSWARE: MUG, GOBLET, OR TUMBLER
AVAILABILITY: SPRING

With a deep, spritely amber base color and a massive whip of craggy foam, Brewery Ommegang's offering brims with all manners of aromas, dancing from partner to partner, starting with a ripe fruit character, a funky dusting of earthy and peppery spice, and tinges of bready malt, all followed by a musty, barnyard funk from the Brettanomyces used in the secondary fermentation. The medium body reveals a light, lively carbonation that helps cut the way for citrus fruit and green apples, nuanced and bready malt sweetness, all finished by a spicy touch from the yeast and hops and a touch of earthy, minerally funk.

Signature Bière de Garde

KREBS BREWING COMPANY
KREBS, OKLAHOMA
WWW.CHOCBEER.COM
ALCOHOL CONTENT: 7.0% ABV
GLASSWARE: MUG, GOBLET, OR TUMBLER
AVAILABILITY: YEAR-ROUND

A burnished copper tone starts things off, followed by a dollop of creamy yet tightly carbonated white foam and rows of soft, biscuity and graham cracker like malt grains, green apples, and a slight hint of earthiness. The resulting sips flush with ripe apples before giving way to decidedly grainy and husky malt sweetness, flanked by additions of caramel malt, followed by a longer, clean earthiness. With its medium body and strong carbonation, each sip ends with a flip of a switch, leaving the palate clean and ready for the next sip.

Schlafly Bière de Garde

THE SAINT LOUIS BREWERY
SAINT LOUIS, MISSOURI
WWW.SCHLAFLY.COM
ALCOHOL CONTENT: 7.5% ABV
GLASSWARE: MUG, GOBLET, OR TUMBLER
AVAILABILITY: YEAR-ROUND

With its hazy orange countenance and soft cascade of big bubbles into an ivory tower of foam, this Bière de Garde is striking in appearance and adds nutty, earthy, and sweet biscuit malt grains next to a residual ripe fruit character and a sharp tartness in the nose. Loyal to the aroma, the beer fills with zesty and refreshing hop and yeast zips, followed by a slight spritzy citrus fruit element and a tangy malt character. With its medium body and light carbonation, the mildly creamy texture finishes clean and a touch earthy.

Avant Garde

THE LOST ABBEY
SAN MARCOS, CALIFORNIA
WWW.LOSTABBEY.COM
ALCOHOL CONTENT: 7.0% ABV
GLASSWARE: MUG, GOBLET, OR TUMBLER
AVAILABILITY: YEAR-ROUND

This Lost Abbey offering starts with a tangerine orange color and a substantial fluffy cascade of white foam, and continues with an earthy, bready, and fruity jumble of aromas, ranging from a slight funk, cinnamon and cardamom spice, followed by apricot and apple notes, and a long caramel and bready malt whiff. The flavor starts with a touch sweet before drying out, with dashes of ripe but distant fruit, a funky and earthy yeast flavor and a zippy hop bite, followed by biscuit malt sweetness. A tad phenolic at times, the medium body carries a lot on its shoulders, arriving at the finish line with a winner.

Oro de Calabaza

JOLLY PUMPKIN ARTISAN ALES
DEXTER, MICHIGAN
WWW.JOLLYPUMPKIN.COM
ALCOHOL CONTENT: 8.0% ABV
GLASSWARE: MUG, GOBLET, OR TUMBLER
AVAILABILITY: YEAR-ROUND

Pouring with a golden amber-orange hue and a self-possessed, towering head of well-laced foam, the aroma begins with a brush of striking tart citrus notes mixed with some deeper fruit hints, followed by a slight earthy funk and a bready malt base. The first sip co-mingles light bready sweetness and citrus fruits followed closely by a reserved black pepper and clove spice, and finishing with a strong burst of carbonation to scrub the palate nearly clean. The mouthfeel is unexpectedly creamy at times, with a light tartness contributing a lasting cleanliness to the proceedings.

Domaine DuPage French Style Country Ale

TWO BROTHERS BREWING COMPANY
WARRENVILLE, ILLINOIS
WWW.TWOBROSBREW.COM
ALCOHOL CONTENT: 5.9% ABV
GLASSWARE: MUG, GOBLET, OR TUMBLER
AVAILABILITY: YEAR-ROUND

A ruddy and hazy orange face gives way to waving brows of white foam in this slight murky beer, suggesting the mélange of funky flavors to come, including notes of cinnamon spice, caramel and bready malt, along with an orange ring citrus tinge. The resulting flavor is smooth and drinkable, with notes of toasted, biscuity malt giving way to a slight earthy and zesty spicy quality, all sprinkled with orange and apricot fruit essence. The finish is a touch hoppy and funky, which adds an additional layer of complexity.

SAISON

A staggeringly complex style that marries a host of flavors, from lightly wheaty Witbiers to funky Lambic and spicy Tripels, Saisons are an increasingly popular offering from American breweries looking to branch out from standard fare summer seasonal beers. Sometimes referred to as Farmhouse Ales, Saisons are light golden to deep amber in color, often bright but sometimes hazy with yeast, and possess a labyrinth of sophisticated aromatics, including spicy yeast phenolics, herbal hops, dusty malt notes, light alcohol hints, and occasional tart or acidic traces. The flavor is correspondingly complex, with spicy, peppery, and herbal notes blending together with a modest tart or acidic quality. A light bitterness fuses with decided citrus fruit qualities, all wrapped around a solid pilsener malt base.

Saison

YARDS BREWING COMPANY
PHILADELPHIA, PENNSYLVANIA
WWW.YARDSBREWING.COM
ALCOHOL CONTENT: 6.5% ABV
GLASSWARE: GOBLET OR SNIFTER
AVAILABILITY: SUMMER

Dull, slightly hazy luminous orange color with a vibrant, puffy, thick white head. The aroma is a mixture of light fruit notes, including banana and Belgian candi sugar, a bit unusual in the nose for the style. Definite hints of warming alcohol. There is sort of an airy, ethereal quality to the European malt notes, not too heavy or light. Flavor goes the complete opposite direction with initial phenolic, peppery notes mixed with a slight tangy funk that glides into a quick dose of sweeter cereal malts and candi sugar, followed by a mild but pronounced and drawn out bitterness that finishes very dry. This seemingly mild-mannered brew that develops to become quite a complex offering.

Red Sky At Night

HEAVY SEAS BEER
BALTIMORE, MARYLAND
WWW.CCBEER.COM
ALCOHOL CONTENT: 7.5% ABV
GLASSWARE: MUG, GOBLET, OR TUMBLER
AVAILABILITY: SUMMER

Pouring with a hazy golden hue and fluffy cast of white foam, this specialty offering in the brewery's Pyrate Fleet line-up pours with an active mélange of citrus fruit, pale malt, a touch of phenolic spice, and considerable funky yeast character. In the glass, the beer turns crisp, with tones of lightly sweet pale malt followed by a mild phenolic spicy quality, citrus fruit, and earthy hops. The medium-bodied experience renders a striking balance, allowing all elements to express themselves without allowing any one quality to overwhelm the palate.

Hennepin

BREWERY OMMEGANG
COOPERSTOWN, NEW YORK
WWW.OMMEGANG.COM
ALCOHOL CONTENT: 7.7% ABV
GLASSWARE: MUG, GOBLET, OR TUMBLER
AVAILABILITY: YEAR-ROUND

This signature offering from Brewery Ommegang pours with a beautiful golden color and a big billowy head of foam and possesses a litany of airy aromatic wonders, ranging from pale malt sweetness, minty touches, and a spicy character from the hops and yeast, all atop a dry wheat base. The flavor is similarly dry in character, with a subtle mixture of wheat and a flash of pale malt sweetness, followed by a warming alcohol, hints of ripe fruit, and a light grassy quality that blends with the spicy yeast and hoppiness for a slightly bitter finish. Tightly effervescent and sharply structured, Hennepin sets the standard for American versions of the classic Saison style.

Saison Athene

SAINT SOMEWHERE BREWING COMPANY
TARPON SPRINGS, FLORIDA
WWW.SAINTSOMEWHEREBREWING.COM
ALCOHOL CONTENT: 7.5% ABV
GLASSWARE: MUG, GOBLET, OR TUMBLER
AVAILABILITY: YEAR-ROUND

Pouring from a cork finished bottle, this Saison starts with a light golden color, slightly hazy, and with a sizable, clean white head, and offers a curious patchwork of mild spicy notes, with cinnamon, ginger, and a touch of citrus fruit playing host. The medium-bodied beer continues the flavor parade of spice covered citrus fruit, with spicy caches of cinnamon, cardamom, and allspice flavors, all nicely attenuated in a dry approach. A dry wheat base element brings order to the spice bazaar, with herbal qualities continuing to counteract the spicier elements.

Saison

BOULEVARD BREWING COMPANY
KANSAS CITY, MISSOURI
WWW.BLVDBEER.COM
ALCOHOL CONTENT: 6.2% ABV
GLASSWARE: MUG, GOBLET, OR TUMBLER
AVAILABILITY: YEAR-ROUND

With its bright golden-orange color and a nice and sizable, pillowy off-tan head, Boulevard's gleefully understated version of the style starts with a slightly funky acidic tartness and farmhouse funk that grooves with banana esters and pale and caramel malts to create a tightly constructed sweetness. Similarly restrained in the body, all of the aromatic elements come together in a wonderfully smooth marriage of flavors, with the funky sides blending well with dollops of pale and caramel malt sweetness and the additions of a mildly grassy and herbal flavor, balanced out by light aspirin bitterness. The hop and yeast characters give off a mild herbal quality along with some slight peppery bitterness that keeps the whole arrangement in check.

Bam Bière

JOLLY PUMPKIN ARTISAN ALES
DEXTER, MICHIGAN
WWW.JOLLYPUMPKIN.COM
ALCOHOL CONTENT: 4.5% ABV
GLASSWARE: MUG, GOBLET, OR TUMBLER
AVAILABILITY: YEAR-ROUND

Another in this creative Michigan brewery's expanding arsenal of funky brands, this bottle-conditioned Saison pours with a cloudy golden hue with orange touches at the edges and a dense billowing pillow of cloudy foam. The bouquet possesses a deep peppery quality that melds with the spicy yeast and contributes a great deal of complexity, along with the orange citrus notes and herbal hop tones. The medium-bodied flavor starts with a toasted malt quality that quickly gives way to a range of fruits, from apple to white grapes and orange peel, along with a rinse of funky yeast flavor accompanied by a touch of acidity. The earthy and floral hops right the ship towards the end, leaving a lengthy and dry finish.

RYE BEER

Continuing along the spice trail, beers made with rye contain a distinct peppery quality that is hard to mistake. Using a percentage of rye grain in the malt bill, brewers can achieve an unusual contrast to sweet malts across a broad range of styles. Rye beers can be made as either a lager or ale, the former resulting in a cleaner beer and the latter a fruitier one. Depending upon the amount used, the aromas can give off a sharp, spicy note like ground black pepper, and the underlying grain aromas can range from fine to husky. The flavor is piquant and often bitter with a spicy quality that dries the palate and should be mixed against a little underlying malt sweetness for balance. German-style Roggenbiers contain large proportions of rye in addition to wheat, resulting in grainy, spicy, and Hefeweizen-like banana fruit esters all mixed together in a husky and unusually phenolic experience.

Red's Rye

FOUNDERS BREWING COMPANY
GRAND RAPIDS, MICHIGAN
WWW.FOUNDERSBREWING.COM
ALCOHOL CONTENT: 6.6% ABV
GLASSWARE: PINT
AVAILABILITY: YEAR-ROUND

This powerfully aromatic and iconic offering from Founders commences with a ruby-amber tone, a strong frothy head of beige foam, and a smack of earthy, zippy, and zesty rye and hop elements mixed over a light citrus fruit quality, slight notes of cream, and grapefruit sweetness. The flavor immediately starts hoppy and bitter, with earthy points mixed in, followed by an herbal quality that is speared by a light, sweet, and toasted malt base that hides far away from the battling forces of complex bitterness. Red's Rye is a more challenging Rye offering for those daring to try something new.

Righteous Rye

SIXPOINT CRAFT ALES
BROOKLYN, NEW YORK
WWW.SIXPOINTCRAFTALES.COM
ALCOHOL CONTENT: 7.2% ABV
GLASSWARE: PINT
AVAILABILITY: YEAR-ROUND

Pouring with a deep, luminous, and hazy ruby orange tone and a cascading off-tan head, this Sixpoint offering starts with wild fruit notes, mixed with bready European malt stretches, followed by a deep spicy herbal quality from the rye malt. The mixture of sweeter toasted malt flavors and sharp, spicy rye notes is quite striking in the glass, calling into focus the value of contrasting elements. The spicy flavor tends to win out, with the malt contributing bready and even vanilla and caramel notes, along with a pronounced and sustained citrusy and bitter hop finish.

Rye Pale Ale

TERRAPIN BEER COMPANY
ATHENS, GEORGIA
WWW.TERRAPINBEER.COM
ALCOHOL CONTENT: 5.5% ABV
GLASSWARE: PINT
AVAILABILITY: YEAR-ROUND

This Georgia brewery keenly uses rye in several of its beers, to great effect, and Rye Pale Ale starts with a modest orange-yellow tone and a sustained and creamy beige head. The aroma imparts a startling array of juicy citrus hops, with grapefruit and orange leading, followed by slight pale malt tints and earthy rye spiciness. The medium-bodied flavor is rich and dense in character, with robust citrus hops cascading around a mellow and dry malt sweetness, followed by a light spicy character in the finish.

Rail Mail Rye

WILLIMANTIC BREWING COMPANY
WILLIMANTIC, CONNECTICUT
WWW.WILLIBREW.COM
ALCOHOL CONTENT: 5.5% ABV
GLASSWARE: PINT
AVAILABILITY: LIMITED RELEASE

This tiny northeastern Connecticut brew-pub specializes in hoppy beers and uses rye to impart spice and bitterness in several of its beers. Rail Mail Rye starts with a hazy amber-orange color and a modest white cap of foam, followed by a considerably earthy and funky aroma of bready malts and sharp rye, along with hints of citrus. The flavor corresponds with citrus and funky Belgian-style yeast gives another layer of character, all while a dried apricot fruit flavor mixes with a bready malt base.

Rye Hopper Ale

FRENCH BROAD BREWING COMPANY
ASHEVILLE, NORTH CAROLINA
WWW.FRENCHBROADBREWERY.COM
ALCOHOL CONTENT: 5.9% ABV
GLASSWARE: PINT
AVAILABILITY: YEAR-ROUND

With its clean amber hue and soft, downy crest of foam, Rye Hopper appears as an easy-drinking beer and the aroma bears this out, with gentle and floral citrus fruit notes matching pine and evergreen asides along with a mild earthy spiciness and a bready caramel component. The flavor starts out a touch sweet before swapping out for a sharp tinge of bitterness that immediately dries out the body before gliding in with a light, slick, and creamy quality. A slight tang from all of the elements washes the palate before finishing dry and slightly spicy.

Full Moon Pale Rye Ale

REAL ALE BREWING COMPANY
BLANCO, TEXAS
WWW.REALALEBREWING.COM
ALCOHOL CONTENT: 5.7% ABV
GLASSWARE: PINT
AVAILABILITY: YEAR-ROUND

This Texas Rye Beer begins with a hazy golden-amber color and a slight cap of white foam and projects a decidedly earthy hop backbone over a base coat of biscuit and bready malt sweetness. The flavor kicks forward with a shot of sharp, zesty hop bitterness followed by a light rinse of caramel sweet malts, accompanied by a quick smack of earthy rye flavor. Very easy-drinking with all of its elements, Full Moon Pale balances the sweeter and zestier notes in a manageable production.

SMOKED BEER

Taking funk to its logical extreme, inquisitive American brewers have returned to the grittier days of brewing when malt was dried over open fires, resulting in smoky, acrid beers. Using small proportions of malts smoked over beech-wood, alder, maple, and other woods, brewers impart maple ham, country sausage, and smoked salmon notes to their beers, sometimes with unsettling results for unsuspecting partakers. Smoked beer, sometimes called Rauch-bier after the German word for smoke, is certainly an acquired taste for most people, but provides a rich experience, pairs beautifully with foods, and can age for many years. Some brewers use only a touch of lightly smoked malt to add depth and complexity to styles ranging from Märzens to hefeweizens, while other employ a heavier hand, resulting in a peaty, pungent experience.

Z Lager

FORT COLLINS BREWERY
FORT COLLINS, COLORADO
WWW.FORTCOLLINSBREWERY.COM
ALCOHOL CONTENT: 5.5% ABV
GLASSWARE: PINT, MUG, OR GOBLET
AVAILABILITY: YEAR-ROUND

The cozy town of Fort Collins is a brewing Mecca, home to a handful of great brew-eries. In order to set its self apart a touch, Fort Collins Brewery focuses on lager beers. Heading in a different direction than many Smoked Beers, Z Lager tends more towards the classic Rauchbier styles of Bamberg, Germany. Brewed as a smoked Amber Lager, this beer starts with a deep amber pitch, a modest off-tan head, and develops mildly smoky malt notes over con-siderable residual caramel malt sweetness. The flavor washes clean and sweet caramel malts over a base fruit character, all with a film of light smoke, and with a slight bitter kick in the finish. Z Lager is a very drink-able offering due to the relatively low alcohol and mild smoke character.

Smoke

O'FALLON BREWERY
SAINT LOUIS, MISSOURI
WWW.OFALLONBREWERY.COM
ALCOHOL CONTENT: 6.0% ABV
GLASSWARE: PINT, GOBLET, OR MUG
AVAILABILITY: YEAR-ROUND

Opening with a light brown to black shade with ruby hues at the extremes and a creamy brown head, the simply named Smoke offers a lightly smoky yet deep meaty nose, akin to homemade beef jerky, not overwhelming or acrid and with ample dark roasted malt notes. The resulting fla-vor infuses touches of clean smoke alongside tiny bits of caramel malt that quickly give way to another round of long, drawn out meaty smokiness and then another round of caramel sweetness, fol-lowed by a round of meaty smokiness. This dizzying round and round experience fin-ishes with a light tart and tangy quality amid the pleasant roasted malt base.

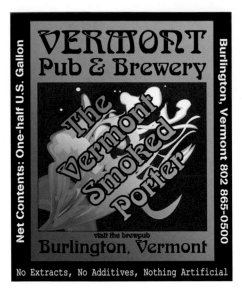

Smoked Porter

VERMONT PUB AND BREWERY
BURLINGTON, VERMONT
WWW.VERMONTBREWERY.COM
ALCOHOL CONTENT: 5.9% ABV
GLASSWARE: PINT, GOBLET, OR MUG
AVAILABILITY: YEAR-ROUND

Every couple of months at the Vermont Pub and Brewery, brewers spend several hours smoking their own malt over maple, hickory, and apple wood chips in a smoker next to the pub. A pioneer in the American smoked beer renaissance, the Vermont Pub's signature beer starts with a deep jet black color and a moderate off-tan to ivory head and delivers a consistently smoky aroma, along with views of the underlying dark roasted malts in the Porter base. The 15 percent smoked malt bill imparts a pleasant and subtle smokiness to the lightly malty and dark roasted flavors swirling through this beer. A substantial bitter hop bite keeps the flavors in check in this classic American tip of the cap to an ancient age of brewing. A real tribute to the pub's founder, the late Greg Noonan.

Alaskan Smoked Porter

ALASKAN BREWING COMPANY
JUNEAU, ALASKA
WWW.ALASKANBEER.COM
ALCOHOL CONTENT: 6.5% ABV
GLASSWARE: GOBLET, MUG, OR SNIFTER
AVAILABILITY: YEAR-ROUND

One of the pioneers in resurrecting smoked beers in America, Alaskan Smoked Porter has won more medals at the Great American Beer Festival than any other beer. Smoked with the local alder wood so common in the area's salmon fishing history, the beer starts with an understated and mildly smoky nose that is balanced by a slightly sweet malt underpinning, a darker roasted malt element, and ending with distinct earthy hop bitterness. The flavor continues with greater Porter qualities, including roasted coffee and chocolate alongside some curious vanilla and oak hints, and then a passive smoked quality. This classic has proven itself considerably age worthy, and the brewery conducts vertical tastings of vintages dating back to the early 1990s.

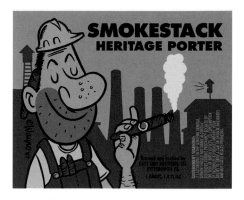

Smokestack Heritage Porter

EAST END BREWING COMPANY
PITTSBURGH, PENNSYLVANIA
WWW.EASTENDBREWING.COM
ALCOHOL CONTENT: 6.8% ABV
GLASSWARE: GOBLET OR MUG
AVAILABILITY: LIMITED RELEASE

This specialty offering, recently resurrected due to popular demand, starts deep brown to black, with ruby hues at the edges followed by a mocha colored foam top. The aroma starts with a toss of dark roasted malt followed by a sweeter layer of toffee, caramel, and iced coffee, all enveloped in a light cloud of meaty smoke. The flavor starts in the reverse, with the smoke starting quick out of the gate and then fading as strong chocolate and caramel malts gallop to take the lead through the wire. Hints of cream and a slick mouthfeel aid the drinkability in this mildly strong offering.

Smoke Jumper Smoked Imperial Porter

LEFT HAND BREWING COMPANY
LONGMONT, COLORADO
WWW.LEFTHANDBREWING.COM
ALCOHOL CONTENT: 9.2% ABV
GLASSWARE: GOBLET, MUG, OR SNIFTER
AVAILABILITY: WINTER

On the stronger end of the spectrum, Left Hand's pitch black offering starts with a deep, creamy dark tan head and possesses a huge and intense smash of smoky and dark roasted malt notes, all drizzled over a slightly sweet caramel and toasted malt quality. The powerful aroma gives way to a slightly less acrid version but is still reminiscent of a liquid campfire rolled in dark chocolate, ashen coffee, and with a dollop of sweeter caramel tossed in for good measure. Despite its smoke and roasted malt character, the bitterness levels remain low and a light nutty quality seeps in towards the finish, leaving a dry and surprisingly drinkable offering in its wide wake.

GRUIT AND HEATHER ALES

In the days before hops took control as the main vegetable ingredient in beer, European brewers used sweet gale, yarrow, wild rosemary, heather, spruce, and seaweed to create unhopped beers. Brewers of Gruit suggested that the beverage possessed mysterious qualities that could stimulate the mind. Tales abound of how politicians and religious leaders feared the potion, which led in the mid-1800s to the rise of hops as a flavoring and preservative agent in beer. It was thought that hops blunts the libido, in a condition unpleasantly referred to as Brewer's Droop.

The Cambridge Brewing Company in Massachusetts has a thing for vegetable beers. In lieu of hops, its Weekapaug Gruit uses sweet gale, yarrow, and wild rosemary, as well as Scottish malts and oats. A hazy amber brown color, it has a dry flavor with light biscuity malt flavors. Cambridge's The Wind Cried Mari Heather Ale is similar in color but smells of toasted malt and a mildly spicy mixture of cinnamon and all-

spice from the fresh heather plant.

From western Massachusetts, the tiny Amherst Brewing Company's award-winning Heather Ale uses a generous dose of heather from Washington State. Bouncing from a tongue-teasing minty flavor to an unexpected, yet pleasing sweet malt finish, the beer remains one of the most approachable and drinkable versions of the style.

The Solstice or Summer Gruit at the Zero Gravity brewery of the American Flatbread chain in Burlington, Vermont, adds Labrador tea, mugwort, and sweet woodruff to the list of old-school brewing ingredients. A copper colored beer with a strongly herbal and piney nose, the Gruit tastes a touch minty and even tea-like, but with a restrained hand on the spicing, all backed by a moderate carbonation level and medium body.

EXTREME TASTES

Once the fringe candidate excluded from the debates, extreme beers are now the toast of the town. The snickering kids in the back of the classroom have taken over and started teaching others about their envelope-pushing brewing ideas. Spawned by a refusal to adhere to rigid and traditional style definitions, these creative brewers employ unusual and fanciful ingredients to achieve curious and remarkable results. The brewers' experiments have evolved from brewing slightly stronger beers to the alcohol arms race pushing beers to 60 proof, from measured additions of a new hop variety to the battle for super hoppy humulus lupulus supremacy, and from careful uses of chocolate or rye to the maniacally gleeful additions of St. John's wort, chipotle peppers, and even garlic.

With the modern craft beer renaissance, the chains are off when it comes to experimentation. Extreme beer is often described not as a category or style but as a movement or state of mind, and it signifies a freedom to experience, to break out of neat little boxes, and to travel new paths. Sometimes it's less spiritual and more about seeing just how much you can get away with. But for the best brewers, extreme beer is the antidote to the blight of blandness and uniformity that has long plagued this nation's beer choices. It's a return to diversity and alternatives, a broadening of our portfolio to match the explosion in our culinary options in America. At its heart, extreme beer is about fun and expanding boundaries. While not every unusual offering will meet with your approval, each extreme beer experience will get you thinking and expand your understanding of what the word "beer" really means.

As with the Lush and Fruity chapter, extreme beers come in many different styles as brewers tweek everything from light Blonde Ale to potent Imperial Stout. Accordingly, some of the listings include a description of the underlying style to assist your selection process.

BARREL-AGED BEER

It often seems as if everyone in the beer industry is trying to jump on the barrel-aging bandwagon. The Barrel-Aged Beer category described here doesn't denote a single beer style, but instead describes a method of injecting new flavor components into a wide range of beer styles. The flavor spectrum and aromas encompassed in this section is vast, ranging from boozy alcohol bombs filled with vanilla esters extracted from bourbon barrels to citric tart and lactic sour bacteria derived from American oak barrels. Often made in extremely small quantities, sometimes only a few barrels at a time, these beers garner great acclaim and can sometimes be very expensive and difficult to find. In making my selections, I've shied away from the trophy beers you would never be likely to find except on eBay.

Redline Imperial Stout

ROCK BOTTOM BREWING COMPANY
CHICAGO, ILLINOIS
WWW.ROCKBOTTOM.COM
ALCOHOL CONTENT: 11.5% ABV
GLASSWARE: SNIFTER OR TULIP
AVAILABILITY: LIMITED RELEASE

Part of the large chain of American brewpubs, this Rock Bottom operation is a standout among many excellent outlets. It has also long had success with a barrel aging program, even before such practices became popular among craft brewers. Pouring with a jet black color with some lighter notes at the ends and a sizable cocoa brown hued cap, the Redline is a picture of stunning through subtlety. Aged in bourbon barrels, the aroma thankfully doesn't seek to strangle you with a noxious vanilla cloud, instead opting for a nuanced approach to the spice, along with chocolate, roasted coffee, and hints of warming alcohol. The flavor starts sharply with a bourbon-based flare, only to quickly and quietly recede, allowing the base Stout's roasted character to shine through. The wood here works as an equal partner with the Stout to achieve a perfect marriage of flavors.

Kentucky Breakfast Stout

FOUNDERS BREWING COMPANY
GRAND RAPIDS, MICHIGAN
WWW.FOUNDERSBREWING.COM
ALCOHOL CONTENT: 11.2% ABV
GLASSWARE: SNIFTER
AVAILABILITY: SPRING

The highly-acclaimed KBS blots out the sun with its imperially black color and menacingly brown foam crest. Brewed with immense portions of coffee and then cave aged in oak bourbon barrels for one year, the aroma announces its arrival with a thunder clap of cold roasted coffee, followed by roasted malt, touches of espresso, vanilla, and fainter hints of bourbon deep in the background. Downright imposing in body, the velvety flavor cascades in waves of deeply roasted coffee, burnt malt sugars, and bourbon barrel influenced vanilla and oak, all with a present but subtle alcohol base. KBS is a masterful Stout that seamlessly blends all of its diverse elements to create an excellent drinking experience.

Pilgrim's Dole Wheat Wine

NEW HOLLAND BREWING COMPANY
HOLLAND, MICHIGAN
WWW.NEWHOLLANDBREW.COM
STYLE: WHEAT WINE
ALCOHOL CONTENT: 11.4% ABV
GLASSWARE: SNIFTER
AVAILABILITY: WINTER

In an American twist on classic strong ale styles, brewers replace up to 50 percent of the malt bill with wheat to create the unusual and potent hybrid style called Wheat Wine. Similar to Barley Wines in their brawny size, but much lighter on the palate in body, these beers also demonstrate honey notes and fruit esters. New Holland's version bears a moderate copper amber color with a wispy off-tan head and an aroma that is strongly of oak, light wheat, and booze from the bourbon barrel aging, with a slightly nutty finish. In the glass, the flavor explodes with big woody and mild vanilla barrel-aged qualities, with some distinctly earthy noble hop bitterness, and then alcohol warms the palate. Light oak flavors pervade the beer and it finishes surprisingly bitter and dry.

Temptation

RUSSIAN RIVER BREWING COMPANY
SANTA ROSA, CALIFORNIA
WWW.RUSSIANRIVERBREWING.COM
STYLE: AMERICAN SOUR ALE
ALCOHOL CONTENT: 7.25% ABV
GLASSWARE: SNIFTER
AVAILABILITY: LIMITED RELEASE

Russian River may be America's most respected purveyor of barrel-aged goodies. Eschewing the ubiquitous flavor experiences of the omnipresent bourbon barrels, and revealing its heritage in the heart of California wine country, the brewery focuses on wine barrels for most of its barrel-aged beers. The brewery's first release, Temptation, remains one of its best. Aged in French oak wine barrels for twelve months, the beer pours with a luminous and attractive golden apricot color and with a sizable off-white head, which gives off a substantial barnyard funk and woody quality that is at once delightfully potent yet reserved. The base golden ale boasts ripe fruits mixed with light spices and a touch of earthy hoppiness, all leading to a drawn out tang from Brettanomyces that puckers on each sip.

Cuvee de Tomme

THE LOST ABBEY
SAN MARCOS, CALIFORNIA
WWW.LOSTABBEY.COM
STYLE: QUADRUPEL
ALCOHOL CONTENT: 11.0% ABV
GLASSWARE: SNIFTER
AVAILABILITY: SPRING

Starting with a base beer of Quadrupel, this beer, named after The Lost Abbey's brewmaster and co-owner, pours a deep brown hue with sprinkles of crimson patches shining through and a light, wheat colored head. A full sniff brings in a substantial waft of fresh sour cherries, a touch of saccharine, and a brimming tartness that hits your jaw even before you sip, all with a slightly hot alcohol note. The beer expands in the snifter to reveal a complex array of flavors, including tart cherries, a measured yet radiating barnyard funk, and a deep presence of dark fruits mixed together, all next to hints of oak, vanilla, and other spices.

La Folie Sour Brown Ale

NEW BELGIUM BREWING COMPANY
FORT COLLINS, COLORADO
WWW.NEWBELGIUM.COM
STYLE: OUD BRUIN
ALCOHOL CONTENT: 6.0% ABV
GLASSWARE: SNIFTER OR TULIP
AVAILABILITY: YEAR-ROUND

The original wood-conditioned beer from New Belgium hails back to the sour red ales of the brewmaster's Belgian brewing roots. A deep and slightly hazy brownish auburn beer with a toasted almond colored head, the aroma fills with sour cherries and dried dark fruits, mixed with a spine-tingling sour and tart character that puckers your jaw, and a long earthy and woody quality. Conditioned in French oak barrels for one to three years and often blended, La Folie's tart qualities are quickly on display, starting with a quick burst of sour cherry puckering followed by a dry fruitiness and mild cherry flavor mixed with hints of European sweet malt, and finishing very dry and puckering in the end.

UNCONVENTIONAL OFFERINGS

Once bound by a fervent dedication to the core four ingredients of beer, anything goes in terms of ingredients in the new American era of craft brewing. Born from the tradition of homebrewing, where everyday household food ingredients were fair game to be tossed into the brew kettle or fermenting glass carboy, the movement towards extreme brewing has included the use of some very odd ingredients, including a disturbingly red beer created with beets. The movement has also led brewers to study up on brewing history and in some instances revert to practices abandoned long ago in search of some ancient flavors. Whether born from experimentation, history, or accident, extreme brewing represents a conscious decision to depart from the safe confines of traditional brewing in hopes of creating something different and unique for adventurous drinkers.

Gingerbread Ale

BISON BREWING COMPANY
BERKELEY, CALIFORNIA
WWW.BISONBREW.COM
STYLE: PORTER
ALCOHOL CONTENT: 6.8% ABV
GLASSWARE: SNIFTER OR TULIP
AVAILABILITY: WINTER

When brewers use seasonal spices to make their winter specialty beers, it can often turn into a Christmas fruitcake nightmare. The Bison Brewing Company manages a steady hand with the spice shaker with its Gingerbread Ale, a holiday Porter brewed with ginger, nutmeg, and cinnamon. Pouring with a deep, dark chestnut color and an off-tan, creamy head, the aroma wafts cleanly with cinnamon, dried fruits, and a lightly sweet, bready malt character that is indeed reminiscent of holiday cookies. Crisp and drinkable in body, the flavor starts with a brief shot of cinnamon, followed by a duet of toasted and roasted dark malts, followed by a long, dry, drawn-out ginger finish.

Sahti

GOOSE ISLAND BREWING COMPANY
CHICAGO, ILLINOIS
WWW.GOOSEISLAND.COM
ALCOHOL CONTENT: 5.6% ABV
GLASSWARE: TULIP OR FLUTE
AVAILABILITY: LIMITED RELEASE

Brewed in the old style of beer of Finland and Estonia, Sahti is a traditional holiday beer made with large portions of rye malt, oats, and then heavily spiced with juniper berries. Goose Island's specialty release pours with a hazy golden amber hue and a mild off-white head. Despite looking conventional enough, the beer's aroma quickly devolves into a wonderland of pine and other deep forest brush scents, with underlying malt spiciness, and a resiny grain base. A slight malt sweetness transitions to a long, dry, and often tart spiciness, slick on the palate, mixed with earthy and minty juniper flavor. Refreshing in body and spirit, this example of an historic and disappearing style is a welcome addition to the brewery's solid lineup.

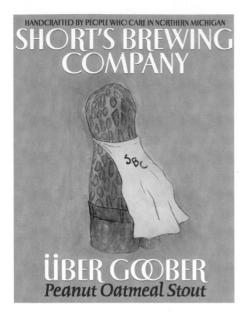

Über Goober Oatmeal Stout

SHORT'S BREWING COMPANY
BELLAIRE, MICHIGAN
WWW.SHORTSBREWING.COM
ALCOHOL CONTENT: 6.5% ABV
GLASSWARE: PINT
AVAILABILITY: WINTER

Tucked away inside Michigan's Upper Peninsula, the Short's Brewing Company makes a madcap kaleidoscope of offbeat beers, including ingredients such as black licorice, Roma tomatoes, and celery seed. For the less faint of heart, its quirky peanut butter Stout, with its jet black color and two fingers of gurgling cocoa head, offers an equally unusual tasting experience. Made with peanut puree, the aroma of crushed and roasted peanuts with touches of chocolate from the Stout contributes the perfect counterbalance. Less obvious touches of creamy peanut butter flash throughout the body, with roasted chocolate notes blending together for an uncommon drinking experience. The brewery's Bananas and Blow Créme Ale, a blending of a cocoa and banana beer, might be the perfect accompaniment.

Bosco's Famous Flaming Stone Beer

BOSCOS BREWING COMPANY
MEMPHIS, TENNESSEE
WWW.BOSCOSBEER.COM
STYLE: AMBER ALE
ALCOHOL CONTENT: 5.5% ABV
GLASSWARE: PINT
AVAILABILITY: YEAR-ROUND

Leave it to the curiosity of the American brewer's mind to tinker with brewing methods that pre-date the Industrial Revolution. At this brewpub chain, the brewer decided to follow the ancient and near-extinct Steinbier and dropped white hot granite stones, heated in the pub's pizza oven, directly into the mash to cause a sudden rise in temperature. When the sugary wort hits the 800 degree stones, it starts to caramelize in ways that normal malts cannot. The resulting beer takes on a decidedly smoky and caramel sweet malt flavor, unlike typical toasted malts, and is balanced by a loose and slightly spicy hop base. Surprisingly dry in the finish, the Famous Flaming Stone Beer shows how taking a stroll through brewing history can lead to pretty interesting results.

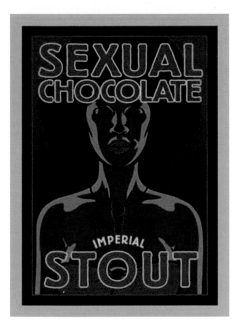

Sexual Chocolate

FOOTHILLS BREWING COMPANY
WINSTON-SALEM, NORTH CAROLINA
WWW.FOOTHILLSBREWING.COM
ALCOHOL CONTENT: 9.7% ABV
GLASSWARE: SNIFTER
AVAILABILITY: WINTER

Drawn in by the name, this Imperial Stout quickly becomes a fan favorite due to its infusion of organic Peruvian cocoa nibs into the brewing process. Close to a black hole in terms of color, the solid light brown creamy cap invites your nose to experience an incredibly rich melody of bittersweet chocolate, black strap molasses, toffee, and dried dark fruit. A stunner in aroma, the flavor is no slouch either, with correspondingly dry bittersweet chocolate notes and some roasted coffee hints that mix with a wondrous pastiche of dark fruits and toffee. Essentially dry-hopped on cocoa nibs, this is not an overwhelmingly sweet chocolate Stout as many are, but instead focuses on a measured and drawn-out chocolate accent to the underlying base beer.

Crème Brûlée Stout

SOUTHERN TIER BREWING COMPANY
LAKEWOOD, NEW YORK
WWW.SOUTHERNTIERBREWING.COM
ALCOHOL CONTENT: 10.0% ABV
GLASSWARE: SNIFTER
AVAILABILITY: SUMMER

This is the most unusual and challenging dessert beer you'll ever likely encounter. Loosen the cap a smidge and so dizzying a force is unleashed that you may think you've just been assaulted by a pastry chef. Immediately greeting your nose is the unmistakable yet jarring aroma of, you guessed it, *crème brûlée*. Pouring a deep brown with auburn highlights and a cocoa colored head, the aroma pops with aggressive vanilla dollops, burnt sugar and egg, and cloyingly sweet malt. Ostensibly listed as an Imperial Milk Stout and brewed with lactose sugar, the beer simply tastes exactly like the dessert from which it derives its name (but perhaps sweeter). You will either love or hate the Crème Brûlée Stout, but if dessert is your favorite meal, you might just consider skipping it for a few sips of this one.

HIGH ALCOHOL BEER

As American craft brewers started to expand their personal definition and understanding of beer, some wondered whether beer should be limited to splashing in the shallow end of the alcohol pool. Few brewers had dared try to advance past the 10 percent mark. Using champagne and wine yeasts, American craft brewers managed to continue fermentation of their high gravity beers far beyond their prior restrictions. In 1994, the Boston Beer Company released their original Triple Bock. Weighing in at 17.5 percent it could hang with cognacs and ports. When it comes to higher alcohol, bigger doesn't necessarily mean better. It takes a talented brewer who appreciates balance and the subtle beauty of alcohol, not just its blunt force power, to create a high-alcohol beer that is rich, complex, and fascinating to experience.

Black Magick

VOODOO BREWERY
MEADVILLE, PENNSYLVANIA
WWW.VOODOOBREWERY.COM
ALCOHOL CONTENT: 15.0% ABV
GLASSWARE: SNIFTER
AVAILABILITY: LIMITED RELEASE

The brewers take a base beer of Imperial Stout with about 12 percent alcohol and then age it in experienced bourbon barrels for a year, where it picks up a few extra points of alcohol. Poured at cellar temperature, the beer opens with a motor oil-like quality, both in color and viscosity, with huge whiskey notes followed by shots of roasted malts, dark and milk chocolate, and vanilla. The bourbon character recedes in the flavor, where a more traditional Imperial Stout flavor emerges, mixed with hints of vanilla and a moderate but not overpowering boozy quality.

3 Guys Off The Scale Old Ale

DARK HORSE BREWING COMPANY
MARSHALL, MICHIGAN
WWW.DARKHORSEBREWERY.COM
ALCOHOL CONTENT: 15.0% ABV
GLASSWARE: SNIFTER
AVAILABILITY: LIMITED RELEASE - SPRING

Brewed once a year by this Michigan brewery and changing a bit each time, it pours with a deep, dark brown hue accompanied by a wispy off-brown head that reveals an aroma of syrupy caramel and toasted malts, rich brown sugar, and a mixture of juicy dark fruits on top of a heady alcohol. The first sip results in a shock of sweet alcohol followed by more caramel malt character and a warming and fruity alcohol burst again, culminating with a balancing structure of lightly spicy hops. The taste is reminiscent of plums and raisins covered in brown sugar, and with a low carbonation level, this is a real enjoyable sipper.

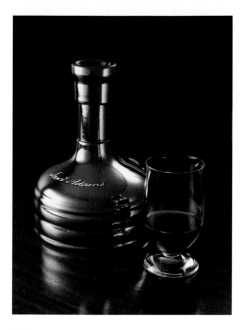

Utopias

BOSTON BEER COMPANY
BOSTON, MASSACHUSETTS
WWW.SAMADAMS.COM
ALCOHOL CONTENT: 27.0% ABV
GLASSWARE: SNIFTER
AVAILABILITY: YEAR-ROUND

The undisputed king of high-alcohol beers, Utopias weighs in at an impressive 27 percent alcohol and doesn't taste like any beer you've ever had. In fact, you could be forgiven for mistaking it for cognac or a tawny port. A rich tawny caramel color with absolutely no head, it looks like a spirit and is best enjoyed a mere two or three ounces at a time. The warm and robust aroma is filled with a complex blend of vanilla, unadulterated sweet caramel malt, oak, and soft but firm alcohol. Served at room temperature, the first sip coats the tongue with the flavors of cognac but with the velvety body of a thick Stout. At around $175 per bottle, Utopias is a beer to be shared on a special occasions among friends and family.

World Wide Stout

DOGFISH HEAD CRAFT ALES
LEWES, DELAWARE
WWW.DOGFISH.COM
ALCOHOL CONTENT: 18.0% ABV
GLASSWARE: SNIFTER
AVAILABILITY: LIMITED RELEASE

What started as a friendly competition between two of the most well-recognized craft brewers, Jim Koch of the Boston Beer Company and Sam Calagione of Dogfish Head, led to a sea change in how brewers perceived the upper limits of their brewing possibilities. In response to Triple Bock and Millennium, Dogfish Head brewed this wistful dark beer. Fermented with a closely guarded and well-cultivated selection of wine and champagne yeasts, the world's strongest dark beer is jet black with a dark chocolate colored head and offers a whirlwind aroma of vanilla, bittersweet chocolate, roasted coffee, and boozy alcohol. Definitely tasting more like a traditional beer, the super-strength Stout boasts molasses, rich dark fruits, and a sticky creamy quality, with rich roasted dark malts alongside a prominent vanilla alcohol touch.

Samael's Oak-aged Ale

AVERY BREWING COMPANY
BOULDER, COLORADO
WWW.AVERYBREWING.COM
ALCOHOL CONTENT: 14.5% ABV
GLASSWARE: SNIFTER
AVAILABILITY: LIMITED RELEASE

Pouring with a deep chestnut color and a very slight head, this oak aged English strong ale is chock-full of woody, oaky notes, alongside vanilla, warm alcohol, and a mild earthy note. Surprisingly smooth to drink, especially considering its 30-proof status, a slow foray into this beer reveals dried light and dark fruits, boozy in nature, along with roasted malt touches, treacle, and an oaky finish. The carbonation level is very light and the mouthfeel remains tacky and thick at times, reminding you that this beer requires time to enjoy.

Arctic Devil Barley Wine

MIDNIGHT SUN BREWING COMPANY
ANCHORAGE, ALASKA
WWW.MIDNIGHTSUNBREWING.COM
ALCOHOL CONTENT: 13.2% ABV
GLASSWARE: SNIFTER
AVAILABILITY: WINTER

If there is such a thing as an Imperial English Barley Wine, perhaps it can be found in the tundra of Alaska. Midnight Sun's ferocious offering is brewed in January and aged in oak barrels for several months before blending and release after Thanksgiving. It snarls at you with a bright copper color with auburn tones and a toffee colored cap that pours forth huge, rich caramel, toffee malt, leafy tobacco, and substantial earthy notes. Very much a malt-focused offering, sticky caramel malt drains from the glass, mixed with waves of earthy tones and hints of vanilla and oak. A mildly velvety drinking experience, the Artic Devil cools your palate while warming your mind.

CHILE BEER

Chile Beers, or those made with piquant spices and peppers, range in terms of colors and textures, but all such offerings have one thing in common: heat. The warmth these beers exude derives not from alcohol, but from the addition of actual hot peppers, extracts, or oils to the beer, either during fermentation or before bottling. The base beers range from simple American lagers to complicated porters and vary in terms of heat and spiciness from mild peppery notes to five alarm throat blazing. The Ithaca Beer Company has gone so far as to age its Smoked Porter in a Tabasco barrel, appropriately rechristening the fiery dark beer "Tastes Like Burning," a *Simpson's* reference.

The Rock Bottom Brewing Company's Boston location offers a spicy, yet pleasant Chile Beer called the Cinco de Mayo Jalapeño Lager. Brewed with actual jalapeños, the beer has a sharply piquant aroma, like nacho cheese, that tingles your nose and offers intense bursts of spiciness that gently needle your throat.

Brewers at the Great Dane Pub and Brewing Company have created a devilish marriage between a solid Pilsener beer and spicy habanero peppers. Taking the oils and juices from smashed peppers, the Tri Pepper Pils skillfully balances the pronounced spiciness with a slightly residual malt sweetness to create a clean, drinkable, and spicy Chile Beer.

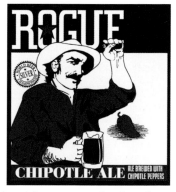

In Fort Collins, Colorado, CooperSmith's Pub and Brewing offers the Sigdas Green Chili Beer, a light and crisp golden ale base into which brewers add Anaheim and Serrano chilies to create a lightly spicy but not overwhelming entrant for those willing to give this unusual style a try.

The Rogue Ales Brewery of Oregon's Chipotle Ale has some light fruit and malt notes in the aroma mixed with smoky pepper touches, and the flavor follows suit with more smoke than heat and a bready maltiness that continues throughout.

Not to be outdone, the Dogfish Head Brewing Company brews its Theobroma, or "food of the gods," with Aztec cocoa powder and cocoa nibs, honey, ancho chilies, and annatto. The resulting beer mixes the unusual elements of chocolate, sweet honey, and peppery spice in the aroma, and the flavor weighs more heavily on the honey side with a constant, continued heat throughout.

CHAPTER THREE

ENJOYING BEER

Now that you've had the chance to learn a little about beer and peruse some excellent examples of familiar flavors, it's time to put it all into practice. With every subject, there comes a time when book learning can only take you so far and that time is especially short when it comes to the thirst-inducing subject of beer. After learning about the history, production, and style of American beers, you can now move on to the user's guide for selecting and enjoying the right beer for the moment. The time has come for a little field research.

In this expansion of the lessons you learned earlier, you'll be able to increase your enjoyment of beer, from buying it to matching it with food, and even check out some great beer bars where you can experience the best craft has to offer in a friendly environment while surrounded by passionate and like-minded beer lovers.

Now, you may bristle at the suggestion that you could use some advice on how to enjoy beer. I mean, come on, it's simply lift, drink, and repeat, right? Far from critiquing your particular beer drinking form, there can be a lot more to enjoying beer than merely drinking it. Starting with selecting the right beer for the right moment, like choosing wine from a lengthy list in a restaurant, standing in front of a refrigerated case stacked high with dozens upon dozens of craft beer selections can be a little daunting. There will be some advice on picking the perfect beer for the right moment and making sure nothing goes awry in the process. You'll be guided through the selection process, including advice on checking for product freshness, reading beer labels, caring for and storing beer (light and temperature), and the prospect of aging beer.

Once you get that beer home, there are several things you can do to enhance your experience beyond just popping the top. These are suggestions for the times you do not feel like drinking straight from the bottle, which certainly has its moments. There are many simple little things you can do to maximize your beer drinking enjoyment, including understanding the importance of temperature and its effects on the flavors of specific styles. Even knowing a bit about the history and variety of glassware available to complement different styles of beer is something that will affect your beer drinking satisfaction. Enjoying beer should be a pleasing experience for all of the senses, including sight, and proper pouring can help elevate your beer's appearance.

After taking some time to consider the beers in front of you, you can begin to give some consideration as to how you can respect beer a little more in a post-macro world. While I am in no way looking to turn beer lovers into pinky extending, air-kissing, label judging snobs, in a world filled with flatulent horse and talking frog ads (and twins!), it wouldn't hurt to have a different perspective on it all.

A great deal of attention has also been paid in recent years to the concept of matching beer and food. Far beyond mere beer can chicken, chefs at top restaurants across the country have realized the majestic pairings that their quality cuisines can offer when matched with beer. After all, restaurateurs had to be embarrassed to offer hundred or thousand dollar bottles of wine next to a single Miller Lite bottle or tap handle. With the help of some top flight beer chefs, you can focus on the pleasing interactions that are possible when beer and food are brought together, including a few recipes and pairings that you can try at home.

Finally, sometimes you just feel like going out for a beer. In the section on 25 Great Beer Bars, you can learn where to head to sample many of the finely crafted beers and diverse styles profiled in this guide. You can also experience beers served in proper glassware, presented with care, in unique environments, and enjoy a dinner prepared with beer or other special events.

BUYING THE RIGHT BEER

A few decades ago, popping to the store for a six-pack of beer would have been no big deal. Depending upon where you lived, the local liquor or grocery store would have offered a dozen or so big named brands, including Stroh's, Schlitz, Hamm's, and the Big Three (Anheuser-Busch, Miller, and Coors). If it was a good store, it might have even included a couple imported brands, such as Lowenbräu. Today, that little selection has been replaced by dozens if not hundreds of different beer labels, each clamoring for a moment of your time and consideration. The selection process can get so overwhelming that you might understandably just reach for what is familiar or even closest. Hopefully with the last chapter under your belt, you can narrow down the styles of beer you feel like drinking. Now that you know whether your mood befits a roasted, brooding Stout or a snappy, zesty

India Pale Ale, it's time to choose the right brand. But wait, before you reach for that six-pack and head to the register, you need to be sure your beer is in the best shape possible.

Freshness Dating

You may have heard of the born-on date, a marking on your beer telling you when it was brewed. For all the flack that it takes, Anheuser-Busch did consumers and the industry a real favor in playing up the importance of fresh beer. Beer will never taste as good as it does in the brewery's tap room, but you should be able to judge how fresh it is and try to avoid stale beer. Beer by its nature is a foodstuff, and is generally meant for consumption promptly after its release. If you miss a certain window of time, your beer won't grow mold or make you ill, but its quality will likely change for the worse. Even the biggest, strongest beers can fall prey to beer's two biggest enemies: oxygen and light. Overexposure to these elements can leave you drinking either a cardboard cocktail or a stink bomb.

You have inevitably experienced both of these unfortunate sensations when drinking beer from clear or green glass bottles. If you sample some of the most popular imported brands when their bottles have not been exposed to light, usually when wholly covered in a twelve-pack container, you'll notice a huge difference from the flavors and aromas you usually get. These beers suddenly possess a stronger malt base and respond as very clean lagers. But let these bottles sit in the light for a few minutes, as happens every day in liquor stores, and the flavors of both beers change dramatically. A light-struck beer is one where specific wavelengths of light interact with the molecular compounds in hop oils to create a photosynthetic reaction, resulting in a skunky aroma and flavor. Avoiding this stinky plague is why most brewers prefer light-resistant brown bottles to store and protect their beers. Careful brewery operations and secure packaging are required to combat that other beer foe, oxygen, which causes beer to taste and smell of cardboard or wet paper.

Both macro and craft brewers have long considered whether and how to date their beer bottles. Despite its importance for consumers, freshness dating is one of those things that many craft breweries avoided for a long time because it led to beer orphaned on store shelves if it did not sell within a specified time period. As craft beer grew more popular and the stability of its packaging increased, however, brewers felt more secure in helping consumers answer the age-old question: "Is my beer fresh?" So now you can tell if your local liquor store cares about the beer it sells. If you see your favorite local brewery's winter beer on the store shelves in July, feel free to say something to the employees. Or better yet, drop a line to the brewery itself. Nobody wins when old beer gets circulated to the public, as the repercussions of a stale beer experience can be long lasting. After getting burned by a three-year-old Winter Warmer, many consumers will simply head back to their staple brands, abandoning craft beer altogether in some cases.

The rule of thumb with the vast majority of beers is the sooner the better in terms of consumption. For most craft beers, a window of up to four months from the brewing or release date is a good measure of a beer's freshness. For styles that rely upon heavy doses of hops, such as India Pale Ales, the subtle hop aromas can start to fade after a month or two, resulting in maltier flavors coming to the surface. For beers that focus on malt-forward flavors, they may continue to mellow in the bottle for several months and are generally less noticeably affected by the passage of time.

Aging Beers

Despite the generalized cautions about older beer, there are some styles and specific brands that beer enthusiasts actually purposefully subject to aging, often in cool basements or dark closets. Beers that possess higher alcohol contents, such as Barley Wine and Imperial Stout, can age for years or even decades. Many cafes and bars in Belgium have bottles in their cellars that date back more than a quarter-century, offering once-in-a-lifetime opportunities to taste rare beers in classic environments. If you have the time and patience, you can easily try this experiment at home by taking a bottle or two and storing it away in a cool, dark, and dry place, preferably near 45-50 degrees Fahrenheit. With larger cork-finished bottles, simply store the bottles standing upright, as the corks don't need to be in contact with the beer to maintain their stability. Try taking a bottle out of your cellar after six or months or a year. Sample it next to a fresh bottle and you will notice how the time has affected its character, softening the hops, accentuating the malts, and letting new flavors shine through. The hardest part is keeping your hands off the resting bottle while time does its work.

What About Awards?

While you are in the store or reading about beer online or in the newspaper, you will often come across claims that a particular brewery has won a medal or two for its beers. The debate over the importance of competitions and medals dates back at least to the 1893 World's Columbian Exposition in Chicago, where more than twenty breweries vied for the top prize. After the judging concluded, Anheuser-Busch's Budweiser and an offering from the Pabst Brewing Company split many of the awards and the competition ended in controversy, with the Pabst beer narrowly besting Bud. More than a century later, the brewery still touts its slender victory with its popular Pabst Blue Ribbon.

Today, brewery medals and awards are as plentiful as caps on bottles. Even as breweries slap countless accolades on the sides of their six-packs, consumers would be smart to consider a competition's judging methods before putting too much stock in a beer's "award-winning" quality. As an inherently subjective commodity, one whose quality cannot simply be determined by hooking up a bottle to a machine, it's difficult to know how to judge beers. In order to bring some sanity to the crazy world of judging beer, two main approaches have developed: everyone picks their favorite or comparison to established style rules. As the results of popularity contests change on a daily basis, breweries usually prefer to tout the awards of structured contests.

At major beer events around the country, including the Great American Beer Festival and the World Beer Cup, both run by the Brewers Association, the sheer number of entrants is impressive (more than 2,400 for the GABF and 2,200 for WBC). In these events, judges employ strict, written style guidelines in a blind process where the reviewers do not know the identities of the brands involved. For participating breweries, these events are among the best opportunities to have trained, experienced industry veterans review and judge their beers against top-flight examples from other breweries. For non-conformist brewers, these competitions are anathema to their creative operations, as it requires them to closely adhere to rigorous rules defining the proper appearance, aromas, and flavors of each style. Enter your beer in the wrong category and an otherwise flawless beer may come home with nothing but a brewer with a bruised ego.

But even when judges follow style guidelines, consumers cannot always blindly rely upon the results. There are many smaller competitions run at festivals and through private tasting companies where only a small handful of breweries compete, with each often entering most of their beers due to the lack of competition. Where there are only four or five beers being judged in a particular style, it's hardly a cage match among the world's greatest beers, and the resulting awards don't offer consumers much substance upon which to rely. Much like a kindergarten talent show where every participant receives an award, the feel-good politics of the judging process may leave everyone but the consumer happy at the end of it all. If, on the other hand, a brewery is able to tout multiple GABF or WBC medals, it's often a safe bet that the lauded beer is a solid if not exceptional representation of its style. Just make sure the accolade in question doesn't date back to the Blue Ribbon days.

SERVING AND TASTING BEER

Most people rightly believe that they don't need any assistance or advice on how to drink their beer. And while this attitude is indeed correct in a mechanical sense, in that you know how to flex your elbow enough to get the glass or bottle from the table to their mouth and back again, you may not be giving much thought to the serving and tasting of your beers. I've long believed that there is a clear distinction between drinking beer and tasting beer, sort of like the difference between hearing music and actually listening to it, or seeing natural beauty and actually taking it in. In a world where one light beer cannot realistically be distinguished from another except in their methods of advertising, the process of selecting, serving, and enjoying a beer is treated with the care given to making a peanut butter sandwich. Knife, bread, peanut butter, consume. The best you might do is add some jelly to the mix, but you don't really give it any thought.

This approach to drinking made a lot of sense in an era when the big brewers treated their products as ubiquitous widgets, essentially interchangeable with any other similarly tasting and appearing widgets. Once upon a time not so long ago, if a bar ran out of kegs of a macro beer, they simply hooked up another brewery's brand and didn't bother to change the tap handle or tell their customers. And no one noticed. But things have changed considerably since those dark days, and you're now surrounded by dozens upon dozens of beer styles, possessing the widest ranging flavors imaginable, unrestricted by anything other than the brewer's imagination. With beers available in all shapes, sizes, colors, and consistencies, you also now have myriad types of glassware to match the diversity of your beers. Subtle changes in the way you serve your beers can also influence their flavors and aromas, in either positive or negative ways. The improvement of available options has also affected the mechanics of how to drink your beer. Instead of treating the pints and bottles in front of you as a tasteless means to a boozy end, you can now pause over your weizen glasses and snifters along the way to experience the bright pastiche of flavors and aromas brewers work so hard to create for you. It's not like you need to extend your pinky out and curl an old-timey moustache before spitting your beers into nearby buckets. But taking a few minutes to think about the ordinary act of drinking beer can literally transform a mundane experience into a brilliant one of actually tasting beer. Here are a few time-tested suggestions on how you can improve your beer drinking experience.

Passing on the Coldest Beer in Town

Americans have been long told by television advertisements that it is their patriotic duty to drink beer as close to the point of freezing as is chemically possible. We chill our glasses in the tundra of bar freezers, cool draft lines down to the point of freezing, and rejoice when bartenders serve slushy pints with little frozen beer droplets along the edges. Macrobrewers have spent countless hours constructing cans that turn different colors, like some creepy Hypercolor T-shirt, when the beer encased within hits the optimal degree of frigidity. While the glacial beer screams out like Han Solo encased in its carbonite sarcophagus, Americans bask in the chill, having achieved the heavily advertised Rocky Mountain cool. The problem is that bars aren't 7-Elevens, and you're not drinking adult slushies. In truth, the only beers that should be consumed ice cold are those that don't taste very good when warmed up.

Very few beers actually express themselves best at near freezing temperatures, and many styles benefit from a reasonable degree of warming. Changing the temperature level can greatly affect the aromas and flavors of most beverages, including beer and wine. When served ice cold, most beers withdraw and their flavors and aromas contract into near non-existence. Serving beer at these frigid temperatures hides delicate, nuanced aromas and accentuates carbonation levels, leaving drinkers with sharp, unpleasant, and unusually bitter results. If you want to make a bitter beer face, simply freeze your beer and then take a few sips, and you'll experience the unpleasantly, prickly sensation that is your beer's cry for help. In contrast, beer tends to open up as it warms, revealing previously hidden aromatic notes and flavors.

Many styles of beer, including those with higher alcohol levels or cask-conditioned offerings, need warmer temperatures in order to assure proper enjoyment. Don't believe me? Then try a little experiment at home. Take two bottles of the same beer and put one in the refrigerator and the other in the freezer. After the bottles have chilled but the freezer bound one has not frozen, take the fridge beer out and let it warm up for a couple of minutes. Then pour both beers into glasses and take a long sniff and taste of the freezer beer followed by the fridge beer. I'm guessing that with the freezer beer you didn't get much of anything, except perhaps some bitter flavors in the body, while the warmer beer opened up a comparative flood of aromas and flavors. I learned this lesson during a visit to the Great Lakes Brewing Company when a tour guide performed the trick for a group of thirsty visitors, including several dedicated macro beer fans. After sampling two different degreed versions of the brewery's classic Dortmunder Gold, audible gasps and mutterings of surprise could be heard from all assembled over the considerable differences between the two samples. Taken straight from the fridge, the beer possessed very little aroma and tasted of tough, bitter flavors foreign to the style. With the simple change of a few degrees, the lager transformed into its usual complex, malty self.

There are also many great beer producing and drinking countries around the world that serve their beers at far warmer temperatures than we would generally ever consider acceptable here in the states. Perhaps the best example, long subject to jokes on American comedy and talk shows, is British cask ale. Also known as real ale, cask ale is defined as beer that is conditioned in the vessel or container from which it is to be served to the public. Brewers add live yeast to each cask, causing a secondary fermentation process, which provides natural carbonation for the beer. Derided as flat beer due to its lighter carbonation levels and warmer temperatures, real ale is alive and flavorful. After tapping the cask, which is traditionally a nine-gallon firkin or an eighteen-gallon kilderkin or kil, the beer quickly changes in flavors and should be enjoyed with a few days.

With its higher serving temperatures, reduced carbonation levels, and absence of excess carbon dioxide, real ales remain among the most expressive and enjoyable beers available. The experience of trying cask ale, while certainly a culture shock the first time, demonstrates the beauty that can be revealed when layers of cold are removed from a beer.

There is no hard and fast rule about finding the right serving temperature for your beer, although many on-line and print resources exist that can give you some suggestions for a particular beer or style. Many breweries include recommended serving temperatures on their bottles, six-packs, and websites if you're interested in pursuing the subject. Otherwise, simply experiment a little at home. Taking a bottle out of the fridge a few minutes before drinking it or noting how the beer's aroma and flavor evolves as it warms in your glass can open a new door to the appreciation of your pint.

Picking the Right Glass for the Right Moment

If you've ever seen a shapely, elegant glass of Hefeweizen pass by, you know the value of serving beer in different glassware. The tall, curvy weizen glass accentuates the gentle gradations of color in the beer, while providing a secure and attractive home for its cavernous, pillowy crown of foam. While taste and smell usually capture all of the limelight when it comes to enjoying beer, the importance of the sense of sight is too often ignored or left as a mere afterthought. With its arresting, multi-colored tones and gravity-defying, craggy heads, beer opens up a seemingly endless vista of visual elements that deliver a new level of pleasure to the drinking experience.

Even when it comes to enjoying tap beer at bars, Americans don't spend much time thinking about the visual side of beer. In the drive for efficiency and order, most bars and restaurants have tended to adopt the utilitarian over the eccentric when it comes to serving beer, opting for the ubiquitous and uninspired Shaker pint glass as the vessel into which they pour nearly all beer. Derided by some brewers as a mere "jam jar," the Shaker pint's appeal lies not in its intrinsic beauty or its ability to accentuate and showcase the style of the beers it contains. Rather, the Shaker pint has come to rule pubs and home bars simply because of its ability to stack evenly on shelves. In addition to its uninspired design, the Shaker pint allows all aromatic esters to escape through its wide-brim, while its inevitable stacking scuff marks quickly kill any head on your beer. When it comes to choosing a glass in which to maximize the enjoyment of our beers, the time has come to send the Shaker pints packing.

In rejecting the culture of apathy that the Shaker pint represents, drinkers can learn that different types of glassware actually influence the aromas and even the flavors in their beer, all while certainly enhancing the ceremony of the drinking experience. In Belgium, the presentation of beer has been raised to a level approaching an art form. Casting efficiency to the side, servers in beer cafes in Brussels thoughtfully locate your beer, choose the matching glassware, carefully present the beer to you, and methodically pour the proper beer, stopping just short of the brim and allowing you to decide if and when to pour the last delicate ounces. These same bars also manage to carry several dozen, if not hundreds, of individual beer brands and their accompanying glassware, all without any storage problems.

While the Belgian approach is certainly impressive, it's unlikely that American bars and home drinkers are likely to stock hundreds of different glasses. Moreover, it's not necessary, as a few staple glasses will well-serve even the most diverse drinking needs.

Start with the basic, everyday drinking glass, the Shaker pint. While it can be a handy option in a pinch, replacing it with the gently sloping Willi tumbler offers a more attractive and functional option. With its taller countenance and narrow brim, this inexpensive, everyday drinking glass better contains the volatile and delicate aromas teeming in craft beers and improves the appearance of beers, all while stacking neatly side by side. Its slender base also limits the transfer of heat that naturally occurs between your hand and the liquids inside your glass every time you grab the glass to take a sip. This glass comes in a variety of sizes, from smaller eight-ounce versions to the preferred seventeen to twenty-two ounce varieties that allow for a vigorous pour without worry of spillage. When referencing pints as the suggested serving vessel in this book, it is the Willi tumbler I recommend using. In a

IMPERIAL PINT

WILLI TUMBLER

pinch, the twenty-ounce Nonic or Imperial Pint glass will also better serve your drinking needs than the American Shaker pint.

For most everyday beer styles with average alcohol levels not requiring specialty glasses, a couple of other glasses can come in handy. A solid mug, with its hefty structure, wide-brim, and sturdy handle helps maintain the head of your beer, allows for deep sips, and completely limits the transfer of heat between your hand and the beer. They are best used for less delicate beers, styles whose strong flavors aren't likely to fade as the beer warms, thus escaping without a trace into the air. The dimpled and ceramic varieties definitely put a serious kink in the ability to see your beer, but can be kitschy fun at times.

The tall, angular Pilsener glass is another familiar sight to many beer

PILSENER

WEIZEN

drinkers and remains a staple in any home bar's beer glass collection for routine use. Precisely tapering from its wide-brimmed top to its fluted bottom, the Pilsener glass enhances the carbonation and striking golden appearances of Pilsener beers, all while directing the aromatics to your nose and providing ample room for the style's prodigious foam head. The glass is best suited for displaying brilliant, bright beers that lack any haze.

Certain styles call out for the use of specific beer glasses, and perhaps no style better captures this indivisible relationship than the Hefeweizen and the weizen glass. As described earlier, the Bavarian weizen glass is king when it comes to capturing and maximizing the visual appeal of beer. Usually about a half-liter or seventeen-ounces in size, the weizen glass slopes from a wide yet tapered top to a narrow and slender base, allowing the colorful hues and immense foam heads of the Hefeweizen style ample room to display their beauty. The glass is designed to capture the substantial head, all while containing the full yet delicate banana, fruit, and spicy phenolic aromas associated with the style.

Not to be outdone by its Bavarian cousin, Belgium's Witbier also commands its own glass, the stout, sturdy tumbler. Almost synonymous with the classic Hoegaarden version, a once style-defining Witbier now brewed by mega-brewer Anheuser-Busch InBev, the workhorse tumbler glass is squat in stature, with a wide top bowl and a narrower base. Thick glass walls line the sides and the style is not so much form as functional, a testament to the everyday utility of the glass as a workingman's way of drinking many Belgian beers, from witbiers to lambics.

In getting a little fancier and less conventional, the snifter is probably familiar to you in the context of watching your grandparents drink ridiculously oversized glasses of cognac and brandy as digestifs. Beyond the caricature of large snifters filled with nearly no booze, endlessly swirling around the base, rounded snifters allow drinkers to vigorously agitate the contents in order to release delicate aromas, which then funnel through the glass's narrow top. American craft breweries and beer bars have picked up on this old-timey practice and have applied it to beers possessing higher than usual alcohol levels. Whether it be a Barley Wine, Imperial Stout, or other strong beer, the snifter naturally slows down your drinking, allowing you extra time and space to experience the aromatics of your beer in an enclosed glass environment.

SNIFTER

GOBLET

In branching out from snifters, a chalice or goblet also works well for stronger beers, especially big, sturdy beers with loads of malt. Similar to the mug in its lack of ceremony, but with greater utility due to a more enclosed opening, the stemmed goblet ranges in shape from robust chunks of glass to delicate, handcrafted works. Gently curving from a wide-mouthed brim to a lengthy stem, the more gentle offerings can resemble flute or tulip glasses. With the addition of intentional scoring in the bottom of the glass, additional boosts of carbon dioxide may be released, continually reinforcing the beer's head.

Long, narrow flutes, like those used for Champagne, help certain beer styles maintain and maximize their carbonation levels. Strikingly attractive and objects of curiosity when containing beer, flutes are tall and thin,

FLUTE

TULIP

with stemmed feet, causing effervescent beers to cascade their bubbles towards the tapered, flared top. Highly carbonated fruit beers display well in flutes, as do American wild ales and even Pilseners.

The final glass is perhaps the most important when it comes to branching out from traditional glassware. With its undulating and chaotic shape—wide-brimmed at the top, trim in the middle, and bulbously squat at the base—the tulip glass is the utility player on the beer glassware team. Capable of containing and improving nearly any style, from routine IPA to fabulously creative Saison, the tulip offers ample room in the base to contain the beer, gently guiding the aromas into a tapered top, all while thoughtfully displaying the contents and encouraging and sustaining the head.

A quick trip to your local home goods store will certainly provide you these options and many more for enjoying any beer you buy. Following the examples set by the Belgians, American craft brewers have also begun to display a greater appreciation for the benefits of diverse glassware, and some have even designed their own glasses in which to serve their particular beers. By replacing a few of your Shaker pints with a Willi tumbler, a tulip glass, and a snifter, you'll have the makings of an excellent lineup of options for improving your beer drinking experience.

Starting Things Off with a Good Pour

When it comes to pouring their beers, Americans generally agree on one thing: they want the most beer possible to fill their glass. Part of this relates to the problems created by the bedeviled Shaker pint, where you can only achieve a full sixteen ounces in the pint you asked for if the bartender fills the glass to the very brim, with no head. It's gotten so bad that most American drinkers consider a frothy head to be a problem to grouse over. Bartenders in many bars invite a tongue lashing if they dare serve their customers with any hint of foam. Considering that people expect to receive what they pay for and they want an actual pint of beer, this situation is somewhat understandable, if sadly lamentable.

You've seen bartenders pour countless beers, often overflowing into the waste drain. You may have even poured beers at a college keg party or during a backyard barbeque. But beyond these infrequent occasions, Americans generally don't bother pouring their beers into any kind of glass, instead opting to simply drink their beer directly from the can or bottle it came in. Frankly, there's nothing wrong with enjoying a beer directly from the bottle during a summer party or sipping from a can during a camping trip. These are the moments that these containers were made for. But there are times when you will want to experience the full range of flavors and aromas in your chosen beers. While fun, drinking directly from a can or bottle, with their narrow openings and opaque appearance, definitely limits how your beer can express itself. You can't enjoy the appearance and look of the beer, the aromas are muted, and the flavors a touch more drab when you lift the can or bottle to your mouth.

Before you get ready to pour your beer, make sure you first have a clean glass. Dirty glasses or ones marred by oils or residue from a previous drink can cause poor head formation and retention. Some beer drinkers prefer to wash their glasses in very hot water or with baking soda as opposed to regular dish soap, which can leave a faint film on the inside of the glass. I've also heard of hard-core beer enthusiasts using mixtures of lemon juice or salt scrubs to get their glasses beer ready. Hot water alone is fine for cleaning most glasses, with an occasional scrub to keep them spotless. Air drying glasses helps minimize the possibility of contaminating glass interiors with head- and lace-deteriorating substances.

Achieving the best looking head often depends upon the type of glass you're using and how you want your beer to end up looking. For the average pint glass or Willi tumbler, simply pouring a bottle at a 45-degree angle down the side of the glass, followed by a 90-degree upright pour into the center of the glass in the final third or quarter of the bottle will suffice to bring forth a few fingers of foam. A more vigorous pour can help encourage beers with somewhat faint heads to foam up, while a steadier, slower hand can handle the highly active beers. For most bottle conditioned beers, or those with yeast still left in the base of the bottle, you should keep an eye on the sediment and avoid pouring it into your glass. The exception to this rule tends to be yeast-rich hefeweizens, which counsel the full pour of yeast. You can use a light source (wine drinkers often use a candle to keep sediment from entering their decanters) below the bottle neck to keep an eye on the yeasty travelers. Towards the end of your glass, consider pouring the rest of the yeast, which is often rich in vitamins and completely digestible, into the glass to sample how it changes the flavor and appearance of the beer.

Spending Quality Time with Your Beer

When you've done all the legwork and finally have a good looking glass of beer in front of you, take a moment to give the experience some thought. Enjoying beer should always be a pleasant experience for all of your senses, including sight. From the striking Hefeweizen glass to the foreboding snifter of pitch-black Imperial Stout, a beer's appearance can tell you a lot about what to expect in the actual drinking. Does the beer present with a nice, well-sustained head, or does it simply fall away due to poor construction or a dirty glass? Is the beer hazy and unfiltered, or can you see straight through its clear, brilliant colors? Does the foam lace down the side of the glass as you drink it, or does it quickly separate and disappear? Always remember that looks can be deceiving when it comes to beer. The intimidating Irish-style Dry Stout may appear sinister, but it actually turns out to be surprisingly light in body, texture, and flavor.

Sticking Your Nose in Your Beer

Your sense of smell makes up a huge proportion of your sense of taste, as the two chemical sensing components are interrelated in your complex nerve system. When aromatic molecules hit your olfactory nerve system deep in your nose, your brain tingles and works to decode their meaning and identity. When you have a cold, your ability to taste many foods and liquids can be substantially diminished. Your brain can process the texture and temperature of what you're consuming, but it doesn't receive the necessary data to process what it's taking in.

While the understandable first inclination when a beer is placed in front of you is to reach out and bring it towards your mouth, keep your inner Homer Simpson in check for a moment. Definitely reach for that glass, but before taking a sip, stick your nose towards the glass and take a deep sniff. Think about what you smell, especially in light of the style of beer you're drinking. If it's an IPA, can you smell fruit, citrus, oranges, sweet malt, or something else entirely? If it's a Stout or Porter, can you pick out dark roasted notes, such as coffee or chocolate? Is the aroma faint or is it strong? Can you detect warmth from alcohol or spiciness from hops or yeast? And do all of the elements please your nose, or do they fail to work well with one another? All of these elements are important in considering the beer in front of you.

Taking time to stop and smell your beer can be a brief but rewarding digression from the actual drinking process. Always remember that beer is a fluid product whose aromas often change from the first pour to the last sip, depending upon changes in temperature and agitation. So every once in a while, swirl your glass, and don't be embarrassed to take a deep whiff.

It Tastes So Good Once It Hits Your Lips

Now that you've endured all these steps to a better beer, it's time for the payoff. Before taking that first sip, remember that the only true guiding principle for enjoying beer is that there are no inviolable rules other than to treat beer and brewers with respect and to follow your own personal taste. In letting your palate be your guide, keep an open mind and think about what you enjoy, what you don't, and why.

For drinkers who are relatively new to more flavorful craft offerings, the common tune of "it tastes like beer" might initially get some repeated airplay. Americans have been conditioned over many generations not to expect their beers to taste different from one another, and that value is so ensconced in their drinking DNA that it takes time to overcome. When you break beers down by flavor, the process of identifying differences becomes a lot easier. If someone tells you to expect coffee or chocolate flavors in Stout or toffee sweetness in Scotch Ale, you'll probably be able to recognize it. Once you've stepped through the gateway of flavor, the distinguishing process draws clearer.

So after taking your first sip, let the beer roll around in your mouth, touching every part of your palate. Think about the beer's mouthfeel, the fancy term used to describe the relative body of how the liquid feels on your tongue. Is the beer thin and watery or velvety and robust? Hops, malt, yeast, water, and a host of other possible ingredients remain at play in your beer, each contributing different flavors and characters. The elements of bitterness and sweetness are the two most notable components, and the best beers achieve a harmony between these competing flavors.

RESPECTING BEER

A long time ago, I wrote that beer was the Rodney Dangerfield of the beverage world, never getting any respect. Since that time, beer has found itself in the pages of the *New York Times,* the *Wall Street Journal,* and the *New Yorker*, on morning and evening television across the country, and in an ever increasing number of high-end food establishments, all with glowing reviews. And while things are far from perfect, beer is finally getting some of the respect that it deserves. Mr. Dangerfield would be proud—and ask that the pitchers keep coming.

The Wit and Wisdom of Craft Beer

Beer possesses egalitarian charms unmatched by other alcoholic beverages, and it remains uniquely capable of bringing people together without pretense. Considering its storied history, rich traditions, and the boundless energy and passion of modern brewers, beer still experiences slights at the hands of wine and spirit drinkers. Battered by stereotypes and a near-constant volley of harmful and demeaning television advertisements, American beer has spent the last decade trying to improve its rundown reputation. Even larger breweries now recognize the folly of their ways and are paying a price for beating up beer's good name. Taking a cue from smaller craft brewers, big breweries have largely abandoned their lampoon-style ad campaigns in favor of focusing on the quality and flavors of the beers they produce. They've even gone so far as to dedicate substantial resources to developing and promoting their own faux-craft brands.

With the growing success of thousands of dedicated craft brewers, the American beer scene is experiencing a true renaissance. From a few dozen brands twenty years ago to thousands today, passionate craft brewers are converting new throngs to their cause of better beer each day, in bars and stores throughout the country. Where you once had to hunt for better beers, they now appear in even the least likely of locations. From airport bars to American Legion halls, craft beers are slowly making inroads and charming their way into new locations with their stories of quality ingredients and dedication to full-flavored beers.

These noble warriors have an easy asset on their side, a beverage able to break down barriers between people and to simplify a complex world for a few minutes or hours. Too often beer fans feel compelled to compare their favored beverage, through a fit of insecurity, to that of wine. To be sure, beer is an incredibly expressive drink and offers flavor opportunities perhaps in excess of what wine can likely offer. Whereas every wine tastes like wine, not every beer tastes like beer. Removed from the restraints of *terroir*, beer benefits from the sweeping flavor palette unique to each brewer, individuals who are capable of mimicking nearly every taste and aroma found in nature. From an iced tea knockoff to finely ground espresso and the keenest cognac, modern craft beer dominates the flavor wheel like no other beverage can.

Away from its funky, experimental angle, beer is also remarkable for its near-complete lack of pretense and airs. Be handed a wine list in a nice restaurant and you can instantly feel the pressure start to build. Despite the growing fascination with beer, ordering a pint will never be as nerve-racking as selecting a glass of wine or as daunting as deciding which bottle to tote along to a party. The accessibility and familiarity of beer are both its advantage and its curse, resulting in a lack of seriousness and respect. And while snobs exist in any subject area, it is recommended that you keep the pinky-extending and judgments to a minimum, all while helping to create a new level of respect for beer.

Learning to Respect Beer

When I talk with people who are interested in learning more about beer, I always start in the same place, by telling them to drink with an open mouth and mind. It is not uncommon for people to carry a few beer prejudices deep within. You may secretly fear dark beers, believe you hate bitterness, or think that all lagers are bland. Left unchecked, these beer prejudices stunt the ability to have a good time and limit the bounty of great beers available for your enjoyment. And while you may not be easily swayed from these prejudices, it's important to tackle them head on from time to time, to try a beer or two out of your comfort zone. Remember, the accessibility of beer is one of its key virtues, and there's perhaps no better quality than the ability to sample a world-class beer for only a couple of dollars. So if you think that you hate porters and stouts, why not buy a couple of bottles the next time you are in the liquor store? A mixed six-pack might run ten bucks, and perhaps you will leave having dismantled a long-standing prejudice and found a new favorite beer.

The more you develop a passion for beer, the more likely it'll be that you'll encounter the dreaded beer snob. A breed that's unfortunately growing more common in beer circles, the beer snob tends to spout judgments about particular beers and breweries. When you encounter these unfortunate souls, just remember to always let your palate be your guide. While beer ratings websites, competitions, and even this guide can suggest beers to try, you should not let any of these dictate which beers you enjoy. If you occasionally enjoy a near frozen, syrupy fruit beer in addition to your super-hoppy IPA or smooth Helles, good for you. If you prefer to add a lemon or orange wedge directly to your Hefeweizen or Witbier, go right ahead. Somebody else might choose a different path, but that doesn't negate your approach. Books, websites, and competitions are not the final word when it comes to beer, and if beer judges or fellow drinkers don't like your favorite beer, don't sweat it. These helpful resources aren't bibles set for worship but are merely tools available to aid your beer explorations.

The more you learn about beer, the more tempted you might become to abandon your roots. And while there are perhaps more flavorful beers out there than those provided by the biggest macrobrewers, try to avoid judging a beer by who brews it. Bashing the big brewers is a favored sport of the beer snob and it really is an unfortunate and out-dated way of thinking. While the big brewers' ad campaigns have damaged the public image of beer and their actions are sometimes unfriendly towards craft brewers, they can brew flavorful beers in addition to their blander offerings. For one, it's difficult to argue that the Blue Moon Belgian White, which many consumers would be surprised to learn is made by Coors, has not introduced many beer skeptics to the joys of better beer. The macrobrewery's promotional efforts for the product could not be more different than its sexualized "Twins" ad. So when a brewery such as Coors creates better beers and treats them with respect, it really is a win-win for beer lovers. In contrast, you need only look at the ridiculous tap handles Anheuser-Busch pushes on bars for its own line of seasonal faux-craft beers to get the uneasy feeling that the brewing behemoth is trying to make a joke out of craft beer.

While Blue Moon fans certainly have a reasonable complaint about the lack of truth in labeling when it comes to this Coors made beer, it doesn't change the fact they probably enjoyed the beer when they tasted it blind to beer politics. In the end, the only question you should ask yourself when judging the pint in front of you is whether the beer is any good. If you like it, the politics will sort themselves out later.

While on your own personal beer journey, remember that lager beer was probably where you started, and you need not run from your heritage. American brewers have undertaken the task of helping to resurrect and redefine many moribund styles, from Porter to Imperial Stout and India Pale Ale. Despite these efforts, many brewers and craft beer fans alike slightly recoil at the idea of giving refuge to ailing lager styles. For at least the last century, lager beer in America has almost uniformly meant derivatives of the classic European Pilsener styles. From before the end of Prohibition, brewers, including Anheuser-Busch, Pabst, Miller, and Coors, have dominated the American beer market, reigning over a long institutional monotony of taste. This uniform tasting experience came to an abrupt end when the craft revolution added a few doses of cheer to American beer. Ever since, lager beer has been left waiting for its invitation to the party. With the exception of Samuel Adams Boston Lager and a small handful of brands from dedicated lager lovers, craft beer in America generally means ale. And while IPA, Hefeweizen, and Stout are ubiquitous, Bock, Dortmunder, and Märzen sadly lack support.

Perhaps due to its association with the bigger brewers, some drinkers rebel against lager beer in favor of ales. Others paint lagers as uncool and lacking in the strong, striking flavors that are more apparent in beers such as Double IPAs. To be sure, the love of lager beer requires an appreciation of subtlety. Drinking a well-crafted lager is a sublime experience that requires patience and consideration, compared to the easily accessible pleasures of ales. For their part, I hope that more craft brewers will eventually embrace this neglected family member and start producing high-quality, traditional versions of classic lager styles. Until that day comes, remember to give some attention to beers such as Victory Prima Pils, Capital Maibock, and Great Lakes Dortmunder Gold, and remember that both ales and lagers, depending upon your mood, deserve a place in your glass.

As you begin to learn more about craft beer, the temptation will inevitably arise to fall prey to some of the bad habits of beer geeks. Here are a few easy rules to help you avoid this unfortunate fate. First off, don't worship exclusively at the altar of big, boozy, and hoppy beers. While big can be beautiful, it's not always better when it comes to beer. The development of the extreme beer phenomenon has led to a quiet and gradual shift in the collective palates of beer drinkers, as brewers seek to capture some of the attention paid to these unusual beers. While some hardcore beer geeks go crazy for unbalanced hop, malt, and alcohol bombs, their rise in popularity has caused a loss of perspective. The truest skill a brewery can display is in the creation of a subtle, gentle beer, in which beauty and complexity flourish without destroying your palate for the next round. While you should certainly think about mixing the occasional Double IPA and Barley Wine into your beer drinking rotation, make it a point to try the lower alcohol beers at your local pub and see what good things come in small packages.

You should also avoid becoming what some beer lovers refer to as a "ticker," a pejorative directed at someone who is too busy checking beers off their personal wish lists to enjoy what they're actually drinking. Far from a solitary beverage, beer at its core remains a sociable drink that requests the company of fellow comrades. While some folks can get lost in the minutiae of beer and brewing, the experience is really about enjoying what you drink. Tracking down a long-coveted beer can lead to a memorable evening, but remember, it's not about hoarding, but about experiencing new beers with friends.

Spreading the Gospel of Better Beer

Once you develop a true taste and appreciation for better beer, why not share your passion with others? If you're lucky enough to have experienced a beer moment, when you realized that not every pint has to taste exactly like the last one, the sociability side of beer counsels that you share your experience with others. Now this is not a recommendation that you start knocking on doors with a cool six-pack in hand, although your neighbors might not complain so much during your next party. Try starting by sharing what you have learned with a few close friends or family members in some easy and fun ways.

To begin, invite some friends over for a small get together where everyone brings a few beers or a different or mixed six-pack. Set out some smaller glasses so that people can sample a few of the beers without being relegated to a single bottle. Provide some cheese or chocolate for mixing and matching and you can really start to experiment with different flavor profiles. This inexpensive way to sample several different beers, all on a budget, remains the most accessible way to learn about beer among friends. Once you find out which flavors your friends enjoy, perhaps having opened their minds to a few new styles, follow-up with a new six-pack the next time you stop by in order to reinforce the experience.

If your friends prefer to move the party elsewhere, try suggesting a local brewpub. Perhaps more than any other place, brewpubs serve as the frontlines in the continuing struggle for hearts and minds in the American craft brewing revolution. And for the price, there is simply no better way to expose your friends to a bevy of beer styles in a safe, friendly environment. A tried and true approach for beer-wary friends is to order a 'safe' beer for your buddy and a sampler for yourself and offer to share a few sips. A brewpub's sampler, which often ranges from three to a dozen or more beers, is the easiest conversion tool you have for helping others get started on their own craft beer journey.

After solidifying the base, turn the learning up a notch with a trip to a local beer festival. With samples of dozens of different beers and styles at a fixed price, these events offer unparalleled opportunities to introduce beer neophytes to the wide world of craft beer. While enjoying the true camaraderie of craft beer fans, beer newbies can sample a wide range of beers without financial or judgment pressure. If they do not enjoy a particular beer, tell them to toss it out and try something new. Beer festivals offer everyone, from novices to self-professed experts, the opportunity to break down their beer prejudices and to try new beers.

Once you settle on a favorite brewery or two, it is time to make a trip out and try the beer at the source. An industry group recently noted that the majority of Americans live within ten miles of a brewery, so it is about time to capitalize on your good fortune. Check the local paper or websites for a list of your local breweries and then give them a call to find out tour times and to schedule a visit. Most breweries welcome visitors and do a great job of educating visitors, thereby courting new customers. A brewery tour is an inexpensive way to spend an afternoon among friends, and it's a great way to support your local brewery. In performing your missionary duties as foot soldiers in the better beer brigade, always be sure to remember the keys to beer evangelism: Never judge or push, and always have fun.

When you've managed to visit all of the breweries and brewpubs in your local area, it's time to pack the car for a road trip. While booze and steering are strictly off-limits, try picking a city where you can visit a few new places, all within easy walking, public transportation, or taxi cab distance. Small towns from Burlington, Vermont, to Bend, Oregon, boast several fantastic breweries and pubs, while bigger towns, from San Francisco to Philadelphia, offer an almost unmatchable range of beer-related opportunities. Travel remains a very important part of any beer adventurer's modus operandi. With few exceptions, beer is a beverage best enjoyed closest to where it's made, and it always tastes better in the presence of the kind souls who brew it. And while it's hard not to let complacency set in if your local beer store carries beers from around the word, armchair beer drinking is no substitute for experiencing beer at the source.

What Bar Owners Can Do to Respect Beer

Consumers are not the only ones who should treat beer with a little respect. As purveyors of alcohol, bar, restaurant, and liquor store owners also possess a responsibility to help build and sustain the public image of beer. As craft beer grows in terms of success and financial importance to these industries, owners should give some thought to the role beer plays in their establishments. Instead of simply choosing the six or twelve most popular beers in your market, a well-planned beer sales and promotion plan can help improve your customers' experience and your bottom line. In the on-premise business, bar and restaurant owners can start by providing beer menus for customers. Finding out which beers are available on tap or in the bottle is a surprisingly difficult question to answer in many places. While some beer bars prefer to use separate, highly detailed menus, a definite selling point for customers, even a rudimentary and up-to-date list, complete with beer names, a single line description, the size, alcohol level, and price, would be a big step forward for many bars. This is especially easy if your beer list does not change much or at all from day to day or week to week.

If your customers occasionally ask you for beers that you do not carry, consider adding a local draft line or two. If your place is like most bars, you offer a few macro standards on tap and round out the selection with some combination of imported brands, such as Guinness, Bass, Harp, or Stella Artois. Why give all your support to cash-flush European mega-giant corporations when you can support your local brewery? Maybe it's time to give one or two a shot and see how your customers respond, and occasionally rotate in a new brand if things go well.

When you get your beer list in good shape, it's time to start training your staff to respond to beer-related questions. Enterprising breweries, distributors, and pub managers know that servers are the frontline soldiers in the war for better beer sales. Yet while managers expect the wait staff to know the food menu backwards and forwards, it is surprising how little these valuable sources know about the beers they serve. Every time a server responds, "We have everything," in response to a beer inquiry, a beer angel loses its wings. Beyond merely asking, "light or dark," servers should understand the beers they sell and be able to offer their customers a brief description of individual brands. This type of service, which often results in upselling on the beer brands involved, comes from solid server training, often planned in partnership with an eager to help local brewery or distributor. Once they get a handle on the beer list, encourage servers to hand out the occasional sample to fence sitting customers. An easy and effective way to interact with customers, offering a sample to those who pause over a beer list is good for business, and tips, and gives the server a chance to shine by displaying their beer knowledge.

Once your establishment is running on all cylinders, consider replacing some of your commonplace and utilitarian glassware with some specialty drinking vessels. Savvy bar owners have slowly learned that the inherent beauty of beer is something they can sell to eager customers. As beer is a multi-sensory experience, the process of promoting beer shouldn't end when the customer orders. In highlighting the showmanship of beer, you need look no further than the turning head reactions caused when a tall, curvy Hefeweizen glass rolls by a table.

You should also consider holding a few events every year specifically focusing on beer. Where such events were once the limited dominion of specialty beer bars, even regular family restaurants can get benefit from focusing on beer sales. Ranging from simple in-house tastings to multi-course beer dinners, breweries and distributors are happy to work with you to plan an event that will also promote their beers.

With a little time and effort, you can both advocate for better beer and raise sales and tips for your servers at the same time.

KITCHEN AND AT THE TABLE

After a long absence, beer is finally returning to its rightful place at the dining table. One of the great contributing forces behind the explosive growth of craft beer in the last decade has surely been the connection brewers and other beer supporters have drawn between their favored beverage and food. It is undeniable that America is in the midst of a food renaissance, one in which many consumers have forsaken processed, homogenized products, including bread that stays fresh in a bag for several weeks, in favor of more full-flavored and natural offerings. This interest is represented in the success of large specialty grocery chains and the growing presence of ethnic eateries in large and small towns across the country. Once limited to takeout Chinese, even some of the farthest reaches of the United States now boast Thai, Vietnamese, and Indian restaurants. The simple meat and potatoes diet of old has been spiced up with dashes of curry, lemongrass, and other exotic spices. Consumer concern for the origin of their foods has also led to the growth of locally sourced materials, resulting in the resurgence of local farmers' markets.

Accompanying this change in the way and substance of what you eat is an alteration in the perception of the world around you and how you interact with it. Instead of passively accepting a limited number of mass-produced products, such as only one or two kinds of cheese, it is now understood that there are countless other offerings that taste, smell, and look different from the staples of our youth. This sea change has also been felt in the world of beer, which has moved from a small handful of available beers to having several hundred or thousand selections available. Even convenience stores, once the well-defended territory of large brewers, now carry a grouping of craft and better beers, creating a veritable chink the macrobrewer's armor.

Long viewed as the exclusive domain of winemakers, restaurants and home dining room tables are increasingly seeing a rise in the presence of craft beers. Chefs at many of America's top restaurants are now working with brewers to learn how beers can be used to infuse new character into their dishes and to pair with their flavors. These chefs, as many winemakers privately acknowledge, understand that beer often pairs very kindly with even the most difficult foods and flavors, whereas wine suffers from several blind spots in the world of culinary match-ups. Once scoffed at in fine eateries, beer dinners are now a more routine offering in top-notch restaurants from Manhattan to Los Angeles. Helping to inform a new generation of chefs, culinary schools are increasingly adding beer tasting and cooking components to their curriculums, as they do with wine.

THE BASICS OF
PAIRING BEER AND FOOD

Once again, when it comes to enjoying beer, your main guide should always be your own individual palate. With that said, here are some starting points and suggestions for your exploration of the possible marriages of beer and cuisine. The first step is to keep in mind what you have already smelled and tasted, both in your pint glasses and on your plates. Understanding the flavors in both what you eat and drink allows you to unlock some of the secrets behind crafting a knock-out coupling. Think about flavors, aromas, and textures in deciding where to start. Is the aroma malty or floral? Is the flavor sweet or bitter, earthy or tangy? Does the beer's texture lightly glide across your tongue before disappearing, or is it bold, lush, and velvety, coating your palate long after the sip is finished? Also consider the intensity of your contenders. If you have a mellow, quiet dish, you don't want to call out your big gunned beers to stomp on the proceedings. When the character, consistency, or intensity of the beer or the dish is overpowering, it's like putting a pee-wee in the ring against Mike Tyson. These are all points to consider when matching up ales and lagers with foods that also possess differing smells, tastes, and consistencies.

Complementing, Contrasting, and Harmonizing

When you taste food alongside liquids that are not part of the dish, your attention is drawn when you sense flavors that mesh well due to their similar flavors, when one offering cuts strongly against the other, or when everything works together in both ways. These classic approaches, in order complementing, contrasting, and harmonizing, are the keys to great pairings.

When it comes to complementing, think about the flavors in your selected foods and then consider beers or styles that possess similar taste qualities. This approach calls for a melding of similar flavors in an easy-going marriage of taste. If you're cooking braised short ribs or firing up the barbeque, you're likely going to caramelize some sweeter flavors along with picking up some darker, roasted, and even smoky notes. These dishes request the company of similarly flavored beers from a wide range of styles, including malty sweet Dubbel, Scottish-style Ale, Brown Ale, and even some lightly Smoked Beers. The earthy, grassy flavors of simple garden salads work well with lightly fruity and earthy Hefeweizen, Witbier, and Kolsch styles. On the dessert front, a creamy, yet slightly burnt dessert of crème brûlée calls for the swirling sweetness of Barley Wine and malty Doppelbock, or the darker, roasted qualities of a Baltic Porter, Porter, or Imperial Stout.

In taking the contrasting approach, think of two quarreling musicians whose off-stage differences result in beautiful chemistry when they're playing together. In considering a contrasting approach, take the flavors you have in your food and consider what beer tastes would cut directly against them, without either being overwhelmed. Restaurateurs have actually long acknowledged the bracing pleasure from pairing a lightly bitter and roasted Dry Irish-style Stout with the earthy, minerally characters of fresh, raw oysters on the half shell. Placing the fruity, citrus notes of American Pale Ale, English-style Bitter, or Alt against the flavors of beef dishes, including Mexican-spiced tacos, prime rib, and beef Wellington, create decidedly different and palate pleasing notes. Sharply hoppy India Pale Ale can also work wonders with aged cheddar cheeses.

Slicing and Dicing
with Hops and Carbonation

A slight derivative of contrasting, but perhaps best considered an element on its own, is the device of using a beer's flavors or carbonation to cut through the bold flavors of a dish. Along the lines of matching beers and foods of similar strengths for the bigger flavored dishes, consider throwing a counter-punch with a highly hopped or tightly carbonated offering. Often left out of the equation is the ability of carbonation bubbles to clear clean paths through otherwise overwhelmingly flavored dishes. For instance, a spicy curry dish from your favorite local Indian restaurant might require the clear-cutting abilities of sharply hoppy but less alcoholic India Pale Ale, German Pilsener, Dortmunder, or even spicy Saison. The malty, sweet flavors of American Amber, Dunkel, and Bock can sooth a palate on its way through spicy dishes as well.

PARTICULAR GROUP PAIRINGS

There are many resources available, both on the Internet and in book form, to provide you with detailed pairings for many beer styles and cuisines, and this essay only hopes to offer you some helpful advice on how to take your first few steps towards a life of pairing beer and food. With that caveat, here are some popular menu categories along with some general beer styles that create interesting pairings.

Salads and Appetizers

Starting with lighter flavors at the beginning of the meal helps to avoid overwhelming the palate before the meal even begins. Offerings from the Easy Drinkers and Cool and Refreshing chapters help bring complementary flavors to garden and Caesar salads, along with tuna dishes, which can also benefit from some lightly hoppy and citrusy offerings, such as American Pale Ale or Kolsch.

Beef and Lamb

Classic English-style ales, such as Bitter, Porter, and Brown Ale, with their diverse flavors, all pair well with robust beef and lamb dishes. Depending upon the method of preparation and the heaviness of any sauces, you could do well with these selections.

Chicken

The great equalizer when it comes to pairings, chicken generally plays well with all styles, including roasted versions with German or Czech Pilsener, American Pale Ale, Lager, or an Irish-style Red Ale.

Fish

The strength and character of flavor of a particular fish helps define the right pairing, with more delicate varieties calling for the slightly tart wheat beers of the Cool and Refreshing section, and more highly seasoned or flavorful offerings calling out for slightly hoppy lagers such as Helles, Dortmunder, or Czech Pilsener.

Barbecue

The smoked flavors and aromas, along with the caramelized malt sugars, provide great opportunities for pairings, including Smoked Beer, many selections from the Mellow and Malty or Robust and Rich chapters, along with the chocolate and coffee tones of the Dark and Roasted offerings.

Pizza

Perhaps the grand-daddy of all beer and food pairings, the red sauce in pizza works well with sweeter, maltier beers such as Cream Ale, Märzen, and Vienna-style Lager, while pesto versions call for spicier offerings, such as Saison, Tripel, or even Rye beers.

Fruit Desserts

From the bullpen, call on the deep bench of Lush and Fruity beers for use with our fruitier desserts, ranging from pumpkin and pecan pies to apple fritters and raspberry tarts. Wheat beer selections from the Cool and Refreshing section also work well with fruit desserts. For a wild card that usually carries the day, considering pairing porters and imperial stouts with your fruit desserts for a contrast made in heaven.

Chocolate and Sweet Desserts

One of the most interesting and inviting areas of pairing relates to the marriage of beer with sweeter desserts, especially chocolate. Depending upon the level of sweetness versus bitterness in the chocolate, nearly anything from the Robust and Rich, Dark and Roasty, or Nightcaps and Nursers sections pair well, especially Scotch-style Ale, Imperial Stout, Milk Stout, Oatmeal Stout, Doppelbock, and Dubbel.

Cheese

Rivaling chocolate for the crown of beer pairings, the perhaps unexpected union of beer and cheese is sacred ground. The strong carbonation in beer, with its clean and crisp brightness and acidity, cuts through the strong and lasting textures of cheese to deliver a powerful punch of contrasting and complementing possibilities. The stronger the cheese, the stronger the flavor of the beer, is a generally accepted concept, with the classic and robust Stilton and Roquefort varieties finding homes in pairings with Tripel, Imperial Stout, and Barley Wine. The softer, zestier edges of earthy cheeses, including Feta and Chevre, blend well with Hefeweizen and American Wheat Ale. Smoked Gouda is a natural match for Smoked Beers and sharp Cheddar, Parmesan, and Romano match with English-style Bitter, India Pale Ale, and Altbier.

RECIPES

The idea of cooking with beer for many people may be limited to the notion of the old Beer Can Chicken recipe, where the cook unceremoniously stuffs a can of macro lager into the hindquarters of poultry before sticking it on the grill or in the oven. The art of cooking with beer, even at the home level, now extends far beyond a single beer ingredient, with some nameless ale or lager, into a realm where the possibilities are limited only by the chef's own creativity. To give you some starting points for your home sessions of cooking with beer, I've asked two leading beer chefs to give you some accessible, yet flavorful recipes to try in your own kitchen.

Beer Chef Bruce Paton's Menu

Long before many other culinary figures started infusing their dishes with beer, two excellent chefs made names for themselves by bringing beer back into the kitchen. Bruce Paton is known in the brewing world as the Beer Chef. Long the executive chef at the now-defunct Cathedral Hill Hotel in San Francisco, Paton hosted a Dinner with the Brewmaster Series, a special event in which he created a distinctive menu of dishes made and paired with a specific brewery's beers. Trained at the California Culinary Academy, Paton worked as a chef in several hotels and restaurants before coming to Cathedral Hill, where he has hosted some legendary beer dinners. The Beer Chef is also the past Chairman of the Board of Directors of The Chefs Association of the Pacific Coast, the San Francisco chapter of the American Culinary Federation, an organization in which he has also been named as Chef of the Year.

After designing countless beer dinners for restaurants, breweries, convention banquets, and private parties, Paton offers you the chance to make your own tasting menu in your home kitchen. He suggests a broad menu of items and some general beer styles that will pair well with his dishes. With his creative yet easily accessible recipes, you can put to use what you learned in The Style and Flavor of Beer to make selections you think will pair well with his chosen dishes.

Dungeness Crab Cakes with Smoked Paprika Butter Sauce

YIELD: 10 SERVINGS

- 1 BUNCH GREEN ONIONS, MINCED
- 1 POUND DUNGENESS CRABMEAT (SQUEEZE OUT WATER)
- JUICE OF 1 LEMON
- 1 TABLESPOON DIJON MUSTARD
- 3 TABLESPOONS MAYONNAISE (OR MORE IF NECESSARY TO BIND)
- 1 TEASPOON OLD BAY SEASONING
- 1/2 CUP BREADCRUMBS (PANKO), DIVIDED
- SALT AND PEPPER

Briefly sauté the green onions over high heat, then let cool. Combine the onions, crabmeat, lemon juice, mustard, mayonnaise, Old Bay seasoning, and 1/4 cup of the breadcrumbs in a bowl. Mix well and form into 2 1/2-ounce "cakes." Coat the cakes with additional breadcrumbs and chill for at least 30 minutes to let the flavors blend. Pan-fry the cakes over medium-high heat until they are crispy, about 5 minutes on each side. Serve with Smoked Paprika Butter Sauce.

Smoked Paprika Butter Sauce

YIELD: 2 CUPS SAUCE

- 1 CUP CHOPPED SHALLOTS
- 1/2 CUP CHAMPAGNE VINEGAR
- 3 CUPS WHITE WINE
- 1 TEASPOON WHOLE BLACK PEPPERCORNS
- 2 CUPS HEAVY CREAM
- 1 TO 2 TEASPOONS SMOKED PAPRIKA TO TASTE
- 8 OUNCES CHILLED BUTTER

Combine the shallots, vinegar, wine, and peppercorns in a saucepan over high heat. Bring to a boil, and then reduce the heat to low and simmer until the liquid is reduced to 1/2 cup. Add the heavy cream and 1 teaspoon smoked paprika. Reduce until thick. Strain out the solids and whisk in the butter. If the smoke flavor is not pronounced enough, add more paprika.

PAIR WITH A RUSSIAN RIVER BLIND PIG IPA OR AN INDIA PALE ALE WITH A CASCADE HOP PROFILE.

Cavatappi Pasta with Fresh Corn, Fennel, and Wild Mushrooms in Garlic Cream

YIELD: 10 SERVINGS

- 3 TABLESPOONS OLIVE OIL
- 2 TEASPOONS CRUSHED RED PEPPER
- 1/2 CUP GARLIC, MINCED
- 6 CUPS FRESH CORN KERNELS (ABOUT 6 EARS)
- 6 BULBS FENNEL, DICED (FRONDS RESERVED FOR GARNISH)
- 1 1/2 POUNDS SHIITAKE MUSHROOMS, DICED
- 1 1/2 POUNDS CREMINI, CHANTRELLE OR OTHER WILD MUSHROOMS, DICED
- 2 TABLESPOONS FENNEL SEEDS, TOASTED AND GROUND
- SALT AND PEPPER TO TASTE
- 8 CUPS CREAM
- 4 POUNDS CAVATAPPI, COOKED AL DENTE
- 3 RED BELL PEPPERS, DICED FINE FOR GARNISH
- ROASTED CORN FOR GARNISH

Heat the oil in a large saucepan over medium heat. Add the crushed red pepper and garlic and cook for 2 minutes, stirring frequently. Add the corn and fennel, stir well, and cook for an additional 5 minutes. Add the mushrooms, fennel seeds, salt and pepper, and cook another 5 minutes. Add the cream and bring to a boil. Reduce the heat and let simmer 20 minutes. Pour over the pasta and garnish with red bell pepper and chopped fennel fronds.

PAIR WITH MOONLIGHT TWIST OF FATE OR ANOTHER MALT-HEAVY ENGLISH-STYLE BITTER.

Shortribs a la Dubbel

YIELD: 4 SERVINGS

- 4 BONE-IN SHORT RIBS
- SALT AND PEPPER TO TASTE
- 2 LARGE ONIONS, PEELED AND CHOPPED
- 1/2 CUP MINCED GARLIC

- 2 CARROTS, PEELED AND SLICED
- 4 THYME SPRIGS
- 1 (750-ML) BOTTLE OMMEGANG FROM BREWERY OMMEGANG
- 2 CUPS CHICKEN STOCK

Thirty minutes before cooking, rub the short ribs with salt and pepper.

Preheat the oven to 300°F. Sear the short ribs in an ovenproof pot over high heat and remove when browned on all sides, about 3 minutes per side. Reduce the heat to medium high, add the onions and garlic, and cook until caramelized, about 3 minutes. Stir in the carrots and thyme and cook for 2 to 3 minutes. Add the beer and chicken stock to the pot to deglaze. Return the short ribs to the pot bone side up. Bring to a simmer. Cover and place in the oven for 2 1/2 hours. Add more stock periodically if necessary. When the short ribs are done, strain the cooking liquid and pour into a saucepan over medium heat. Reduce the by half, skimming the fat as it cooks, or until a sauce consistency. Pour the sauce over the ribs and serve with mashed potatoes or soft polenta.

Mascarpone Soft Polenta

YIELD: 10 SERVINGS

- 2 CUPS WATER
- 3 CUPS (1 1/2 PINTS) HALF-AND-HALF
- 3 CUPS MILK
- 2 CUPS POLENTA
- 1 POUND MASCARPONE
- 4 TABLESPOONS BUTTER
- 1/2 CUP CREAM
- SALT AND PEPPER TO TASTE

Combine the water, half-and-half, and milk in a large saucepan. Bring to a boil and sprinkle in the polenta while whisking constantly. Let the mixture come to a boil and then cover and reduce the heat to low. Stir every 10 minutes or so until completely cooked, about 35 minutes. Stir in the Mascarpone, butter, cream, and salt and pepper and mix well.

PAIR WITH A MALTY AND SPICY DUBBEL FROM THE ROBUST AND RICH CHAPTER.

Butterscotch Bread Pudding

YIELD: 30 SERVINGS

> 6 CUPS $1/_2$-INCH CUBES BRIOCHE BREAD
>
> 7$1/_2$ CUPS (JUST UNDER 2 QUARTS) HALF-AND-HALF
>
> 6 TABLESPOONS UNSALTED BUTTER
>
> 1 TEASPOON SALT
>
> SEEDS FROM 2 VANILLA BEANS
>
> 1$1/_2$ CUPS PACKED DARK BROWN SUGAR
>
> 6 LARGE EGGS
>
> 6 LARGE EGG YOLKS

Preheat oven to 350 degrees F. Butter 30 ramekins. Place the bread cubs in a large mixing bowl and set aside.

In a saucepan, combine the half-and-half, butter, salt and vanilla and heat through over medium heat. In a bowl, whisk together the sugar, eggs, and yolks. Whisk in a tablespoon of the hot half-and-half mixture to temper the eggs; then in a stream, slowly whisk in the remaining half-and-half mixture. Pour over the bread cubes. Spoon the mixture into ramekins. Bake in the middle of the oven 25 to 30 minutes, or until puffed and golden.

PAIR WITH ROGUE OLD CRUSTACEAN, A BARLEY WINE, OR A BOURBON BARREL-AGED BARLEY WINE WITH A LOWER HOP FINISH.

Sean Z. Paxton's Menu

Primarily a self-taught chef, Sean Z. Paxton's focus has always been to create quality dishes with cooking techniques and styles drawn from across the globe. He has worked for several restaurants and hotels, along with catering, in his efforts to share his demonstrable passion for food with others. Along with his love of food, Paxton is inspired by the craft of beer making and with the science of brewing techniques. He is an accomplished homebrewer who draws upon his knowledge of cooking to create new flavors in the beers he brews himself and in collaboration with a few craft breweries. With an extensive knowledge base firmly rooted in both culinary and brewing sciences, Paxton realized early on that each craft shares similar parallels that, when brought together, could result in previously unexplored depths of flavor.

Paxton writes extensively about beer and food for trade and consumer beer publications, as well as running his own website, www.homebrewchef.com, where he shares his knowledge and experience of food and beer. As the Executive Chef for HomebrewChef, he collaborates with pub owners and craft brewers around the country to host exclusive multi-course beer dinners. He is also well-known among hard-core beer enthusiasts for the incredible dinners he has hosted at Ebenezer's Restaurant and Pub in Maine, an establishment profiled in the 25 Great American Beer Bars section to follow. True to his nickname, Paxton is an active board member of the Northern California Homebrew Organization.

Paxton's menu gives you the opportunity to explore several different dishes, depending upon your mood and level of hunger. Not intended as a tasting menu but as independent dishes that you can cook at your leisure, these easy-to-follow offerings provide a punch of flavor. From his take on the classic beer pretzel to his sizzling Chipotle IPA chicken breasts and his holiday Winter Warmer spice cake, the dishes pack tremendous flavor into easy to follow recipes.

———

Allagash White Clam Chowder

YIELD: 8 TO 10 CUP OR 6 TO 8 BOWL SERVINGS

 4 BACON STRIPS, PREFERABLY APPLEWOOD SMOKED, CUT INTO SMALL LARDONS

 1 LARGE ONION, YELLOW, PEELED AND CHOPPED (ABOUT 1 CUP)

 2 POTATOES, RUSSET OR YUKON GOLD, CHOPPED

 1 CELERY RIB, SLICED THIN

 1 TABLESPOON ALL-PURPOSE FLOUR

 12 OUNCES ALLAGASH WHITE ALE

 6 OUNCES CLAM JUICE

 8 OUNCES ($1/_2$ PINT) HEAVY CREAM

 20 OUNCES CLAM MEAT (FRESH OR CANNED)

 1 TO 2 TABLESPOONS CHOPPED ITALIAN LEAF PARSLEY

 SALT AND PEPPER TO TASTE

 PAPRIKA FOR GARNISH

 BUTTER

In a large pot over medium-low heat, add the sliced bacon and render out the fat, stirring till the bacon is lightly browned, about 10 minutes. Remove the bacon from the fat and reserve.

Add the onions to the pan and increase the heat to medium high. Cook the onions until they are transparent, about 5 minutes. Add in the potatoes and cook for another 5 minutes. Add the celery and cook another minute. Add the flour and mix well, cooking about 3 minutes. Add the white ale and clam juice and bring to a boil. Reduce the heat to low and simmer for 15 to 20 minutes, or until the potatoes are tender. Add the cream and clam meat, stirring to heat through, and then turn off the heat. Stir in the parsley and adjust the seasoning with salt and pepper. Serve into cups or bowls and garnish with a sprinkle of paprika and a small pat of butter and cooked bacon.

PAIR WITH A SAISON, SUCH AS HENNEPIN FROM BREWERY OMMEGANG, OR A MILDLY SPICY BIÈRE DE GARDE FROM THE FUNKY FLAVORS CHAPTER.

Alaskan Smoked Porter Chili

YIELD: 8 HEARTY SERVINGS

 OLIVE OIL, AS NEEDED

 6 POUNDS BEEF SIRLOIN (OR PORK BUTT), CUBED INTO 1-INCH CUBES

 2 TO 4 DRIED ANCHO CHILES, STEMMED AND SEEDED

4 CUPS SLICED YELLOW ONIONS (ABOUT 3)

1 RED BELL PEPPER, ROASTED

1 YELLOW BELL PEPPER, ROASTED

1/2 CUP CHOPPED GARLIC (ABOUT 2 BULBS)

2 TO 4 ADOBO CHIPOTLE PEPPERS, MINCED

1 (28-OUNCE) CAN FIRE-ROASTED CRUSHED TOMATOES

44 OUNCES ALASKA SMOKED PORTER, STONE SMOKED PORTER, OR
ROGUE CHIPOTLE ALE

2 TABLESPOONS CORN FLOUR, CORNMEAL, OR POLENTA

SPICE BLEND:

2 TABLESPOONS CUMIN SEEDS

2 TABLESPOONS CORIANDER SEEDS

2 TABLESPOONS SEA SALT

2 TABLESPOONS PAPRIKA

2 TABLESPOONS CHOPPED FRESH OREGANO (OR 1 TABLESPOON DRIED)

1 TEASPOON CAYENNE PEPPER

In a large Dutch oven over medium heat, add enough oil to coat the bottom of the pan. In small batches, brown the beef until golden brown on all sides. Be careful not to over crowd the pot or the meat will steam instead of brown. Place each batch of cooked meat into a large bowl and repeat until all the meat is cooked. Set the beef aside.

Put the dried ancho peppers in a small glass bowl, cover with boiling water, and seal with plastic wrap. Let the pepper soften, about 15 minutes.

Meanwhile, place the Dutch oven with the pan drippings over medium heat. Add enough oil to coat the bottom and add the onions. Stir to coat evenly in the oil, then stir every 3 to 4 minutes until the onions are a dark brown, about 15 minutes. While the onions are cooking, roast the red and yellow peppers over an open flame (or under a broiler), turning once each side is black, until all sides are black. Place the peppers into a plastic bag and seal. (This will capture the steam, helping to remove the burnt skin.) Once cool enough to handle, remove the skin and seeds and slice into strips. Add to the meat bowl.

Once the onions are caramelized, add the garlic and cook for another minute. Then add in the meat, ancho chile peppers, and tomatoes, stirring well. Drain the ancho chipotle peppers, put in a blender, and top off with the beer. Purée until smooth. Add the chili beer mixture to the Dutch oven and deglaze the pan, removing any drippings from the bottom of the pan.

Bring the chili to a simmer.

In a skillet over medium heat, add the spices and toast until they become fragrant. Remove from the pan and place into a spice mill or blender and pulse until a fine powder. Add half of the spice mix to the simmering chili. Add more beer or water, if needed, to have a medium thick chili. Cook for 1 to 2 hours on low heat, checking consistency and stirring every 15 to 20 minutes. The last 15 minutes, add the remaining spices and, if needed, the corn flour (a thickener). Stir in well and let simmer. Check seasonings and adjust with salt, pepper and more spices if needed.

This chili can be made a day in advance and the flavors will meld, making a more flavorful chili the next day.

PAIR WITH SMOKE JUMPER SMOKED IMPERIAL PORTER FROM LEFT HAND BREWING COMPANY.

Sierra Nevada Pale Ale and Mustard Pretzel

YIELD: 8 PRETZELS

8 OUNCE SIERRA NEVADA PALE ALE OR STONE IPA

1/4 CUP DRY MALT EXTRACT* (DME) OR SUGAR

2 TABLESPOONS MUSTARD

1 TEASPOON INSTANT YEAST, RAPID RISE

3 1/2 CUPS BREAD FLOUR

2 TEASPOONS SEA SALT

2 TABLESPOONS COARSE SALT

MAKING THE DOUGH: In a small bowl, combine the beer (and any yeast slurry at the bottom of the bottle), DME, mustard, and yeast, mixing to combine. If you have an electric stand mixer, add the flour and salt to the bowl and add beer-yeast mixture. Using a dough hook, mix on low speed to combine the ingredients and then increase the speed to medium for about 5 minutes. If you are doing this by hand, add the dry ingredients to a large bowl, making a well in the center, and add the beer-yeast mixture and combine. Remove from the bowl onto a floured work surface and knead the dough for at least 5 minutes, until the dough elastic and smooth. To either preparation, if the dough is dry, add 1 teaspoon of beer to bring it together. If the dough is too moist, add flour, 1 teaspoon at a time, until the mixture is not sticky.

Transfer the dough to a lightly greased (with either butter or oil) large bowl and cover with plastic wrap. If you would like your pretzel to have more of a sour dough quality, place the bowl in the refrigerator for 8 to 12 hours or overnight. The cooler temperature will slow down the fermentation, allowing the yeast to develop more flavors. If time is not on your side, let the dough sit in a warm (72°F) place for 1 to 1^1/$_2$ hours, or until it has doubled in size.

MAKING THE PRETZELS: Transfer the risen dough to a lightly floured surface. Depending on your liking, the pretzels can be made small or large. Each recipe can make 6 large or 12 small pretzels. Divide the dough equally and roll each piece into a long rope, making sure each dough ball is rolled out to the same length. Thicker ropes will take longer to bake, thinner ropes shorter baking time. Now, take one end of the rope in each hand and make an upside down U. Cross the ends over, giving a twist and bring each end back up to the top, pressing the end into the dough with enough pressure to stick together. Place onto a parchment paper–lined sheet tray and cover with a clean damp towel for 30 minutes.

BAKING THE PRETZELS: Preheat the oven to 425°F. In a medium-size pot (not aluminum), add 4 cups of water and ^{1}/$_4$ cup of baking soda and bring to a simmer. Carefully place a pretzel onto a wide flat spatula and slowly dip the dough into the water. Poach each side for one minute. Remove the pretzel from the water and place back onto the sheet tray. If your pot is large enough, add two or three pretzels at a time to the water. Once all the dough as been boiled, sprinkle salt (or whatever topping you prefer) evenly over the pretzels. If you like a crispier crust on your pretzels, brush the dough with an egg wash (1 egg beaten with 1 tablespoon water) before sprinkling the toppings. Bake the pretzels 12 to 18 minutes, depending on the size. If you like hard pretzels bake 20 to 25 minutes.

PAIR WITH VICTORY LAGER FROM VICTORY BREWING COMPANY OR ANCHOR STEAM FROM ANCHOR BREWING COMPANY.

Chipotle IPA Marinated Chicken Breasts

YIELD: 4 SERVINGS

12 OUNCES UNION JACK IPA, FIRESTONE WALKER BREWING CO.

2 NAVEL ORANGES , FRESHLY SQUEEZED ($^1/_2$ CUP) AND ZESTED

1 LIME, FRESHLY SQUEEZED ($^1/_4$ CUP) AND ZESTED

$^1/_4$ CUP OLIVE OIL

4 GARLIC CLOVES, ROASTED AND PEELED

2 TO 4 CHIPOTLE PEPPERS IN ADOBO SAUCE (DEPENDING ON YOUR HEAT TOLERANCE)

2 TABLESPOONS WILD FLOWER HONEY

$^1/_2$ BUNCH CILANTRO, WASHED, STEMS REMOVED

SALT AND FRESHLY CRACKED BLACK PEPPER

4 CHICKEN BREASTS, BONE IN AND SKIN ON

In the pitcher of a blender, combine the IPA, orange juice and zest, lime juice and zest, oil, garlic, chipotle peppers (and extra sauce if you crave more intensity), honey, and cilantro, and season lightly with salt and pepper. Purée the mixture till smooth. Rinse the chicken breasts in cold water and pat dry. Marinate the chicken in the chipotle mixture in the refrigerator for at least 4 hours or overnight.

When ready to cook, prepare a hot grill. (I prefer wood coals to gas.) Remove the chicken from the bag (reserving the marinade) and place on the grill. If using gas, add a foil package of IPA-soaked wood chips that have been submerged for 30 to 60 minutes. Place it above the burner but under the grate. Place the breasts over the package and close the lid. Cook skin side down for 4 to 5 minutes, watching for flare ups.

Meanwhile cook the marinade in a saucepan over medium heat. Reduce by half. Flip the chicken breasts and baste the skin with the simmering sauce. Cook for another 5 to 6 minutes until the internal temperature is 160°F with an instant read thermometer. By using the bone in breast, this will protect the meat from drying out and also add lots of extra flavor. Remove from the grill and let rest for 5 minutes before deboning the breast, then slicing for service. This poultry dish is great in an arugula or spinach salad, over a Southwestern style polenta, on a Tex-Mex inspired pizza, or a roasted corn salad. Serve with the sauce.

PAIR WITH RACER 5 FROM BEAR REPUBLIC BREWING COMPANY OR ANOTHER CITRUSY OFFERING FROM THE HEAVENLY HOPPY CHAPTER.

Avery Old Jubilation Spice Cake with a Holiday Ale Frosting

YIELD: 8 TO 12 SLICES

OLD JUBILATION APPLE SPICED CAKE

1 TEASPOON GROUND CINNAMON

1 TEASPOON GROUND GINGER

3/4 TEASPOON SEA SALT

1/2 TEASPOON FRESHLY GRATED NUTMEG

1/2 TEASPOON BLACK PEPPER

1/4 TEASPOON GROUND CLOVES

1/4 TEASPOON GROUND ALLSPICE

1/4 POUND (1 STICK) UNSALTED BUTTER

2 CUPS CAKE FLOUR

1/2 TEASPOON BAKING POWDER

1 TEASPOON BAKING SODA

1/4 CUP SOUR CREAM, AT ROOM TEMPERATURE

1/4 CUP OLD JUBILATION HOLIDAY ALE

3/4 CUPS PACKED DARK BROWN SUGAR

1/2 CUP BLACK STRAP MOLASSES

2 LARGE EGGS

1 CUP APPLE SAUCE, CANNED OR FRESH

1 TEASPOON VANILLA EXTRACT

HOLIDAY ALE FROSTING

1/2 CUP OLD JUBILATION FROM AVERY BREWING CO OR ANCHOR XMAS ALE

8 OUNCES MASCARPONE CHEESE

12 OUNCES CREAM CHEESE

1/4 POUND (1 STICK) UNSALTED BUTTER

2 TEASPOONS VANILLA EXTRACT

2 TO 3 CUPS CONFECTIONERS' SUGAR

TO MAKE THE CAKE: preheat the oven to 350°F. Coat two 8-inch cake pans with nonstick spray or grease with butter. Set aside.

In a bowl, combine the cinnamon, ginger, salt, nutmeg, pepper, cloves, and allspice; mix well. In a small saucepan over medium heat, add the butter. Tilt and rock the pan until the butter has melted and starts to foam. Keep a close eye on the butter. Once the foam starts to break down and turn a light caramel color, the butter will start to smell almost like toasted nuts. This is browned butter. Remove from the heat and add the spice mixture, mixing well, letting the spices toast and flavor the butter. Set the pan aside to cool, while the rest of the ingredients are measured out.

In a bowl, sift the cake flour with the baking powder and baking soda. Set aside.

In a liquid measuring cup, combine the sour cream and Old Jubilation. Mix together and set aside.

In the bowl of an electric mixer, combine the brown sugar, molasses and cooled browned spice butter. Using a whisk attachment, whip until the mixture is combined and sugar is almost dissolved on high speed for 3 to 4 minutes. Add one egg at a time, beating the mixture well. Add the pumpkin and vanilla, mixing for another 30 seconds. Turn the speed to low, add the flour and sour cream mixtures. Mix until just combined, leaving no lumps or wet patches. Divide the cake batter evenly into the prepared cake pans. Place into the center of the oven and cook for 25 to 30 minutes, or until a toothpick inserted into the center comes out clean . Remove from the oven, and let rest for 15 minutes. Then, using a knife, trace the edge of the inside cake pan to loosen it. Invert the cake onto a wire rack and let cool completely. This cake can be made 4 hours to 3 days ahead. Once fully cooled, wrap in plastic wrap and place in the refrigerator, till ready to decorate.

TO MAKE THE HOLIDAY ALE FROSTING: In a saucepan over a medium heat, add the spiced beer. Reduce the beer by a quarter, till it measures 2 tablespoons. In the bowl of an electric mixer, combine the mascarpone, cream cheese, and butter. Beat with a whisk attachment till light and fluffy. Add the vanilla, confectioners' sugar, and beer reduction. Whip until fully combined and the frosting is light and fluffy.

Once the cakes have cooled, place the first cake down upside down on a cake plate, and spread about 1 cup of frosting on top. Using a spatula, level it out, spreading the frosting to the edges of the cake. Place the remaining cake upside down on top to have a flat top to the cake. Starting in the center, add the remaining frosting to coat the top, then using the spatula and spinning the plate, frost the sides. If the frosting is too warm, it will melt off the cake; if the frosting is too cold, it will not want to stick to the cake.

PAIR WITH JUBELALE FROM DESCHUTES BREWERY OR A WINTER WARMER FROM YOUR FAVORITE LOCAL BREWERY.

25 GREAT AMERICAN BEER BARS

Now that you're equipped with enough beer knowledge to get into some fun trouble, why not put your reading to work with a visit to one of America's great beer bars? For those publicans who expend every effort in the promotion of better beer, a visit to their establishments often comes as a much anticipated occasion. To achieve the level of Great American Beer Bar, a pub must balance and achieve a rare execution of diverse elements. I define a "beer bar" as a place that is first and foremost very selective in its offerings, with heavy reliance on high-quality American craft beers. Beyond merely providing a fantastic selection, a top-tier beer bar also dedicates itself to improving the quality of beer enjoyed by its patrons and hosts educational events, such as beer dinners, to encourage experimentation.

From major metropolitan cities to small towns across the country, passionate publicans are dedicating their attention and efforts to matching their customers up with fine craft beers. Often bitten by the good beer bug themselves, these hard-working bar owners love to sell a wide-range of different beers, from hoppy IPAs to soulful imperial stouts, funky smoked beers and zesty Saisons.

The Great American Beer Bars listed herein set themselves apart as being among the best places in the country for lovers of good beer to visit, because they excel in the crucial respects. They include humble neighborhood pubs and dens of beer geekdom, as well as upscale gastropubs and places that only serve popcorn. These noteworthy establishments provide an extraordinary selection of craft beers, respect their clients in terms of keeping prices fair, hold events promoting craft beers, make American craft beer key to their business, and also offer true character as pubs. In these profiles, I introduce you to twenty-five top-notch beer bars that you should plan to consider visiting on a special occasion, the next time you're in town, or frankly, within a few hundred miles.

Armsby Abbey

144 NORTH MAIN STREET
WORCESTER, MASSACHUSETTS
(508) 795-1012
WWW.ARMSBYABBEY.COM
PROPRIETORS: ALEC LOPEZ AND SHERRI SADOWSKI

The hard scrabble town of Worcester in central Massachusetts might be one of the last places you'd expect a world class beer bar to open shop. With its tall ceilings, dark wood bar, and exposed brick interior, Armsby Abbey is definitely a fitting environment for comfortable yet upscale drinking. With twenty-two rotating taps and a lengthy bottle list, including many cellared offerings, this establishment hosts a series of beer events every month, from vegetarian beer dinners to brewer meet-and-greets and new product releases. Its fine menu specializes in locally sourced materials, and the chefs frequently integrate beer into their dishes.

Blind Tiger Ale House

281 BLEEKER STREET
NEW YORK CITY, NEW YORK
(212) 462-4682
WWW.BLINDTIGERALEHOUSE.COM
PROPRIETORS: ALAN JESTICE, DAVE BRODRICK, AND TIM REINKE

Settling into its second location, long delayed due to problems with the local governing council, Blind Tiger has renewed its efforts to promote great craft beer in lower Manhattan. The pub looks like your average corner bar in the city on the outside, and the warm wood interior and wrap-around bar is a pleasant place to have a pint in quieter moments. When American craft breweries decide to enter the competitive New York City market, the first place they call is Blind Tiger, which hosts dozens of brewer events each year. Firmly set in its promotional role, the pub can offer a wide-range of craft beer options from around the country, with twenty-eight draft lines, more than fifty bottles and vintage beers, and several cask beer offerings. Blind Tiger is also noted for its small but well chosen list of upscale sandwiches.

Brick Store

125 EAST COURT SQUARE
DECATUR, GEORGIA
(404) 687-0990
WWW.BRICKSTOREPUB.COM
PROPRIETORS: DAVE BLANCHARD, MIKE GALLAGHER AND TOM MOORE

Three buddies from Athens, Georgia, decided to open a pub, and the rest is history for this Decatur favorite. Comfortable and quirky, with exposed brick and wood and spread over multiple levels, Brick Store serves up seventeen draft beers in its main bar. With the passage of a law allowing Georgia bars to sell beers above 6 percent alcohol, Brick Store kicked its efforts into a new gear with the opening of its Belgian bar, with eight more tap lines that also serve Belgian-style American craft beers. The beer is served in proper glassware and backed by the knowledgeable staff. The pub hosts a monthly beer and cheese tasting and hosts cask beer as well as other events throughout the year.

Brouwer's Cafe

400 NORTH 35ᵀᴴ STREET
SEATTLE, WASHINGTON
(206) 267-2437
WWW.BROUWERSCAFE.COM
PROPRIETOR: MATT VANDENBERGHE

Located in Seattle's quirky Fremont neighborhood, the striking Brouwer's Café serves sixty-four draft beers and more than 300 bottles in a vaulted, open, and multi-floored circular space. A huge, straight bar welcomes drinkers to gaze into the vast coolers and tap lines of beer. The restaurant specializes in decidedly upscale Belgian fare and the staff can suggest particular pairings. The massive beer list nods towards the restaurant's Belgian roots before taking a huge turn in favor of West Coast American offerings. Brouwer's Café runs dozens of brewers' events throughout the year, as well as organizing its own mini-festivals, including a Hopfest, a wood-aged beer event, and the ever popular Hard Liver Barleywine Fest, where attendees vote on their favorite big alcohol entrant.

Cock & Bull Pub

975 CATTLEMEN ROAD
SARASOTA, FLORIDA
(941) 341-9785
WWW.THE-COCK-N-BULL.COM
PROPRIETORS: DAWN AND HOWIE HOCHBERG

Far from the upscale environs of downtown Sarasota, an abandoned looking roadside shack serves up some of the Sunshine State's best beer in a friendly environment. The rickety Bayou style building opens into a well-worn room with vaulted ceilings, wood beams, and various beer signage. The refinished bar area showcases a glimmering cooler displaying hundreds of beer bottles in addition to the surprisingly diverse list of tap beers. Venture out back where the deck opens into a massive yard with a fire pit where folks gather to drink and talk. Filled with folksy charm and dedicated staffers, the Cock & Bull shows just how widespread the enthusiasm for craft beer has spread in America.

Ebenezer's Restaurant & Pub

44 ALLEN ROAD
LOVELL, MAINE
(207) 925-3200
WWW.EBENEZERSPUB.NET
PROPRIETORS: JEN AND CHRIS LIVELY

In a cottage at the end of a golf course in the middle of nowhere, eastern Maine, lurks the Walt Disney World for beer geeks. In his sleeping devil of a beer bar, owner Chris Lively goes all out to provide the ultimate adventure for true beer enthusiasts who visit him deep in the Maine tundra. The pub itself isn't much to speak of, basically a run-of-the mill 19th Hole joint, but golfers have never before seen such a tap and bottle list. A big fan of eBay and with several mammoth cellars worth of aged goodies, Lively excitedly leads his customers through bounties of unexpected offerings, both listed on the menu and on reserve if you know to ask for them. A trained chef, Lively also integrates beer into many dishes and plays host to what are likely the most expensive, indulgent beer dinners ever held.

Falling Rock Tap House

1919 BLAKE STREET
DENVER, COLORADO
(303) 293-8338
WWW.FALLINGROCKTAPHOUSE.COM
PROPRIETOR: CHRIS BLACK

In the center of Denver's rejuvenated Lower Downtown district, Falling Rock serves nearly seventy different beers on tap, with many more available in the bottle—all in a cozy space. With couches and booths flanking the center of the long upstairs bar, the space feels like someone's living room, while the lower level feels like a recreation room. In late September and early October, Falling Rock becomes the unofficial headquarters for thousands of craft beer fans and brewers from around the world who have made the pilgrimage to the annual Great American Beer Festival. The bar focuses on American beer and often receives specialty kegs and experimental beers due to its longstanding support of the industry, which are released at special events throughout the year.

Father's Office

3229 HELMS AVENUE
LOS ANGELES, CALIFORNIA
(310) 736-2224
WWW.FATHERSOFFICE.COM
PROPRIETOR: SANG YOON

In see-and-be-seen Los Angeles, the craft beer scene centers around this humble but upscale craft beer bar and restaurant. With thirty-six taps and a handful of bottle, all served by knowledgeable staff in proper glassware, the pub serves up an excellent craft beer experience. But many visitors come here simply for the food, which helped define gastropub on the LA dining scene. Amid the slick and polished wood paneling, foodies and hipsters rave over chef and owner Sang Yoon's gourmet burger, a dry-aged strip steak served with blue cheese, arugula, and onion compote on French bread which goes for nearly $20. A new outlet for the popular pub opened in Culver City in 2008, taking some strain off this tight yet well-executed space.

Fat Head's Saloon

1805 EAST CARSON STREET
PITTSBURGH, PENNSYLVANIA
(412) 431-7433
WWW.FATHEADS.COM
PROPRIETOR: GLENN BENIGNI

A local neighborhood joint in Pittsburgh's historic South Side, Fat Head's serves up hearty American fare to match its smashing list of forty-two craft beers and cask-conditioned line. While a few Belgian, German, and British brands dot the list, the selection is overwhelmingly dominated by American beers from all over the country. The bar uses its Frequent Flyer Beer Tour to encourage reluctant customers to try beers from all over the world, and it offers a mix and match bottle shop called Upstairs at Fat Head's. Cask beers make an appearance during Firkin Fridays, and the bar hosts a series of other entertaining events throughout the year. Branching out from its home, Fat Head's has also opened a brewpub operation under the same name in Cleveland, Ohio.

Freakin' Frog
4700 SOUTH MARYLAND PARKWAY
LAS VEGAS, NEVADA
(702) 597-9702
WWW.FREAKINFROG.COM
PROPRIETOR: ADAM CARMER

Tucked away in a rundown strip mall a few miles from the glowing neon of Las Vegas's Disney-esque hotels and monster casinos, the location definitely doesn't prepare you for a great craft beer experience. Across from the University of Nevada's campus, this is the grittier local side of Vegas that many visitors don't get to see. Come in from the bright desert sun and a row of well-maintained, cold taps awaits you. Pause a second over the extensive bottle list and the bartender will suggest a refreshing guided tour of the bar's well-stocked cooler, complete with explanations of offerings you pass along the way. Promoted as an intellectual, adult alcohol sanctuary, don't come here expecting glitz, beer bar pretension, or a gastropub. Simple and functional on the interior, the long-bar also has a small room upstairs that stocks more than 600 whiskeys and 300 specialty tequilas. A short cab ride from the Strip, Freakin' Frog serves as a welcomed beer oasis when visiting Sin City.

The Ginger Man
301 LAVACA STREET
AUSTIN, TEXAS
(512) 473-8801
WWW.GINGERMANPUB.COM
PROPRIETOR: VONNIE BALLENSKY-MARRERO

Long a Texas institution, The Ginger Man chain of pubs first opened its beer-friendly environs in Houston in 1985. The chain quickly spread to some other locations, including the popular Austin outlet. Considered by many to be the first multi-tap, an establishment that specializes in large numbers of draft offerings, The Ginger Man offers a solid lineup of local beers, as well as seasonal and imports. With eighty draft lines, the Austin pub is impressive, and holds a few beer tasting events and specials every month. Each location is a little different but each is dedicated to providing a wealth of draft opportunities that is nearly unmatched by any other large pub operation.

The Hopleaf Bar

5148 NORTH CLARK STREET
CHICAGO, ILLINOIS
(773) 334-9851
WWW.HOPLEAF.COM
PROPRIETORS: MICHAEL ROPER AND LOUISE MOLNAR

Developing from a small neighborhood bar into a world-class gastropub, the Hopleaf is a jewel in Chicago's beer crown. Located on the city's far north side in the Andersonville neighborhood, the unassuming Hop Leaf is holy ground for lovers of beer and food. The small, square front room serves as a classic tavern space, with a couple of booths and tables spread out. When you arrive, take a look at the helpful beer menus, which descriptively lay out the range of draft offerings at your choosing. The list is heavily weighted in favor of Belgian and local and Midwestern offerings, with occasional West Coast beers tossed in. The soaring ceilings of the back room, upstairs, and outdoor spaces give diners the opportunity to enjoy conversation and the excellent, upscale cuisine. The mussels cooked in Witbier are a house specialty, but you'll leave happy after any sampling from the creative, hearty menu.

Horse Brass Pub

4534 SE BELMONT STREET
PORTLAND, OREGON
(503) 232-2202
WWW.HORSEBRASS.COM
PROPRIETOR: DON YOUNGER

In the wide world of beer, there's no one quite like Don Younger, owner of the iconic Horse Brass Pub. Always seen with a cigarette in one hand and a beer in the other, Younger and his bar supported craft brewers long before they even had a name for their efforts. A central and revered figure in the vibrant Portland beer scene, Younger also co-owns the local New Old Lompoc Brewery. Horse Brass looks like a cottage-style British pub at times, replete with tons of old brewing and historical memorabilia. The beer soaked menus let you know this isn't some nouveau beer bistro, but an old school joint that just happens to feature great beer. Proudly serving more than fifty taps, with most dedicated to West Coast craft breweries, Horse Brass frequently rotates its list to maintain the undivided attention of loyal pubgoers.

Humpy's Great Alaskan Alehouse

610 WEST 6TH AVENUE
ANCHORAGE, ALASKA
(907) 276-2337
WWW.HUMPYS.COM
PROPRIETORS: BILLY OPINSKY AND JAMES MAUER

Even in Alaska's most populated city, things can get pretty bleak and quiet in the frozen winter months. The locals who know better understand that this is the best time to visit their favorite watering hole, a loveable spot called Humpy's. A bit dark and roughed up on the interior, Humpy's is comfortable and inviting, even for tourists, during the warmer months. In some of the farthest reaches of America, craft beer dominates the impressive list of fifty different taps. Even more impressive is that a large proportion of these offerings are dedicated to local, Alaskan-brewed beers. A friend to live music, Humpy's also gladly plays host to the crazy folks who venture to Anchorage every January for the annual Great Alaska Beer and Barleywine Festival.

Lucky Baldwin's

17 SOUTH RAYMOND AVENUE
OLD TOWNE PASADENA, CALIFORNIA
(626) 795-0652
WWW.LUCKYBALDWINS.COM
PROPRIETORS: DAVID FARNWORTH AND PEGGY SIMONIAN

For a place that sells itself as an authentic British pub, Lucky Baldwin's spends a lot of time flirting with American craft brewers. Of its sixty-two tap lines, a considerable number favor American offerings, with a fair boast of Belgians added to the mix. Located in the old town section of Pasadena, its warm and welcoming environs serve up hearty English classics as well as some British atmosphere. Lucky Baldwin's also sponsors a series of popular mini-festivals, including an IPA event and a Christmas in July celebration of winter warmers and strong ales.

The Map Room

1949 NORTH HOYNE AVENUE
CHICAGO, ILLINOIS
(773) 252-7636
WWW.MAPROOM.COM
PROPRIETORS: MARK AND LAURA BLASINGAME

Located in Chicago's Bucktown neighborhood, this classic Chicago-style long bar bills itself as a traveler's tavern. Bedecked in old National Geographic issues and with world murals and flags dotting the walls, the Map Room and its twenty-six well-chosen taps also encourages an exploration of the world's great beer styles. The bar specializes in pairing beers with their proper glassware, carefully rinsing each in front of you before pouring your beer. The tavern also hosts monthly beer school events, in which a local brewer walks thirsty students through the brewing process and ingredients in a particular set of styles. Always busy but never overwhelming, the Map Room manages to seamlessly integrate its beer enthusiasm into a local neighborhood bar atmosphere.

Monk's Café

264 SOUTH 16TH STREET
PHILADELPHIA, PENNSYLVANIA
(215) 545-7005
WWW.MONKSCAFE.COM
PROPRIETORS: TOM PETERS AND FERGUS CAREY

One of the grand-daddies of Great American Beer Bars, Monk's balances a love for all things Belgian with its dedication to American craft beer. The heart and soul of the burgeoning Philadelphia beer scene, the bar's owners also run a handful of other local establishments, including the nearby Nodding Head brewpub. With a dark and sometimes cramped interior, the front bar serves a handful of Belgian and American taps along with a healthy bottle list, heavy on local Philly craft beers. The pleasant back bar runs sixteen changing taps and often plays host to monthly beer dinners and brewer meet-and-greets. When drinking at Monk's, you're likely to run into brewers and beer enthusiasts from around the country who have come to enjoy *cuisine a la biere* and a few pints of craft beer.

The Muddy Pig

162 DALE STREET NORTH
SAINT PAUL, MINNESOTA
(651) 254-1030
WWW.MUDDYPIG.COM
PROPRIETORS: MARK VAN WIE AND PAUL SCHATZ

Ensconced in an old brick building in the one-time downtrodden Selby-Dale section of Saint Paul that has long housed bars and restaurants, The Muddy Pig has retained a lot of the old time charm of previous establishments. Warm, dark stained wood fills the nooks and booths, and the back room has an especially well-worn, vintage feel. The square front bar features a frequently rotating split mix of forty-eight Belgian and American crafts on tap, with many local favorites, including Summit and Surly, available. Quickly becoming a major beer destination in the Twin Cities, the bar hosts dozens of events throughout the year, including beer release parties.

Mugs Ale House

125 BEDFORD AVENUE
BROOKLYN, NEW YORK
(718) 486-8232
WWW.MUGSALEHOUSE.COM
PROPRIETOR: ED BERESTECKI

With its unassuming exterior, you'd never guess that the bar at Mugs Ale House serves up a stirringly diverse list of beers in a pro-beer but no-nonsense tavern environment. With thirty taps and two hand pumps for cask-conditioned beers, this humble neighborhood pub serves locals and beer geeks alike. The front room is character filled, while the background serves as a slightly quieter dining spot for the bar's small kitchen. The taps often favor local beers, including specialty batches from the nearby Brooklyn Brewery. Be sure to check out the unexpectedly deep vintage bottle list as well. Despite heady competition from many worthy nearby contenders, including Barcade and Spuyten Duyvil, Mugs wins out for its long-standing dedication to American craft beer, its steady stream of beer events (including the Split Thy Skull high alcohol festival), and its incredibly reasonable prices in this trendy Williamsburg neighborhood locale.

O'Brien's Pub

4646 CONVOY STREET
SAN DIEGO, CALIFORNIA
(858) 715-1745
WWW.OBRIENSPUB.NET
PROPRIETOR: TOM NICKEL

Taking cues from old school saloons, O'Brien's is a no-nonsense pub that calls itself the Hoppiest Place on Earth, a moniker well-suited for a bar located in the heart of southern California's hop heaven. The pub offers a well-chosen spread of twenty West Coast-heavy taps and a hundred or so bottles. Instead of spreading itself too thin in an attempt to touch many geographic bases, the draft offerings tend to offer multiple beers from a smaller number of brewers, so you can really get to know a producer. A slave to the hop, O'Brien's hosts an annual Wet Hop Festival, which serves fresh, hoppy beers brewed with recently picked hops. A former award-winning brewer himself, owner Tom Nickel is hooked into the local beer scene and often secures special release offerings for his grateful customers. A haven for soccer fans, the bar runs international matches and hosts monthly beer and cheese pairing events.

The Publick House Brookline

1648 BEACON STREET
BROOKLINE, MASSACHUSETTS
(617) 277-2880
WWW.EATGOODFOODDRINKBETTERBEER.COM
PROPRIETORS: DAVID CICCOLO AND AILISH GILLIGAN

In the upscale Washington Square neighborhood in this Boston streetcar suburb, the owners and staff bring high-quality food and beers to their mixed audience of beer lovers and neighborhood dwellers. The main bar divides its twenty-six selections into Belgians, Here, and There, with beers in the 'Here' category focusing on domestic craft offerings. An addition to the busy main bar and dining room called the Monk's Cell offers a quieter, more contemplative experience. Run by a former brewer, The Publick House serves beers from across the country and in proper glassware to accompany its beer-infused cuisine. The pub sponsors a few events throughout the year, including brewer meet-and-greets as well as its popular HopHead Throwdown, a charity event showcasing some of the region's most tongue blisteringly bitter beers.

Romans' Pub

3475 SOUTH KINNICKINNIC AVENUE
MILWAUKEE, WISCONSIN
(414) 481-3396
WWW.ROMANSPUB.COM
PROPRIETOR: MIKE ROMANS

Despite being home to some world class craft breweries and producers of its share of excellent ales and lagers, Milwaukee was a bit slow to embrace the beer bar craze. So it was welcome news when this owner decided to start serving high-quality, specialty beers. Propped up on the city's south side, far from the downtown action, Romans' is a neighborhood tavern that endeavors to bring great beer to regular, working-class folks, with little pretension but no drop in quality or service. Built in 1885, the building originally served as a roadhouse and stage coach stop before transitioning into its lengthy career as a neighborhood saloon. The ever-rotating list of thirty taps gleams with American craft offerings, with a heavy nod towards small Midwestern breweries. Romans' Pub helps Milwaukee's craft beer lovers celebrate their city's earned reputation as one of America's great brewing cities.

Rustico Restaurant and Bar

827 SLATERS LANE
ALEXANDRIA, VIRGINIA
(703) 224-5051
WWW.RUSTICORESTAURANT.COM
PROPRIETORS: MICHAEL BABIN AND NEIGHBORHOOD RESTAURANT GROUP

Located just outside the trendy downtown area of historic Alexandria, the original Rustico location boasts a diverse list of thirty draft beers as well as a teetering array of 300 bottled beers. The upscale gastro-pizzeria pub's decor mixes brick, tall ceilings and wood floors to create a lively, attractive, and upscale eatery. The kitchen's menu offers an impressive selection of wood-fired pizzas along with a highly creative and elegantly inviting bar appetizer menu, all presented beautifully. And then there's the beer list, which creatively breaks down the beers by flavor, suggesting crisp, hop, malt, and roast offerings along with fruit and spice and tart and funky categories. With selections covering the entire country and occasional imported offerings, Rustico seamlessly blends great food with top-notch craft beer to create a lively and reverential gustatory experience.

Toronado

547 HAIGHT STREET
SAN FRANCISCO, CALIFORNIA
(415) 863-2276
WWW.TORONADO.COM
PROPRIETOR: DAVID KEENE

The Toronado is another legendary pioneer in the promotion of American craft beer. Run by David Keene, the small confines of this Haight-Ashbury district pub focus solely on great beer. A rotating list of more than forty draft offerings, mainly split between Belgians and a well-chosen selection of American crafts, is displayed on an elevated board in the center of the pub. You'll often see visiting beer geeks staring in awe at the many hard-to-find yet reasonably priced offerings listed on the board. The pub, which now has a sister location in San Diego, also hosts a series of beer geek events throughout the year, including a Stout fest and its popular Barleywine Festival, which features more than fifty strong ales from around the country.

Tria

123 SOUTH 18TH STREET
PHILADELPHIA, PENNSYLVANIA
(215) 972-8742
WWW.TRIACAFE.COM
PROPRIETOR: JONATHAN MYEROW

Promoting itself as Philly's wine, cheese and beer café, Tria plays up the artisanship of the people behind the products it serves. In a narrow and attractively appointed space, take a seat at the short bar to watch the bar staff carefully handle and nicely present your drink orders as well as make creative bar snacks. The bar focuses on bottle service, with about a dozen taps sprinkled into the list. The list is divided into some intriguing categories, including invigorating, profound, friendly, and extreme. The nearby and popular Tria Fermentation School offers people the chance to enhance their appreciation of the pub's focal points with classes run by experts in their respective fields, including brewmasters and cheesemakers. The helpful staff is quick to make suggestions and will help guide you through possible pairings.

GLOSSARY

ALCOHOL. A fermentation by-product that occurs when yeast eat the sugars in the wort. Expressed as a percentage of volume (ABV) or by weight (ABW). A misunderstanding of these two measurement tools underlies the common misconception that Canadian beer possesses greater strength than American beer. Canadian brewers generally use the ABV designation, while larger American brewers traditionally relied upon ABW. Craft brewers most often employ the ABV standard for measuring alcohol. A beer with an ABV of 5 percent has an ABW of 3.98 percent, as alcohol weighs slightly less than 80 percent as much as water.

ADJUNCT. A fermentable element substituted for cereal grains, often relating to rice and corn, both of which are used by larger breweries to lighten the bodies of their beers. Adjuncts comprise between 30 and 40 percent of the ingredients found in many popular American beers. Viewed with great disdain by beer geeks who believe their use reduces the quality of the final product.

ALE. One of the two main branches of the beer family tree. Ales are initially distinguished from lagers by their use of Saccharomyces cerevisiae, an aerobic yeast that settles at the top of a fermentation vessel. Ale yeasts generally prefer warmer temperatures, which help contribute to their often fruity, estery characters.

BARLEY. This is the most traditional cereal grain used in the mash of the brewing process. Brewers use dozens of varieties of malt, kilned to different temperatures, in order to achieve different flavor profiles in their beers. Barley typically comprises the majority of the fermentable materials found in craft beer.

BARREL. A unit used to measure amounts of beer. The total volumes found in a barrel differs between the American and metric systems of measurement. A barrel in the metric system contains 36 imperial gallons or 163.7 liters, while an American barrel holds 31.5 gallons or 119.2 liters. An American barrel contains approximately two traditionally sized kegs.

BEER. Any beverage alcohol produced by the fermentation of cereal grain, usually malted barley.

BEER GEEK. An avid enthusiast and consumer of all things beer-related. Running the gamut from respectfully passionate to disturbingly obsessesed, these enthusiasts stroll past the taps upon entering every restaurant, pass through nearby liquor stores to peruse their offerings, and generally take an interest in beer as a hobby. The term is sometimes used in a derogatory fashion towards those individuals who take beer too seriously.

BOTTLE-CONDITIONED. A process of secondary fermentation by which brewers add or allow live yeast to enter the delivery vessel, typically a bottle, to feed upon remaining sugars. The practice creates new aromas and flavors and can help carbonate the final beer by trapping carbon dioxide in the bottle. You can sometimes denote a bottle-conditioned beer if there is sediment in the bottom of the bottle.

Brewers Association. A Boulder, Colorado-based trade organization whose purpose is to advocate on behalf of craft brewers and to promote craft beer. This group sponsors and organizes the annual Great American Beer Festival.

BREWHOUSE. The system, including the brew kettles, upon which a brewer makes beer.

BREWPUB. A pub or restaurant that produces its own beer on-site and sells at least 25 percent of its own beer on the premises. The beer is often served directly from the pub's storage tanks. Where allowed by law, brewpubs sell beer to go and even distribute it to off-site accounts.

BREWERY. A facility that mainly produces beer for sale off-premise at restaurants, bars, and package stores.

CASK-CONDITIONED. Similar to the process of bottle-conditioning but which takes place in a cask or metal keg.

CONTRACT BREWING. A business and brewing arrangement in which one brewery produces beer on behalf of another brewery or company. Some smaller breweries contract out the production of their beer, often in bottles or cans, to larger breweries that have the benefit of larger scale brewing operations. Sometimes considered to be a controversial practice among beer geeks, this arrangement can also result in the production of excellent beers.

CRAFT BEER. A beer that is produced in limited quantities, often using traditional methods, and without adjuncts whose use is designed to lighten the body and flavor of the final product. Where appropriate for style, a brewer may substitute a percentage of malted wheat, rye, or other ingredients to improve the flavor profiles of their beers.

CRAFT BREWER. A somewhat controversial term whose membership, as defined by the Brewers Association as being limited to American brewers that are small, independent, and traditional. The association's definition of "independent" requires a craft brewer not be more than 25 percent owned or controlled by a beverage alcohol company that is not itself a craft brewer. For purposes of this book, a craft brewer is defined as one whose primary focus is brewing and selling craft beer.

DRY-HOPPING. A process by which brewers add hops to fermenting or conditioning beer in order to increase hop character and aroma.

EXTREME BREWING. The name given to the craft brewing trend towards unusual, experimental, and often high-alcohol or highly hopped beers.

Fermentation. The conversion of sugars into alcohol and carbon dioxide, created through the addition of yeast.

GREAT AMERICAN BEER FESTIVAL (GABF). Held annually since 1982, this event is one of the largest and longest-running beer festivals in America. Hosted by the Brewers Association in Denver, Colorado, the GABF offers 1600 beers on tap from 350 American breweries. The association also holds a well-regarded, blind-tasted competition and awards highly coveted medals for the top finishers in more than 65 style categories.

GROWLER. A container of beer, traditionally a half-gallon (64 ounces) in size, in which brewers bottle and sell their products. Growlers are popular methods for selling beer at brewpubs, yet are not legal in all states. Many brewpubs charge a small deposit for the bottle and will refill it at discounted rates upon return. Depending on how the containers are filled, the beer usually should be consumed within a short time after purchase. A great device for sharing beer with friends.

HOPS. A flowering plant (Humulus) used as a primary flavoring agent in beer. Often added to boiling wort or fermenting or conditioning beer in order to impart bitter flavors or aromas. The many varieties of hops each possess distinctive characters and contribute different influences to beer. Hop resins contain two main acids, called alpha and beta. Alpha acids act as preservatives and contribute bitterness early in the boil, flavor in the latter part of the boil, and aroma in the final minutes of the boil. Bitterness is determined the by the degree to which the alpha acids are isomerized during the boil and are expressed in International Bitterness Units (IBUs). Beta acids do not isomerize during the boil, have a negligible effect on beer flavor, but contribute to the aroma.

INTERNATIONAL BITTERNESS UNITS (IBU). A standard system for calculating and expressing the hop bitterness in beer. An IBU is one part per million of isohumulone and the higher the number, the greater the level of bitterness. American light lagers generally have 5 IBUs, while souped-up IPAs can exceed 100. Many experts believe that people cannot taste and differentiate between beers with more than 100 IBUs.

HOMEBREWING. The small-scale brewing of beer for personal consumption. As legalized as part of a bill signed by President Jimmy Carter in 1978, homebrewers are generally allowed to produce between 50 and 100 gallons of beer per year without taxation. Many craft brewers started as homebrewers before stepping up to commercial-scale production.

LAGER. The second of the two main families of beer. Lagers are distinguished from ales by their use of Saccharomyces uvarum or Carlsbergensis anaerobic yeasts that settle to the bottom of the fermentation vessel. Lager yeasts generally prefer cooler temperatures, which tend to soften the edges of the resulting products and provide crisper beers after aging.

MASH. A mixture of hot water and crushed cereal grain, usually barley or wheat, which occurs during the early stage of beer production.

MALT. A process by which cereal grains, often barley, are steeped in water, causing them to germinate. The germination process is quickly stopped when the resulting product is kilned to convert the starches to sugars. Maltsters dry beers at various temperatures in order to create different types of malted barley.

MACRO-BREWERY. A brewery that produces more than 2,000,000 barrels of beer per year. The name given to larger breweries, including Anheuser-Busch InBev and MillerCoors, yet generally excluding large craft breweries, such as the Boston Beer Company. Beer geeks often refer to the beers produced by these breweries as "macro brews" or "macros."

MICRO-BREWERY. A term technically used to describe a brewery that produces less than 15,000 barrels of beer per year. Popularized in the early days of craft brewing and applied to all craft breweries, the term has largely fallen out of favor as craft breweries started to substantially increase the size of their brewing operations. Larger craft breweries producing more than 15,000 barrels per year, but less than 2,000,000 barrels, are called regional breweries.

NOBLE HOPS. A label given to certain European hop varieties that distinguish themselves from other hop varieties in their low bitterness levels and substantial aromatics. While subject to some debate, the group usually includes Hallertau, Saaz, Spalt, and Tettnanger. These hops generally offer distinctly zesty and herbal notes.

REINHEITSGEBOT. The so-called German Purity Law, adopted in 1516 by William IV, Duke of Bavaria. The law once applied to all German brewers and limited their ingredients to grain, hops, and water. When scientists discovered the role of yeast in beer, it was added to the list of ingredients. An exception was also later added for wheat beers. One of the oldest existing food regulations, the law has been severely undercut by Germany's involvement in the European Union. Many brewers voluntarily comply with the law out of a sense of tradition.

SESSION BEER. A beer with a relatively low alcohol-level, usually 3 to 4 percent alcohol by volume, that allows the drinker to enjoy several pints in one sitting without becoming intoxicated. Many English-style ales set the standard for such beers.

WORT. The liquid solution created when sugar water is strained from the spent cereal grain in the mash tun. Wort turns into beer through the process of fermentation.

YEAST. A fungus found in the genus Saccharomyces, this micro-organism feeds on the sugars found in wort and creates alcohol and carbon dioxide as byproducts. Many yeast strains contribute distinct flavors to beer and are used to brew specific styles.

IMAGE CREDITS

Unless otherwise noted, all images are courtesy of their respective breweries. All images used by permission.

Author photo: Jennifer Cox

Photographs on pages: 54 (l), 56 (l), 76 (r), 77 (l), 78 (r), 82 (r), 87 (r), 90 (r), 91 (l), 97 (r), 100 (r), 102 (l), 102 (r), 116 (l), 120 (l), 127 (l), 133 (r), 136 (l), 146 (l), 167 (l), 167 (r), 169 (r), 172 (l), 178, 187 (l), 190 (l), 196 (l), 207 (r), 210 (l), 214 (l), 219 (l), 224 (l), 227 (l), 230 (r), 235 (l),
© 2010 Steve Legato.

Pages 10, 12–13, 46–47, 244–245: Courtesy of Dogfish Head Brewery.

Pages 14, 24, 28, 30: Courtesy of the author.

Pages 15, 21: Courtesy of Boston Beer Company.

Pages 18–21: From the Library of Congress.

Page 22,23: Courtesy of Boulder Beer Company.

Page 29: Courtesy of Stone Brewing Company.

Page 70: Dreamweaver photo by Steve Stoltzfus.

Page 70: Gumballhead photo by Lindsay Gallup Photography.

Page 74: Hoffman Weiss photo by Bill Lee Imaging.

Page 79: The Ramstein Classic photo by Gehrig Photography.

Page 80: Leavenworth Dunkelweizen photo by Leavenworth Biers.

Page 83: Ramstein Winter Wheat photo by Gehrig Photography.

Page 93: McIlhenney's Irish Red Ale photo by Nick Nacca.

Page 100: Dunkel Lager photo © 2010 VFC, Inc. www.virtualfarm.com.

Page 103: Isle of Skye Scottish Ale poster developed by Chuck Skydeck.

Page 113: Bayern Dopplebock art by Monte Dolack and designed by Eileen Chontos.

Page 120: Maibock Lager art by Todd Davies.

Page 122: Tasgall Ale photo by John Warner. Head Brewer: John Lyda.

Page 127: Alpha King Pale Ale Lindsay Gallup Photography.

Page 146: Headwall Alt photo by Craig Harrison.

Page 152: Torch Pilsner graphics by Shapiro Walker Designs.

Page 163: Kozlov Stout photo by Ryan Salat. Brewer: Brenden Dobel.

Page 164: Faricy Fest Irish Stout art by René Greff. Brewer: Matt Greff.

Page 169: Milk Stout photo by Alyson Dratch.

Page 184: Raspberry Strong Ale art by Todd Davis.

Page 175: Black Noddy Lager label by Boost Creative Services.

Page 177: Coffeehouse Porter art by Todd Davies.

Page 182: The Mad Elf Holiday Ale photo by Steve Stoltzfus.

Page 202: Old Guardian Barleywine photo by StudioSholz.com.

Page 218: Brute photo by Andrew Gillis. Brewer: Jeff O'Neil.

Page 219: Supplication photo by Custom Culture Images and Todd Jenkins.

Page 228: Rye Hopper Ale art by Evan Dahm.

Page 235: Temptation photo by Custom Culture Images and Todd Jenkins.

Page 238: Famous Flaming Stone Beer poster developed by Chuck Skydeck.

Page 214: Dark Lord Russian Imperial Stout by Lindsay Gallup Photography.

INDEX OF BEER STYLES

INDEX OF BEERS

INDEX OF BREWERIES

Squatters Pub and Brewery, 133
St. George Brewing Company, 52, 156
Starr Hill Brewery, 94, 106
Stoudts Brewing Company, 66, 97
Sudwerk Restaurant and Brewery, 112
Summit Brewing Company, 33, 96, 157, 296
Sweetwater Brewing Company, 127, 187, 212

T

Terrapin Beer Company, 178, 227
Tap Brewpub, The, 57, 84
Thirsty Bear Brewing Company, 163
Thomas Hooker Brewing Company, 64, 160
Three Floyds Brewing Company, 70, 127, 214
Tröegs Brewing Company, 70, 182
Tuckerman Brewing Company, 146
Two Brothers Brewing Company, 63, 78, 222

U

Uinta Brewing Company, 128
Uncommon Brewers, 117
Upland Brewing Company, 76
Upstream Brewing Company, 218

V

Vermont Pub and Brewery, 33, 230
Victory Brewing Company, 65, 82, 119, 149, 285
Voodoo Brewery, 240

W

Wachusett Brewing Company, 186
Weyerbacher Brewing Company, 81, 141, 189, 191
Willimantic Brewing Company, 136, 227
Willoughby Brewing Company, 185
Wolaver's Brewing Company, 165

Y

Yards Brewing Company, 223
Yazoo Brewing Company, 72, 164

By State

Alaska

Alaskan Brewing Company, 54, 230
Midnight Sun Brewing Company, 208, 242
Silver Gulch Brewing Company, 104

Arizona

Four Peaks Brewing Company, 101, 197
Nimbus Brewing, 203
Papago Brewing Company, 159

Arkansas

Diamond Bear Brewing Company, 92

California

Alesmith Brewing Company, 126, 212
Anderson Valley Brewing Company, 167
Alpine Beer Company, 93, 143
Anchor Brewing, 4, 23, 67, 110, 204, 285
Ballast Point Brewing Company, 88, 154
Bear Republic Brewing Company, 137, 142, 286
Bison Brewing Company, 237
Bruery, The, 77, 84, 207
Drakes Brewing Co., 59
Eel River Brewing, 201
Firestone Walker Brewing Company, 131, 286
Green Flash Brewing Company, 139, 210
Lagunitas Brewing Company, 55
Lost Abbey, The, 221, 236
Lost Coast Brewery and Café, 166
Mad River Brewing Company, 171
Marin Brewing Company, 196
Moonlight Brewing Company, 151, 176
Moylan's Brewery and Restaurant, 122
North Coast Brewing Company, 115, 163
Pizza Port Brewing Company, 107
Port Brewing Company, 27, 153–154